IMAGES
of America

BLOWING ROCK REVISITED

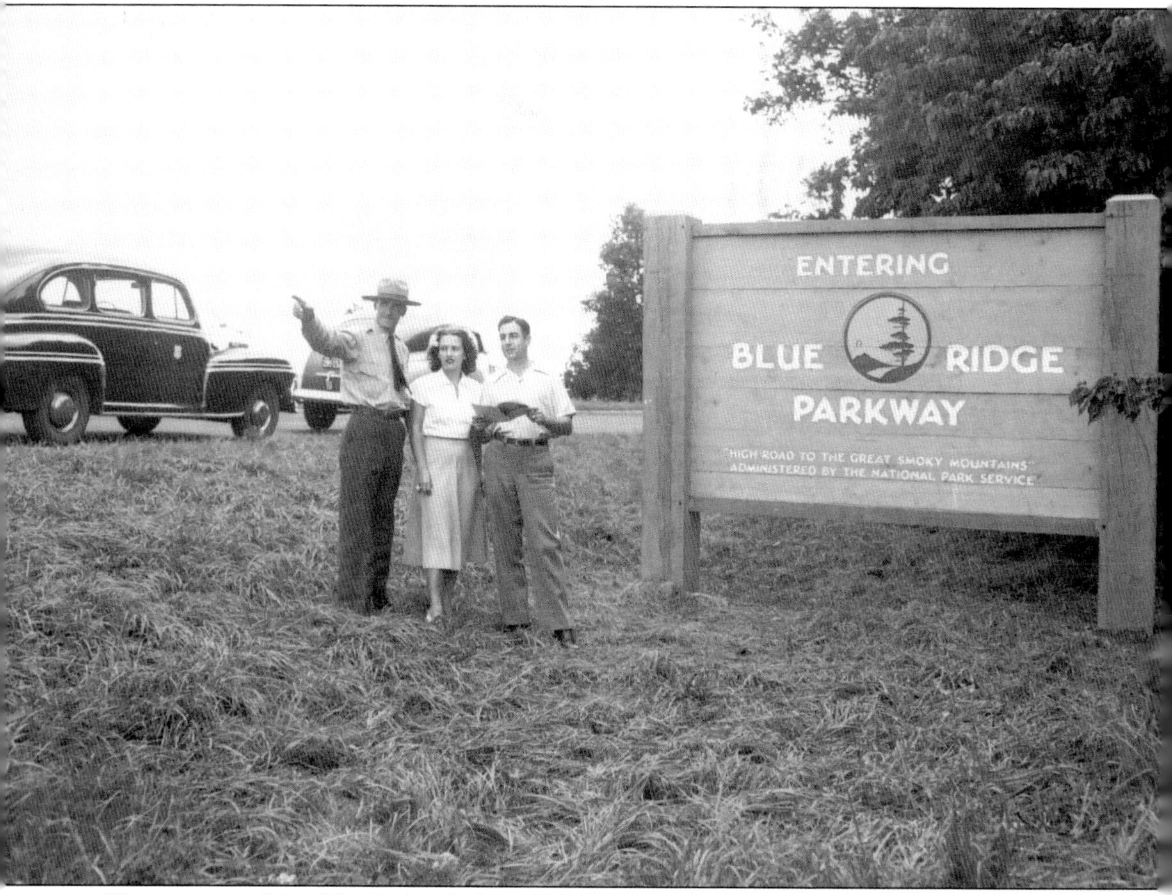

The opening of the Blue Ridge Parkway's Blowing Rock section in 1938 created strong local opinions concerning who would cater to the needs of travelers. Some feared the federal government would step in and provide accommodations if the businesses of Blowing Rock were not prepared to handle increased visitors. With two exits into Blowing Rock along the parkway, motorists gained easy access to the town.

On the Cover: The position of the horse show ring and spectators at the Blowing Rock Charity Horse Show has remained unchanged for its near 100-year history; this image dates to 1937. While other horse shows temporarily shut down during World War II and the Great Depression, Blowing Rock's went on and is the oldest continuous outdoor horse show in America. (Courtesy of the Blowing Rock Historical Society.)

IMAGES
of America

BLOWING ROCK REVISITED

Trent Margrif for the
Blowing Rock Historical Society

ARCADIA
PUBLISHING

ISBN 978-1-4671-3474-3

Published by Arcadia Publishing
Charleston, South Carolina

Printed in the United States of America

Library of Congress Control Number: 2015942369

For all general information, please contact Arcadia Publishing:
Telephone 843-853-2070
Fax 843-853-0044
E-mail sales@arcadiapublishing.com
For customer service and orders:
Toll-Free 1-888-313-2665

Visit us on the Internet at www.arcadiapublishing.com

To my wife, Andrea, and daughter, Amelia, who are among the many that have enjoyed Blowing Rock

Contents

ACKNOWLEDGMENTS

All images appear courtesy of the Blowing Rock Historical Society. This collection primarily came from the late Jerry Burns, longtime editor of the *Blowing Rocket*. His images clearly show the history of a small town he dearly loved and a community better for his efforts. It is hoped that a majority of the 10,000 images in this collection will be found on the website of the historical society in the future. Burns naturally gravitated toward nature, animals, and events; that children were frequently in these images was an additional plus. All of the author's proceeds from this publication will go to support the efforts of the Blowing Rock Historical Society.

Melissa Pickett is my strongest supporter and was gracious in making sure my scanning of these images in Edgewood Cottage was trouble-free. Janice Burns, Marcia Quinn, Ginny Stevens, and Rita White were all very helpful in sharing information on images and general encouragement. A big thank-you also to my former student Marty Tschetter, who initially began the scanning and realized that this work was important and should continue.

Outside of the Blowing Rock Historical Society, many thanks and appreciation to Gary Boye, Greta Browning, Andrea Burns, Steven Burns, Maurice Ewing, Steven Kidd, Ralph Lentz, Pam Mitchem, Mardi Sumrell, and Charles Watkins. The staff of the Blowing Rock Art and History Museum (BRAHM), specifically Ethan Brooks-Livingston and Dianna Louglin, were extremely helpful and the exhibit on the photography of Jerry Burns timely and terrific. A special thank-you goes to Basil's Fresh Pasta and Deli, where a majority of this text was written and to the Blowing Rock Memories public group on Facebook. The assistance of Ginny Rasmussen at Arcadia Publishing was essential in the completion of this work. I would like to thank the patience and understanding of my students at Appalachian State University, who were unclear why they were asked to analyze images of the town instead of our normal discussions on everything from architecture to Martian invasions.

INTRODUCTION

Blowing Rock has held many titles and received multiple recognitions: Year-Round Vacation Paradise, the Crown of the Blue Ridge, in the Heart of the North Carolina High Country, Ohwassah the Beautiful Land of God, and most recently, the Prettiest Town in North Carolina. The community blends a perfect combination of nature and scenery, humanity and architecture, and history and heritage, too.

The first travelers to the region were Native Americans, and primarily residents of Lenoir rode horses up to Blowing Rock as early as the 1840s with the completion of the Lenoir-Blowing Rock Turnpike. The first summer home likely dates to the 1850s, and after the Civil War more permanent residences were established in greater number. It was not a vast number of visitors, but the resort industry also began after the Civil War in Blowing Rock. The construction date of the Martin House of 1870 is one example of this as well as the many other smaller boardinghouses that once stood. The importance of the incorporation of the town in 1889 is significant, if nothing else for land values. Before incorporation, land was $5 an acre, after $250. By the 1890s, Blowing Rock was no longer simply a summer colony of Lenoir, and investors, visitors, and permanent residents appeared from all over.

The completion of the Green Park Hotel represented this new era of tourist travel. It is also important to note its construction required additional workers and the beginnings of a service industry that also would increase residents. An 1897 tourism brochure indicated a year-round population of 300 and 1,000 seasonal. Although Mayview Manor would eventually replace the Green Park Hotel as the center of local social activities, Green Park had the town's only golf course in an era when golf was the major sport of the professional men and women who came to summer resorts. The area known as Green Park was once a larger community than Blowing Rock. It was the first major settlement at the top of the mountain.

Livery stables, bowling alleys, drugstores, churches, a bank, long-distance and local telephone lines, and several physicians are all noted as amenities by the 1910s. This growth made the conception of McCrae's Linville community as a summer resort area also possible, as well as an accompanying turnpike connecting with Blowing Rock. The chestnut-bark construction in Linville exceeds the number in Blowing Rock currently, but at one point they may have been equal. The competition between Linville and Blowing Rock is made clear by the 1930s, with golf tournament challenges, highlighting traveling theater companies, and simply advertising Linville extensively in the *Blowing Rocket*.

The publication of *In Cloudland* added significantly to increasing tourism to the area in the early 20th century, in addition to promoting Walter Alexander's Mayview Park development. *In Cloudland* featured the area in all seasons except for winter, stating "all are delightful, yet each distinctive." Golf is first and foremost in this publication, but also noted are horse riding, pleasure driving, walking, swimming, trap shooting, tennis, fishing, and dancing. Many of the same activities are popular today and depicted through these images in *Blowing Rock Revisited*. The link between tourism and commercial growth was firmly established when the chamber of commerce was organized in 1934, with Mayor Robbins as the first president. He went around the state to promote Blowing Rock, and highlighting attractions back home carried into the decades that followed.

Around 1919, Col. Tom Coffey was responsible for lighting the village's only gasoline street lamp at night. Following the devastating fire of 1923, stone construction proliferated downtown as well as bathrooms, with completion of a city sewer system and ultimately the first paving of Main Street in 1929. Sunset Drive, previously called Boone Street, was resurfaced with crushed stone in the 1930s. These improvements were necessary for the major changes to take place in the 1930s that brought more visitors locally; these included joint promotion of the area undertaken by both Boone and Blowing Rock, the founding of the *Blowing Rocket*, the construction of the Blue Ridge Parkway, the beginnings of the Blowing Rock Country Club, and the development of the Blowing Rock itself as a privately run tourist attraction. The amount of overuse and garbage collection at this latter attraction cannot be overstated, and not all were ready for this change, as a 1933 *Blowing Rocket* comment humorously requested there not be a nudist colony behind the new fence at the rock.

The female campers of Camp Yonahlossee took a trip from Boone to Johnson City on the Tweetsie Railroad in the summer of 1938, taking cameras and making frequent stops along the way. All of North Carolina celebrated Tweetsie Homecoming Day in May 1956, when the more than 60-ton locomotive returned to the state and a year later traveled up the mountain to Blowing Rock. A year after this, the Wild West theme park was established, and Mystery Hill opened nearby. Campers and residents could still visit attractions, but tourist families and visitors became the dominant group, and promotion and marketing of Blowing Rock followed this promotion. The chamber of commerce heavily promoted tourist weekends in autumn in 1961, and the opening of what became the Appalachian Ski Mountain in winter 1962 solidified a year-round destination. Businesses for winter sports appeared, though retail and commercial operations in downtown Blowing Rock remained largely seasonal. The opening of the outlet mall on US-321 in the 1980s eventually created downtown businesses catering to a similar clientele to the point where commercial operations today have more influence locally than before.

A proliferation of hotels, motels, and similar operations in Blowing Rock and on the US-321 bypass also played a significant role in growing the tourism industry, as the only real competition was on East King Street in Boone, evidenced by listings in telephone books from the 1950s to 1980s. Passage of a referendum for legal beer and wine sales and establishment of an ABC store in August 1965 also gave Blowing Rock an advantage for tourist growth and again in March 1986, allowing the sale of mixed drinks in hotels, restaurants, and other establishments. Blowing Rock continues to strike a balance for visitors both young and old, domestic and international alike.

The renovation of Edgewood Cottage by the Blowing Rock Historical Society, opening of the Blowing Rock Art and History Museum (BRAHM), and celebration of the town's 125th birthday in 2014 have kept the history and heritage of the community at the forefront. Effective community growth can be done with respect to the past, and it is comforting that the "sweet smelling air in Blowing Rock" that author John Preston Arthur noted a century ago is still enjoyed today.

One

ATTRACTIONS

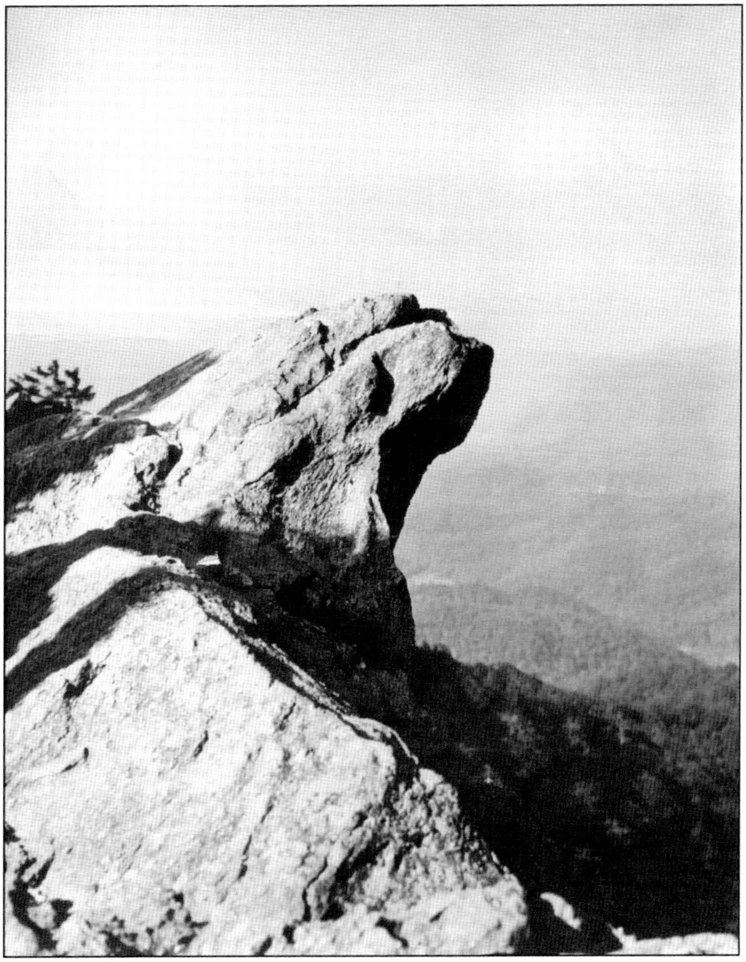

The name of the geological formation itself, officially called the Blowing Rock Gneiss, has beckoned visitors since the mid-19th century. The town is named for this popular curiosity and accompanying legend. The "real" Blowing Rock is over one million years old. Access to the feature was unrestricted until the 1930s, when it became privately run and operated, with the title of "North Carolina's Oldest Travel Attraction."

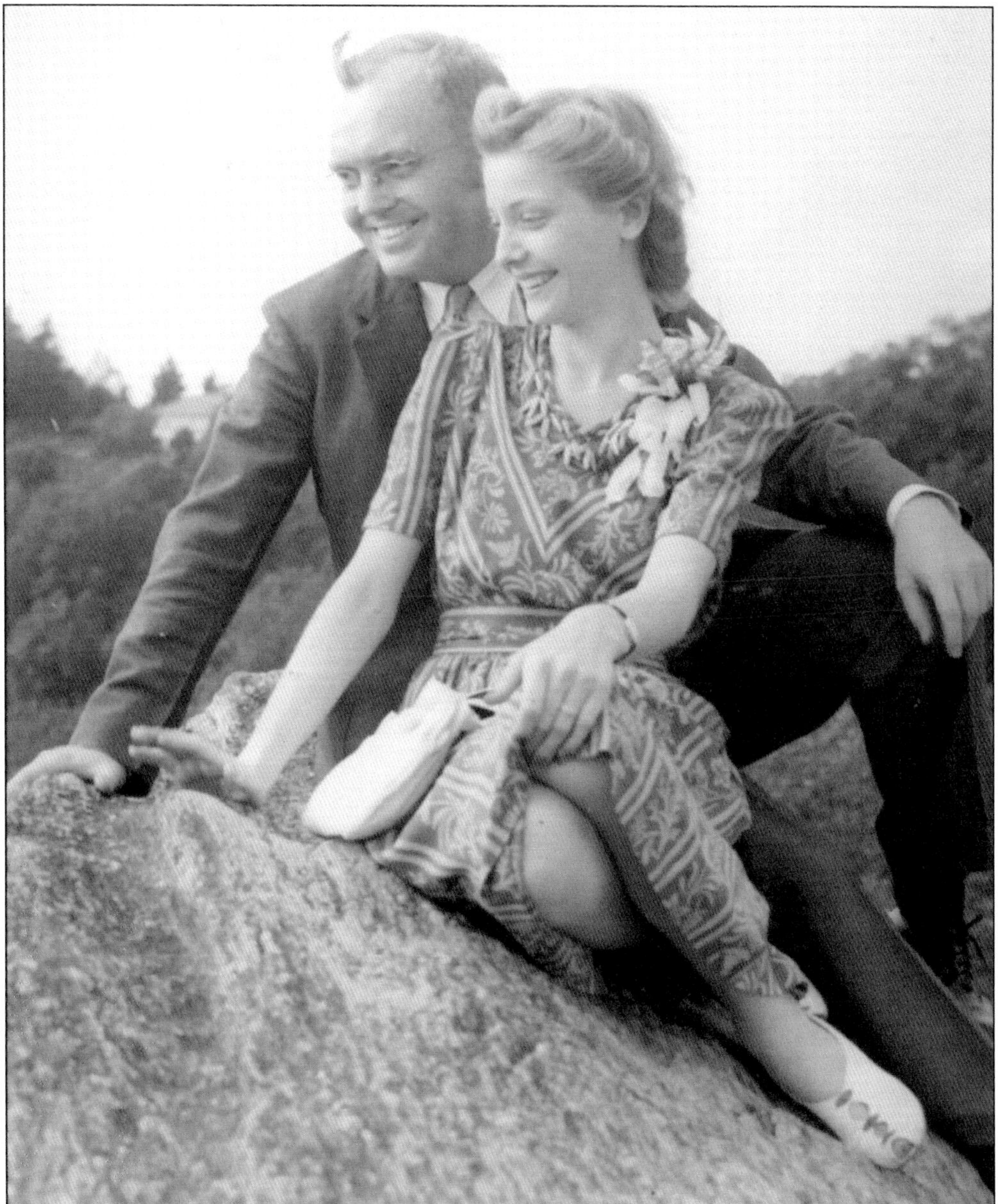

Couples continue to find the Blowing Rock a popular attraction, with marriage ceremonies, honeymoons, and gatherings at the site. The Rock Tavern, opened by Grover Robbins in 1935, became the reception center and gift shop, effectively controlling public access to the attraction. Today, the building's arched entryway and giant stone chimney also house a photograph gallery of local tourist sites. The list of attractions in Blowing Rock constantly changes, yet the Tweetsie Railroad, Mystery Hill, Appalachian Ski Mountain, and the Blowing Rock have all been staples for well over 50 years. Grandfather Mountain, Linville Caverns, the Land of Oz, and the ski mountains in neighboring Avery County were also noted frequently in connection with Blowing Rock tourism. The individuals identified in this image have the last name of Keys, and could very well be related to Dr. Walter K. Keys, reverend of the Rumple Presbyterian Church in the 1940s and 1950s.

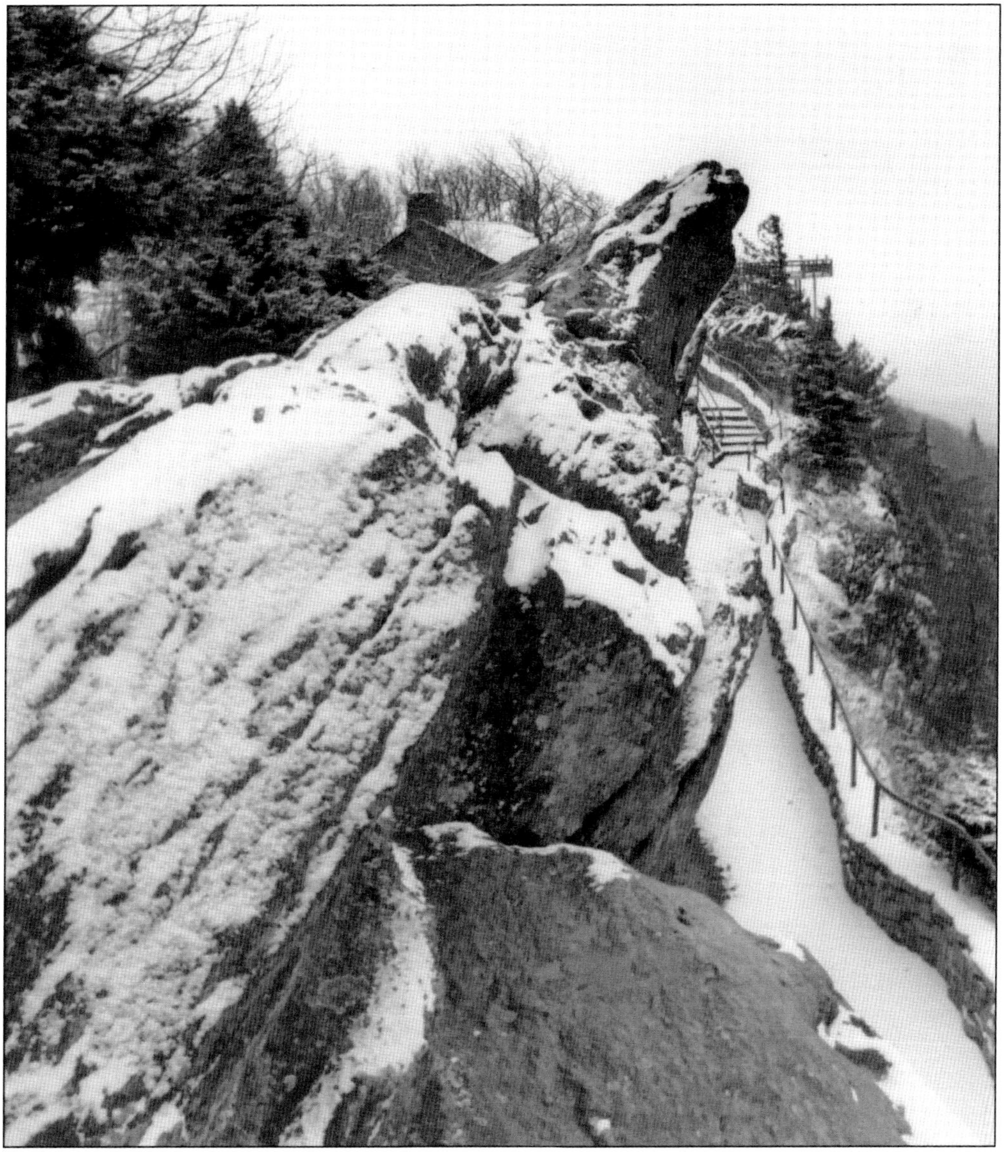

Blowing Rock is the only place in the world where snow falls upside down, according to a *Ripley's Believe It or Not* cartoon. In 2004, the Weather Channel filmed on location and confirmed this phenomenon. Lighter objects cast over the cliff 4,000 feet above sea level have the ability to return with a northwest wind. Most recently, the film *Goodbye Solo* also played off this phenomenon. Hawksbill Mountain, Table Rock, Grandfather Mountain, and Mount Mitchell (highest peak east of the Mississippi River) all are visible from the rock. The forbidden courtship between the daughter of a Chickasaw chieftain and Cherokee brave, torn by duty or love, ultimately ends with the brave leaping to his death. The maiden prays for the Great Spirit to blow her lover back into her arms from the valley below. The legend of the Blowing Rock is enough reason for some to explain why the snow can blow upward.

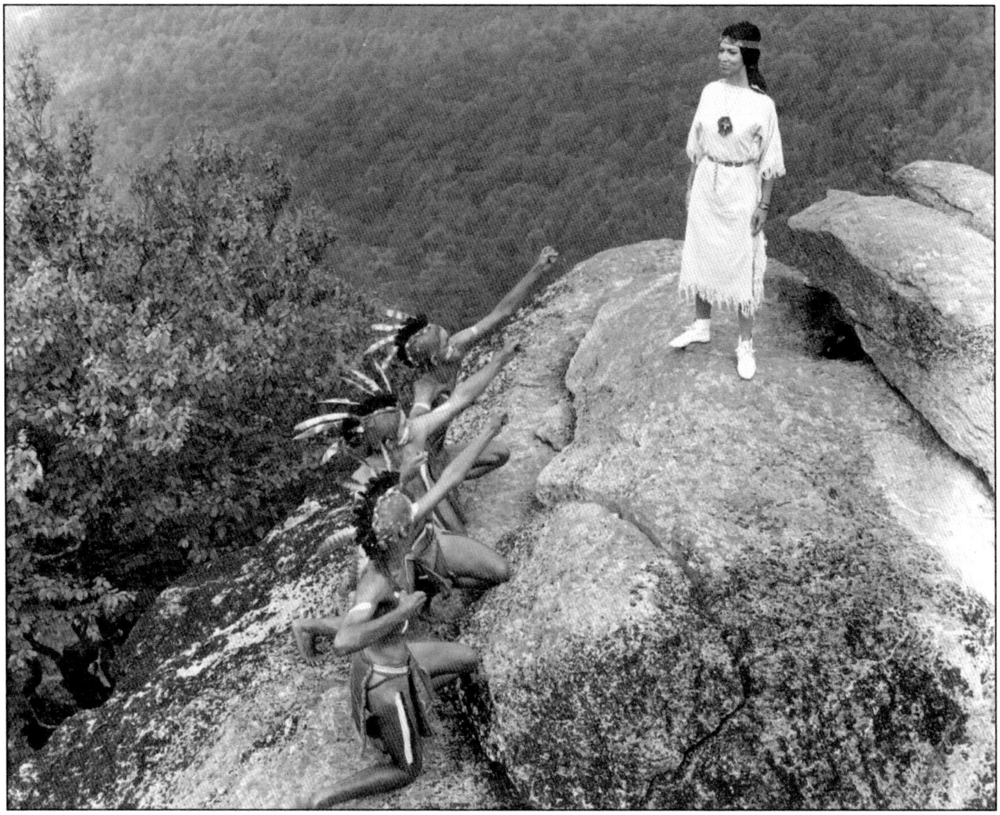

Though located in Boone, the *Horn in the West* production was often featured in the *Blowing Rocket* newspaper, travel publications about the general area, and related promotional shoots at multiple local attractions. Produced since 1952 by the Southern Appalachian Historical Association, North Carolina's Revolutionary War history, featuring Daniel Boone, continues reenactment in this outdoor theater. Despite a cold rainy season, attendance was 21,500 when this photograph was taken.

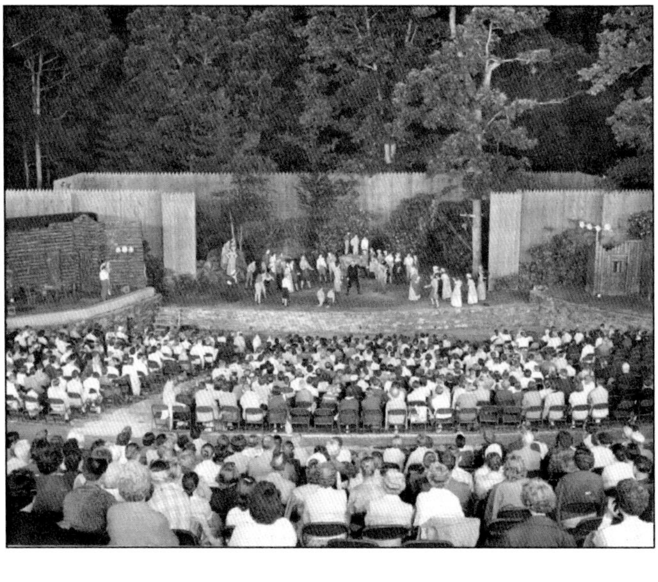

This production of the *Horn of the West* captures a unique moment. Professional and amateur photographers, including Hugh Morton, converged on the Daniel Boone Theatre to "ride in" on the gigantic flash shot set up by Sylvania Electric Corporation. The equivalent of over 60,000 household bulbs were set off simultaneously to light up the entire 2,500-seat venue.

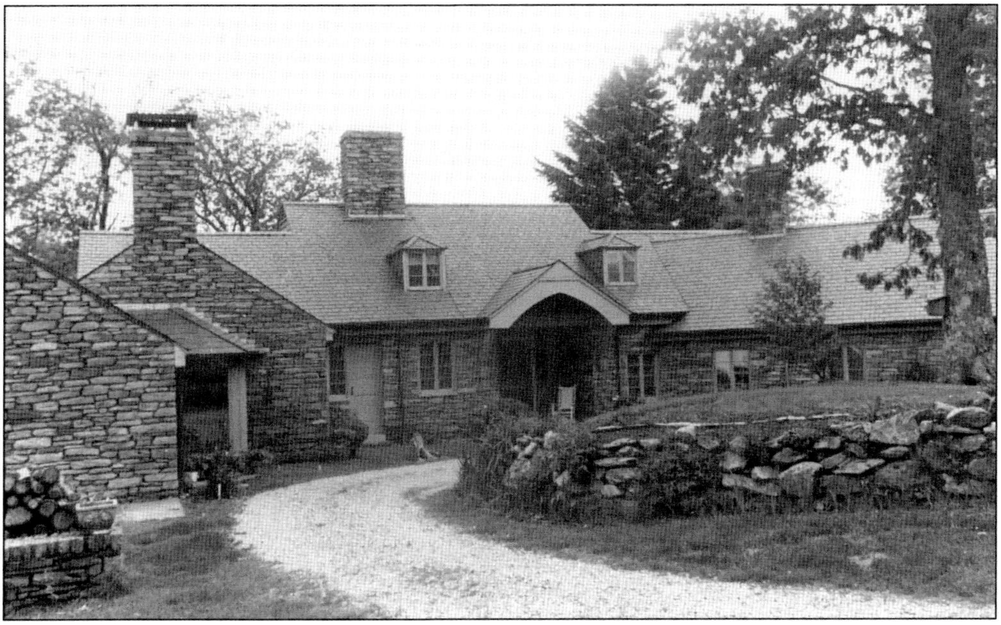

The Gideon Ridge Inn, formerly the home of playwright Norman Lindau, carries on a tradition of residential homes turned into bed-and-breakfasts. The house is built of Grandfather Mountain stone, which is no longer quarried. The grounds were once the location of a portion of the Moses Cone estate orchards, giving some idea of how large this estate once was.

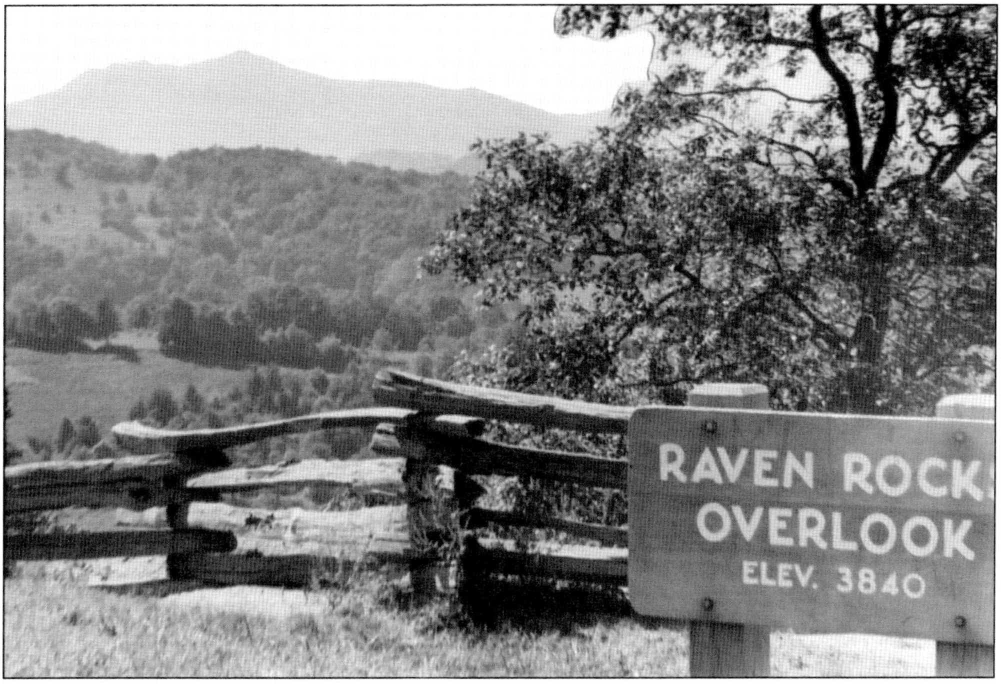

The Raven Rocks Overlook remains a preferred place to watch the sun set. People sometimes gather at overlooks farther west along the parkway after sunset, hoping to catch a glimpse of the Brown Mountain Lights. The Friends of the Blue Ridge Parkway have an adopt an overlook program to help the National Park Service care for these cherished views.

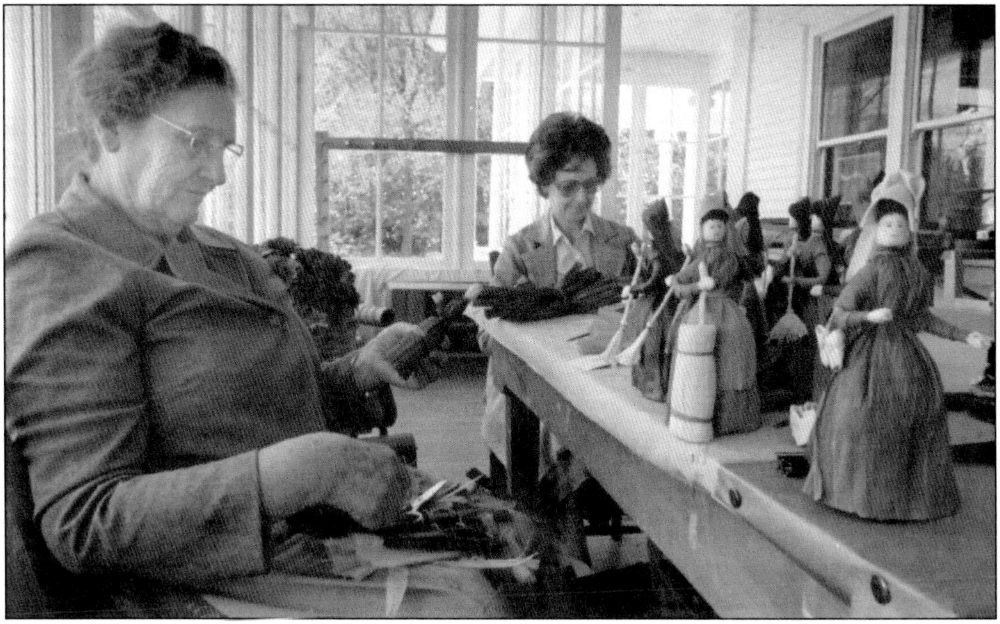

The Southern Highlands Craft Guild operates the Parkway Craft Center at Flat Top Manor. The guild formed in 1930 to preserve, improve, and help market the best in Southern mountain craft. Advertisements for the center are aimed toward summer guests, specifically noting live artistic demonstrations. Lila Marshall and her daughter Phyllis Combs, both from Virginia, are featured at their craft in this 1970s image.

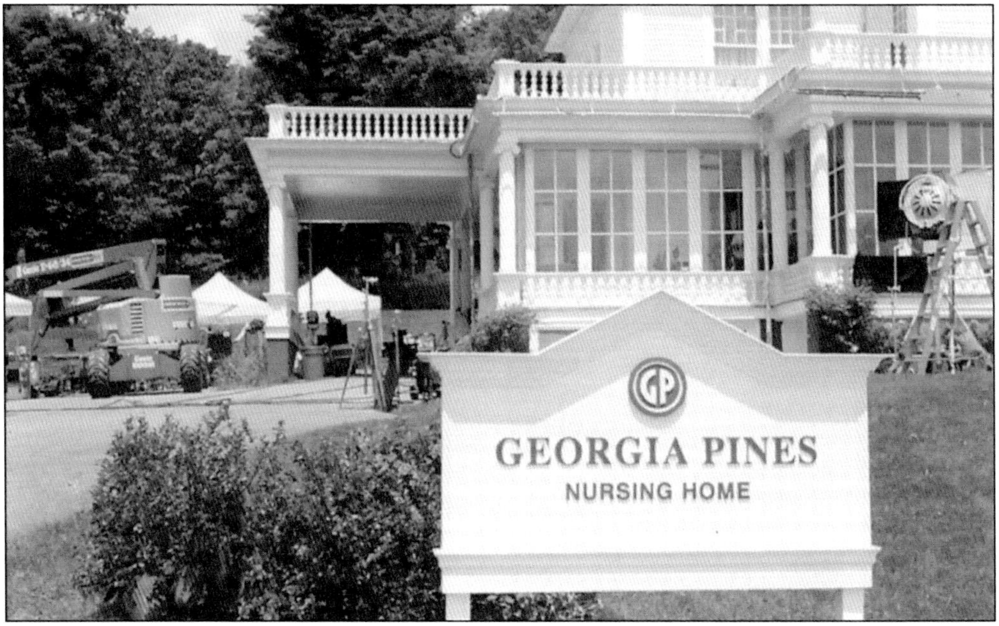

Moses H. Cone Memorial Park, operated by the National Park Service along the Blue Ridge Parkway, originally contained more than 3,600 acres and today includes 25 miles of trails. The architectural features of this Colonial Revival mansion garner attention from residents, visitors, and even filming scouts. Flat Top Manor was renamed the Georgia Pines Nursing Home for opening scenes used in the 1999 film *The Green Mile*.

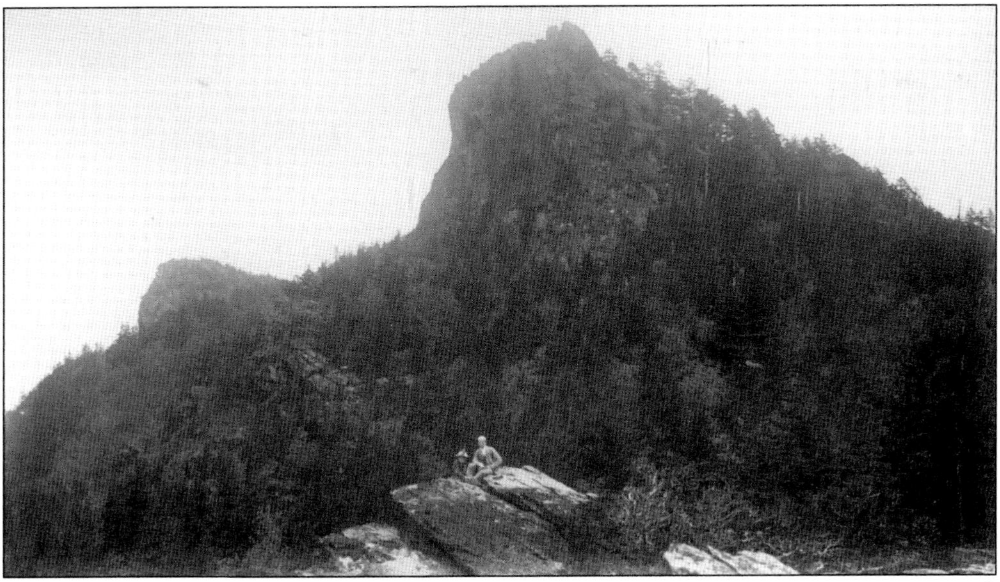

The following is an excerpt from John Preston Arthur's 1915 *History of Watauga County, North Carolina*: "Off to the left from Blowing Rock, seen between near green knobs, the shoreless seas of the lowlands reaches away to leave the edge of the sky. And looking to the right, there lies the calm and noble form of the Grandfather Mountain, its rocky top drawn in a series of curves against the western sky."

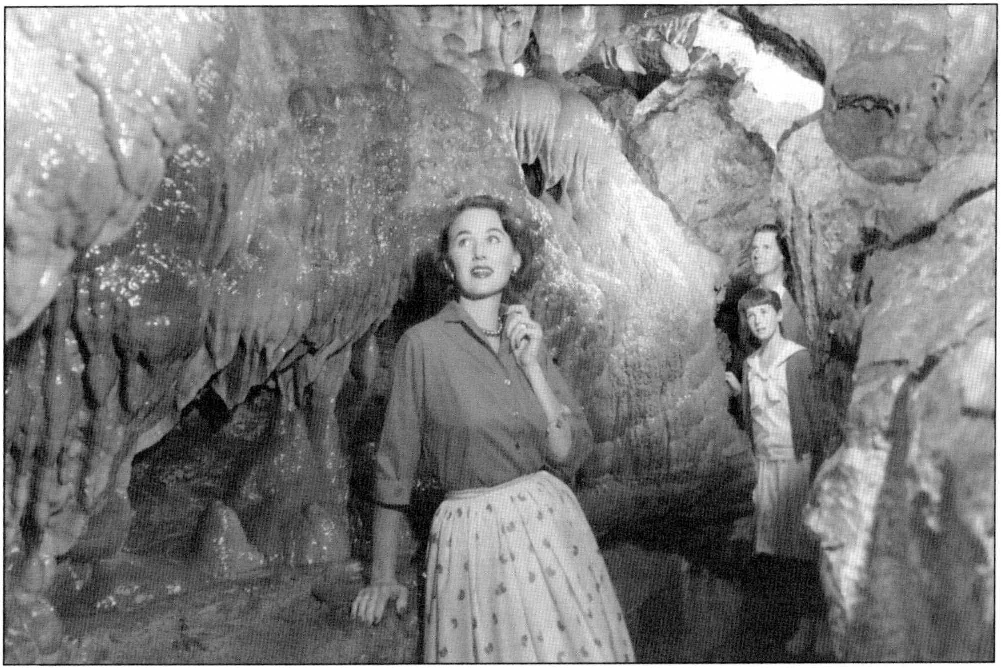

Linville Caverns, located in Avery County along with Grandfather Mountain, also became part of a larger group of regional attractions. Eseeola Lodge, Pinnacle Inn, and the Grandfather Mountain Cabin were just some of the neighboring accommodations featured in the *Blowing Rocket* in the 1930s. Each summer, Linville and Banner Elk hosted traveling performances by the Barter Theater.

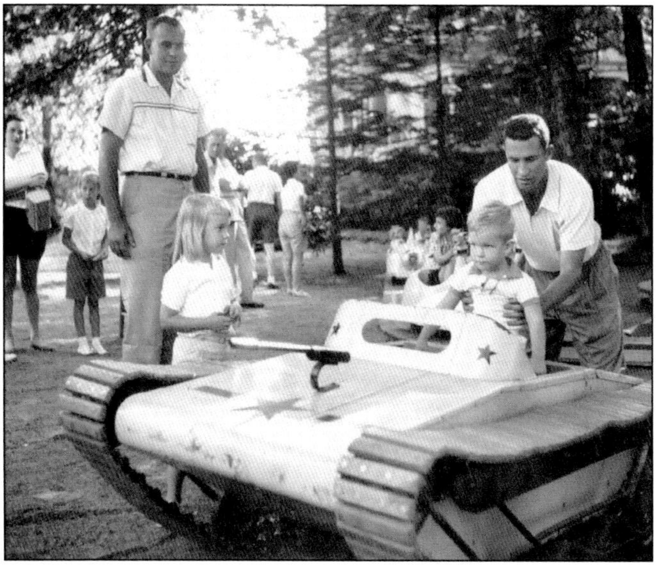

Carter Lentz places a child in a ride at the Skyland Amusement Park, once located near the Blowing Rock. Small but popular, it once included a Ferris wheel in addition to the cars, tanks, and boats on tracks. With the post–World War II baby boom, families vacationed in Blowing Rock and sought out entertainment for all ages.

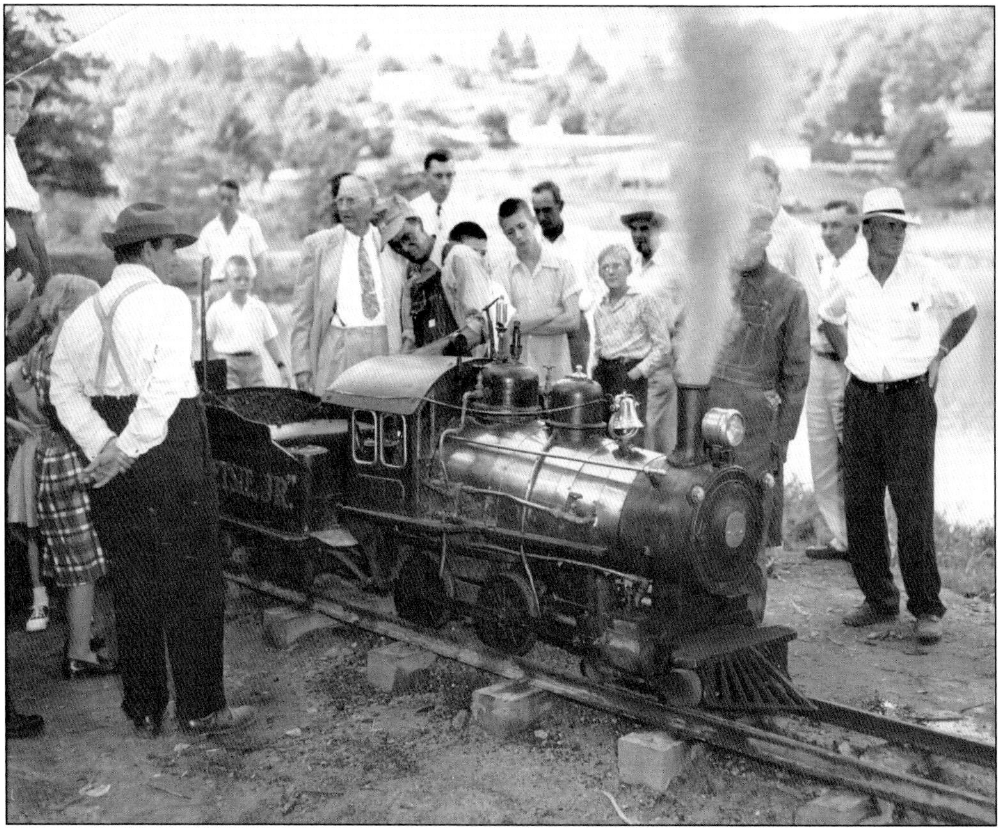

Grover Robbins (in suit and glasses) is among those standing next to the Tweetsie Jr. train, which followed the current walkway around Broyhill Park. Lettering on the side of the train included "Town of Boone's Fork" and "Town of Aho," small communities neighboring Blowing Rock. The former home of Grover Robbins on Park Avenue now fittingly houses the Blowing Rock Chamber of Commerce.

In July 1964, this sign indicated the sights to be seen at Mystery Hill, including "the Revnoor, Grandpa's Cabin, Spooky Spigot, over 250 antiques, and more fun than you can shake a stick at plus the mystery house." Promotion of this attraction always included exotic features, including a past exhibit titled "the valley of little men."

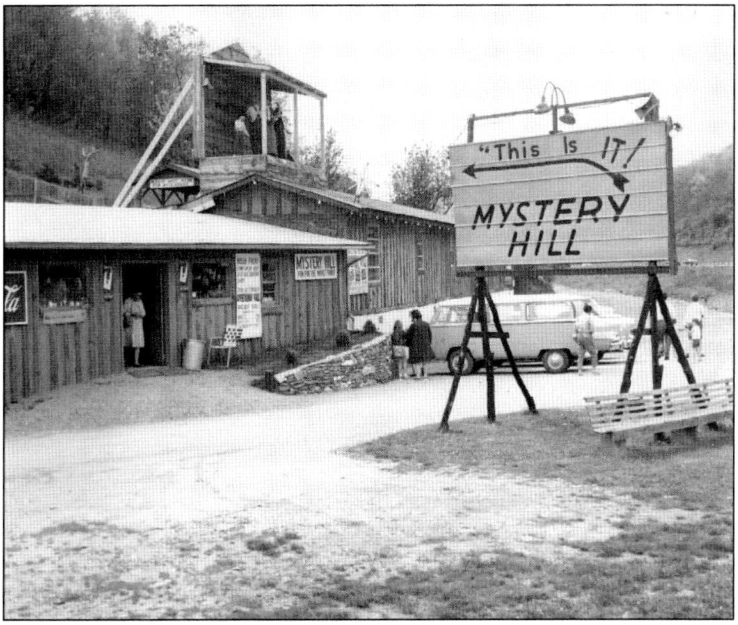

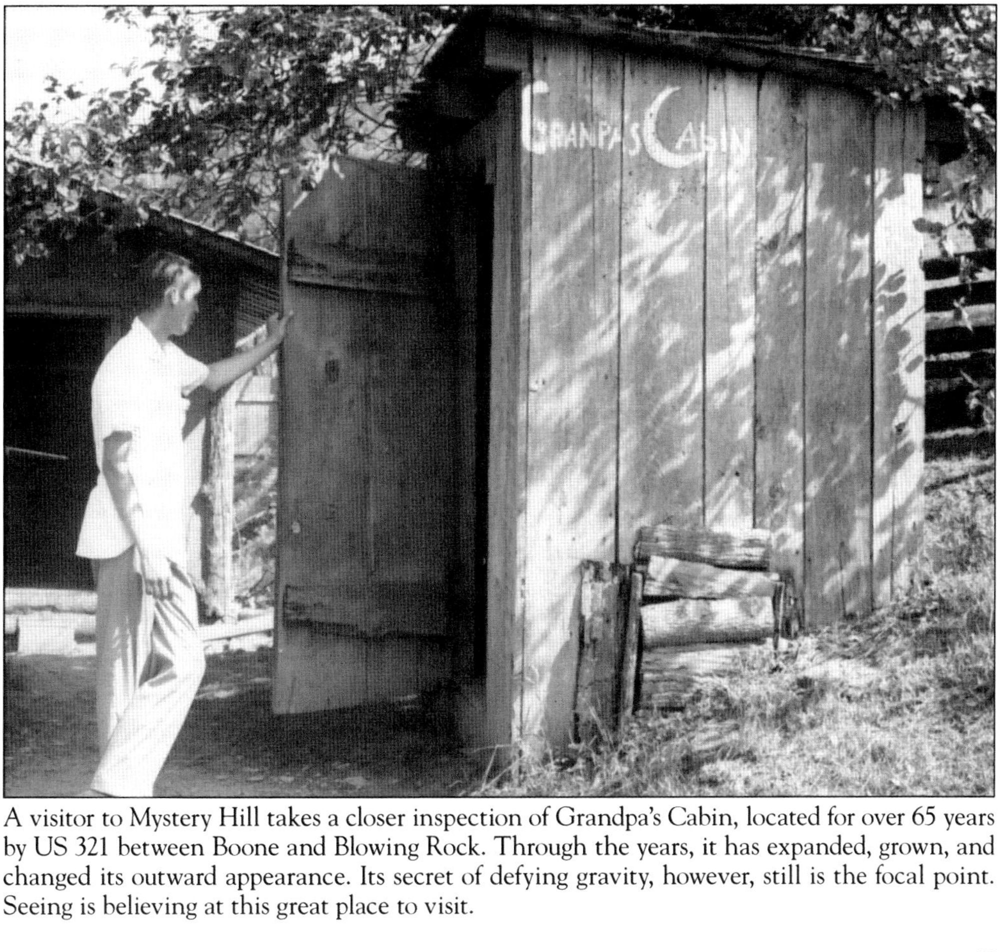

A visitor to Mystery Hill takes a closer inspection of Grandpa's Cabin, located for over 65 years by US 321 between Boone and Blowing Rock. Through the years, it has expanded, grown, and changed its outward appearance. Its secret of defying gravity, however, still is the focal point. Seeing is believing at this great place to visit.

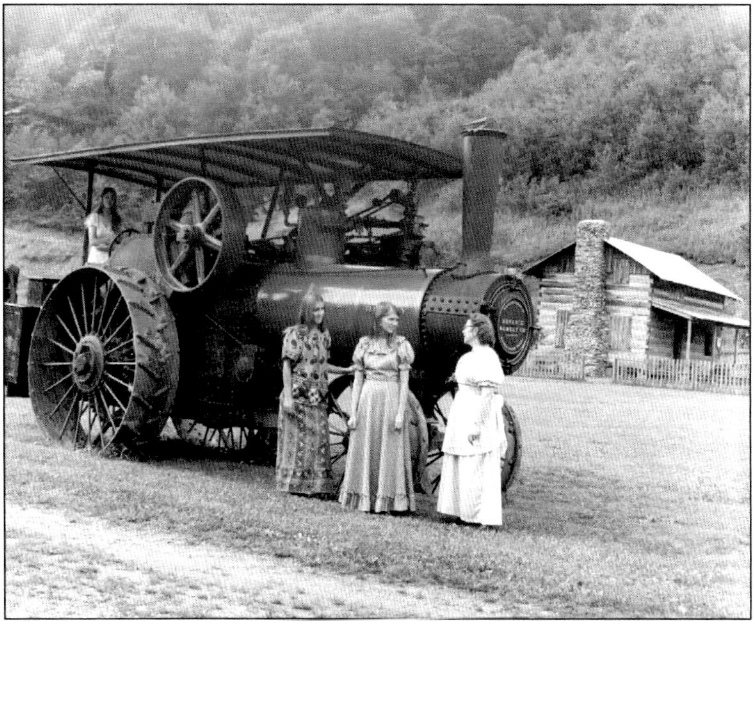

The open fields near the Tweetsie Railroad and Mystery Hill have been utilized in the past for various historical interpretations, including frontier life, Civil War reenactments, and assemblages of old machines. An antique automobile museum started by J.H. Griffin was noted opening near Tweetsie in 1961, with its promotion "let the kiddies ride thc fire engines."

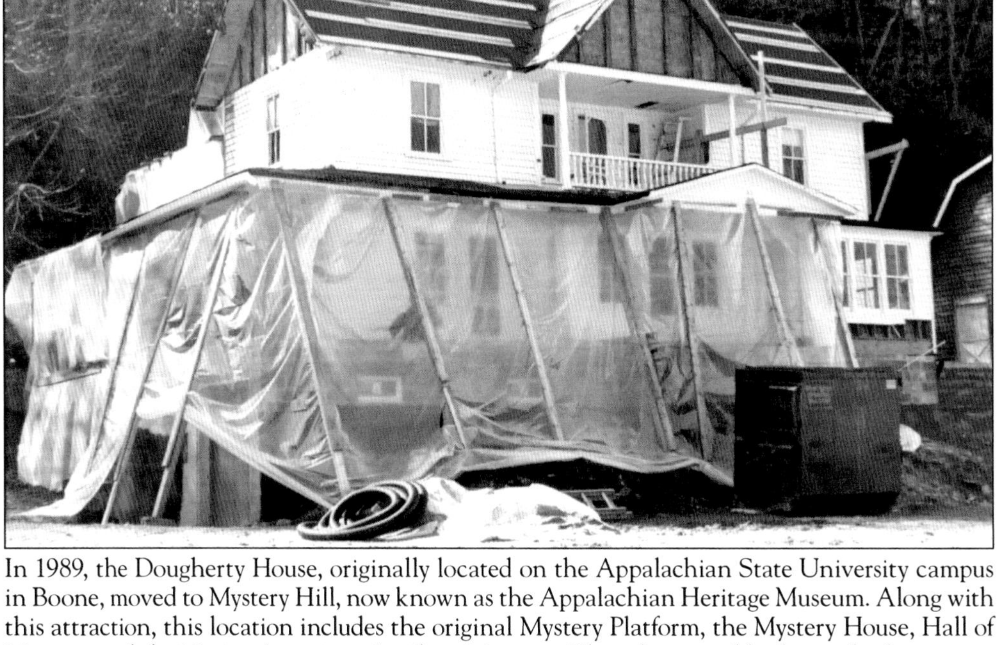

In 1989, the Dougherty House, originally located on the Appalachian State University campus in Boone, moved to Mystery Hill, now known as the Appalachian Heritage Museum. Along with this attraction, this location includes the original Mystery Platform, the Mystery House, Hall of Mystery, and the Native American Artifacts Museum. Though ravaged by fire multiple times in its history, Mystery Hill remains.

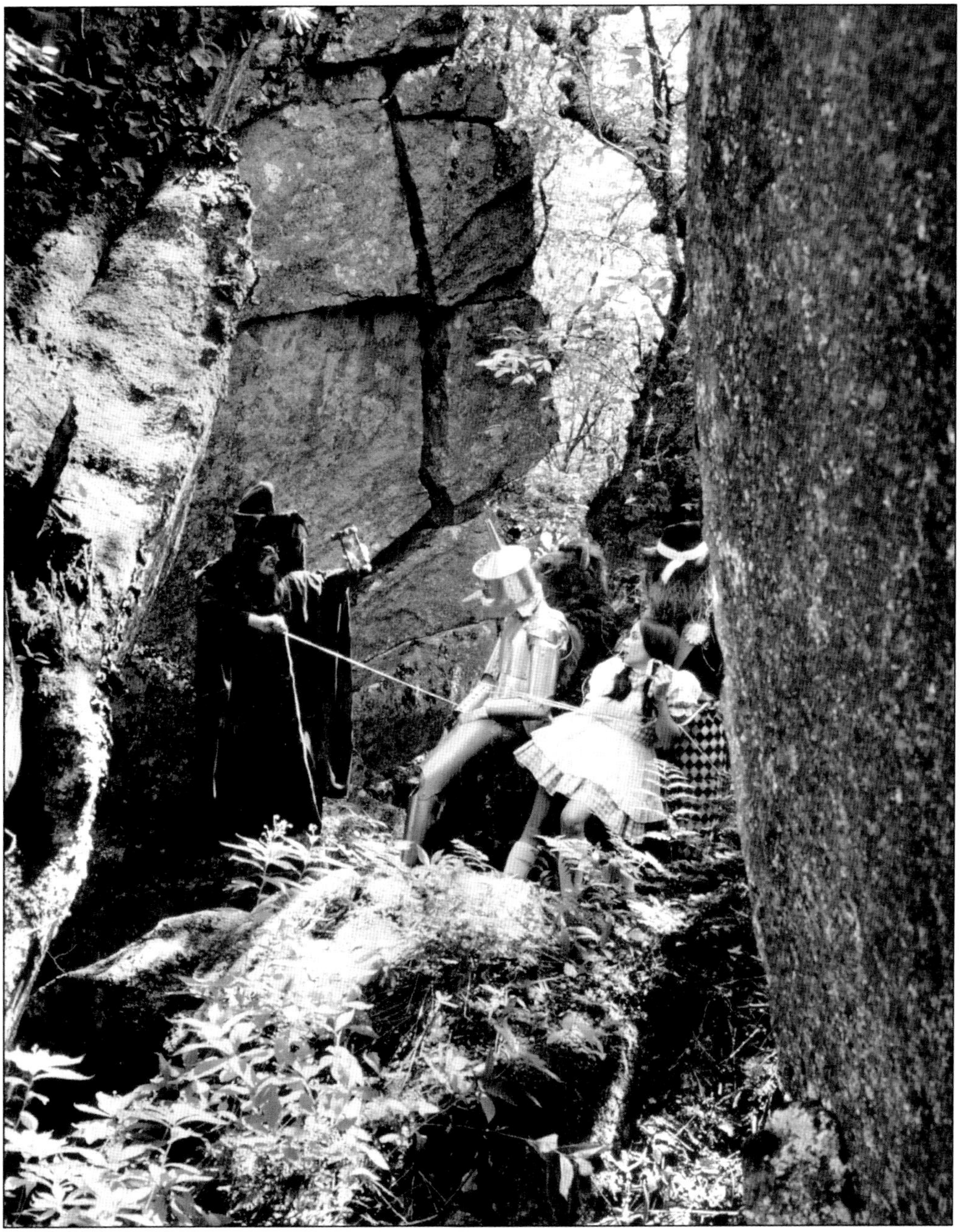

"I'll make stew out of you" says the Wicked Witch, as she temporarily traps those famous Oz characters, Tin Man, the Cowardly Lion, Dorothy, and Scarecrow. The fates of all involved changed by the end of the production, and the Land of Oz became another large-scale area attraction. Grover and Harry Robbins developed the theme park, and ample promotion was given to Blowing Rock guests. By the 1970s, the substantial amount of family fun attractions began to increase visitations by those across North Carolina and the entire South. Thoughts of second homes in the mountains versus the Atlantic coast were beginning to receive equal consideration, and real estate marketing of the time period reflects this. Parts of the park remain on top of Beech Mountain, and visitors can take a nostalgic stroll during Autumn at Oz and other event weekends.

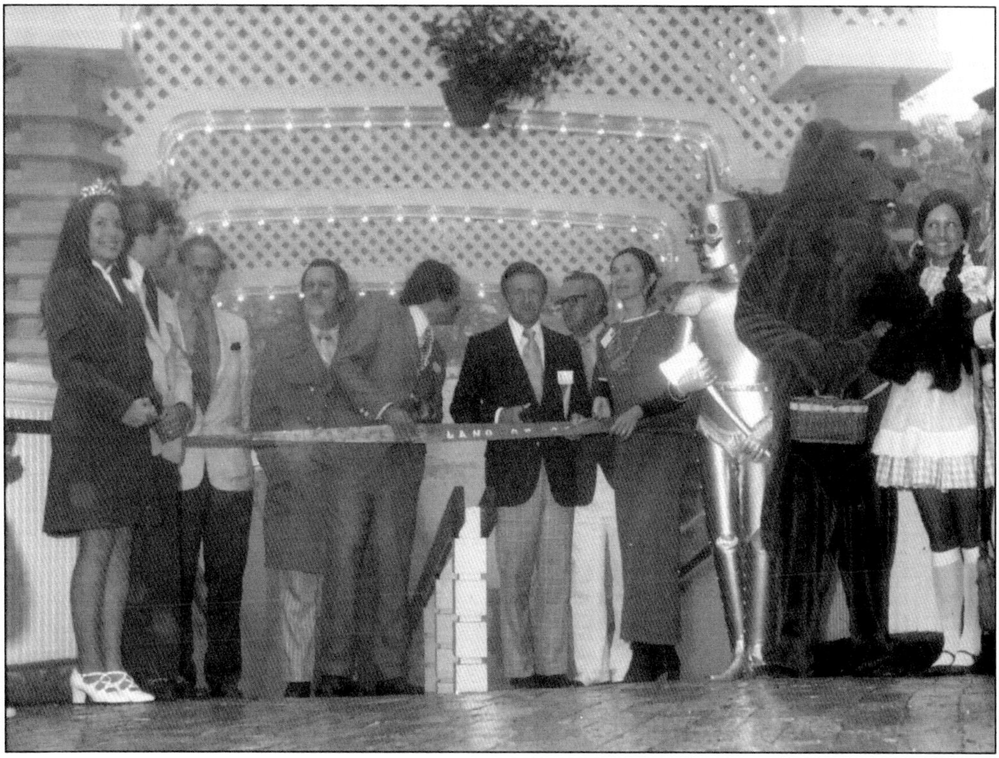

The year 1972 marked the third season opening for Beech Mountain's Land of Oz; the last would be in 1980. Officials and guests of the Carolina Caribbean Corporation are, from left to right, Ms. Watauga County Susan Isley, Oz operations manager Ernie Rhymer, composers Alec Wilder and Loonis McGlohon, designer Jack Pentes, CCC board chairman Harry C. Robbins, writer Kays Cary, choreographer Alice Leggett LaMar, and the costumed characters.

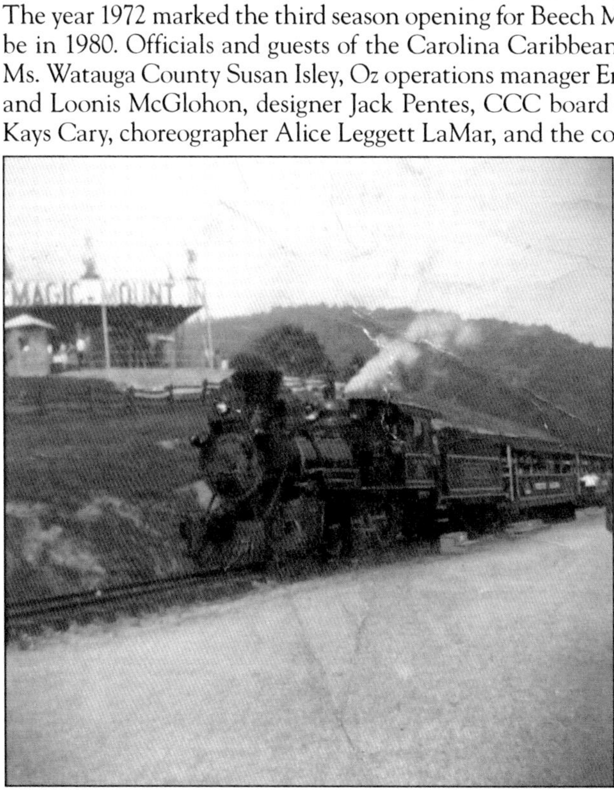

Engine No. 12's path to Blowing Rock included the 40 miles from Hickory and a climb of over 3,000 feet by flatbed truck. In 1961, a total of 200,000 visitors were estimated at Tweetsie, and its Wild West theme was firmly established with the Golden Nugget saloon, stagecoach, Wells Fargo office, village, fire engine museum, marshal's office and jail, authentic blacksmith shop, tintype photography studio, and country store.

Fred Kirby stands in the lower left corner with a large group of visiting foreign-exchange students arranged through the local Rotary. A state television star, he began as Tweetsie sheriff in 1959. His classic red cowboy shirt with white fringe, a cream-colored Stetson hat, leather gun holster with silver buckle, and initialed leathered boots and saddle were some of the items lost in a Tweetsie Museum fire.

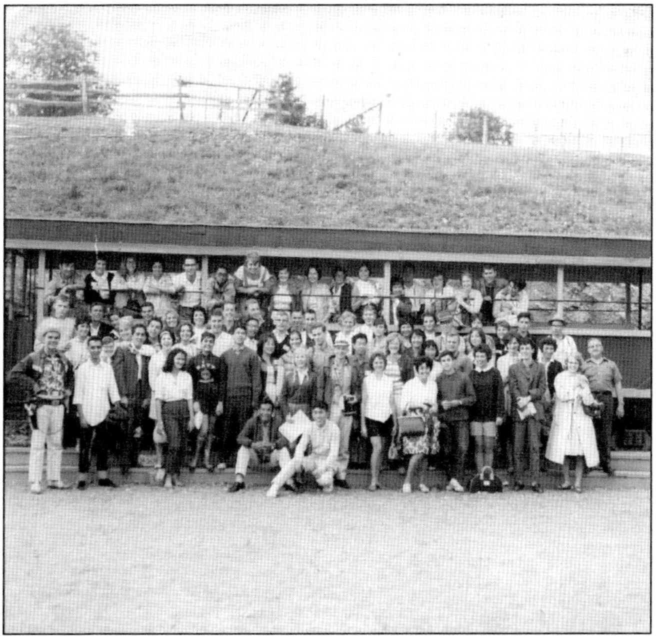

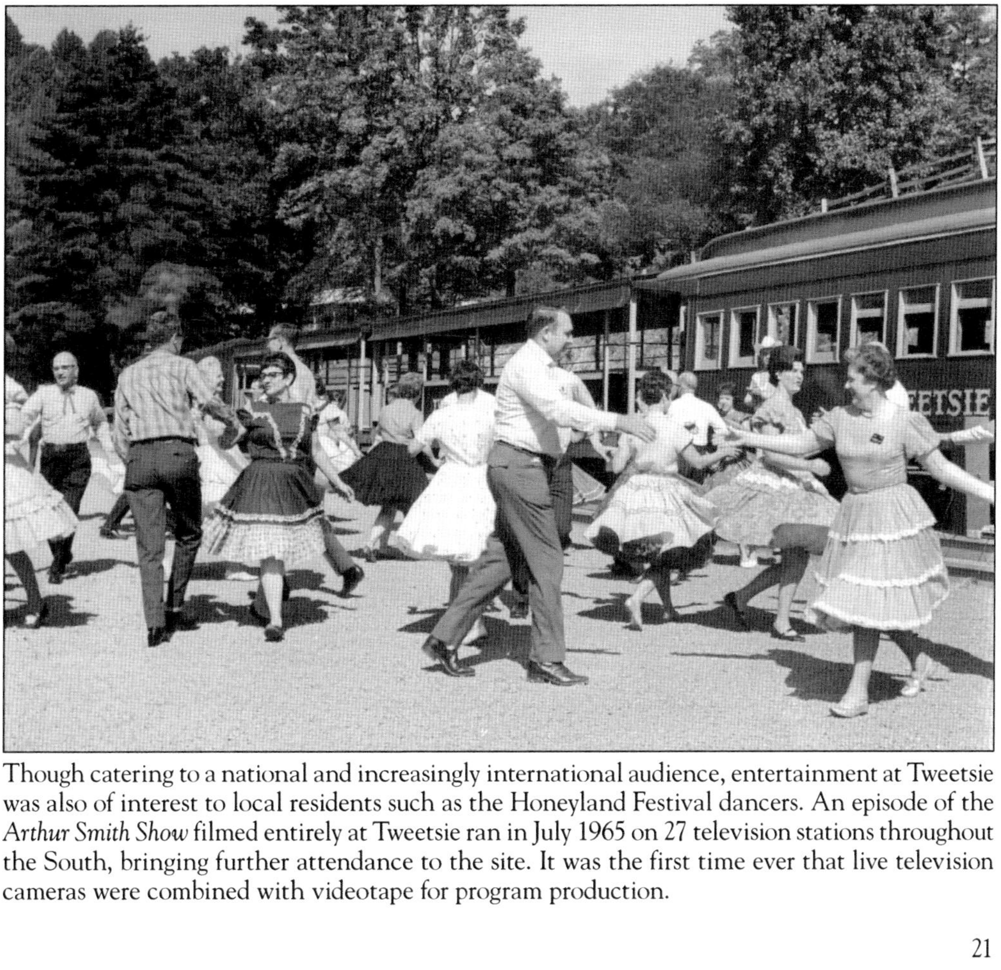

Though catering to a national and increasingly international audience, entertainment at Tweetsie was also of interest to local residents such as the Honeyland Festival dancers. An episode of the *Arthur Smith Show* filmed entirely at Tweetsie ran in July 1965 on 27 television stations throughout the South, bringing further attendance to the site. It was the first time ever that live television cameras were combined with videotape for program production.

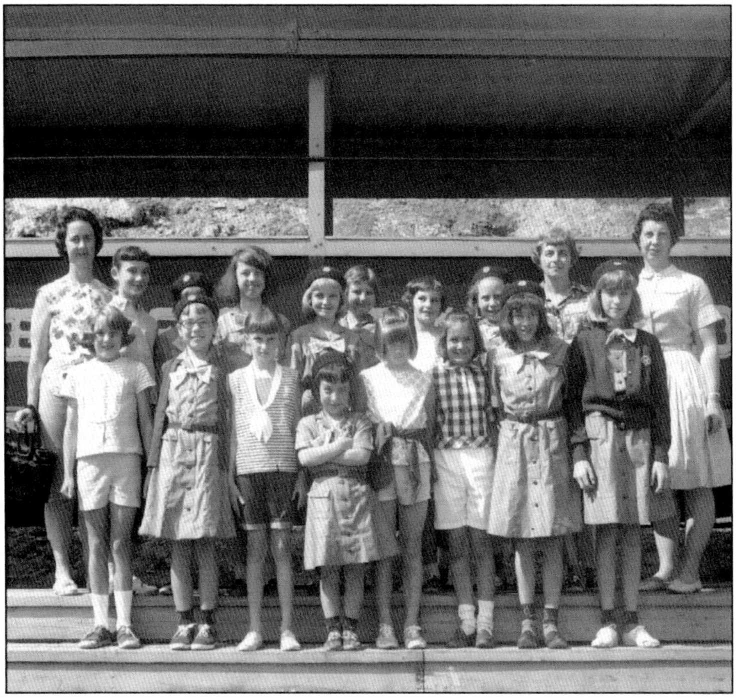

This Junior Girl Scout troop spent the day at Tweetsie in 1965. From left to right are (first row) Nancy Pitts, Louise Hansen, Kay Walker, Mel Hartley, Vicki Coffey, Deborah Walters, Cathy Castle, and Ella Greene; (second row) Mrs. George Baker, Joy Dale, Vivian Baker, Martha Tyson, Debbie Presnell, Mary Ann Brooks, Beverly Grindstaff, Anne Greene, Mrs. Vaughn Hartley, and Mrs. Jay Greene.

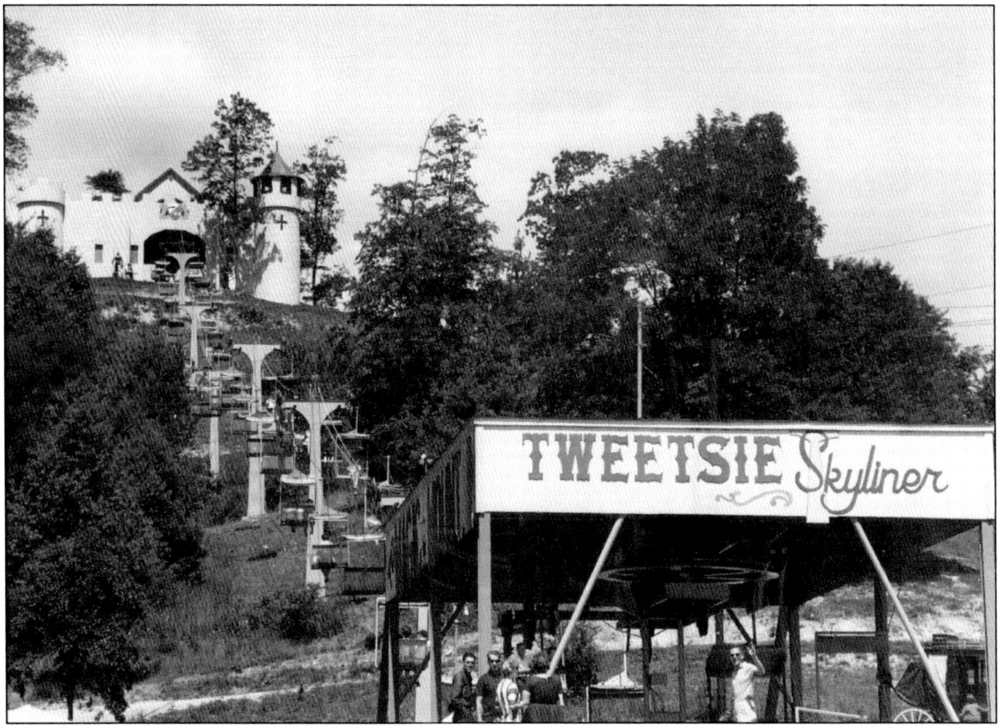

Advertising in 1962 said the Tweetsie Palace Steak House served the best steaks east of Kansas, with "can can girls, barbershop quartet, brass band, folk singers. " A chair lift was constructed to Magic Mountain (later renamed Miner's Mountain), and the park expanded with additional amusement rides. Visitors discovered a sleeping snoring giant as the resident of this pink castle.

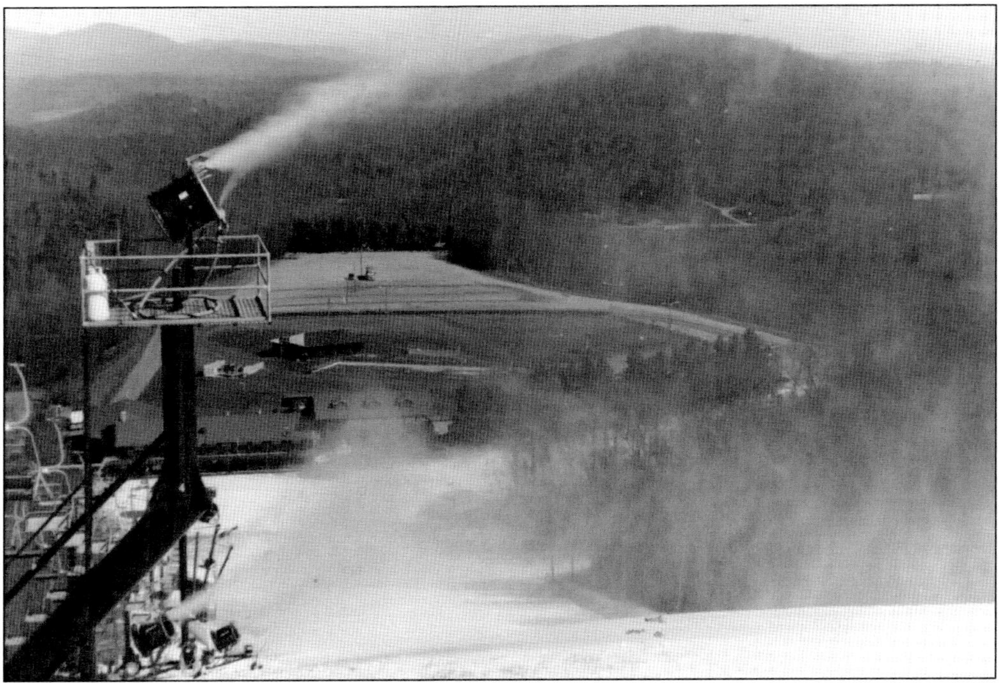

It does not matter that there is no naturally falling snow in the background; the original equipment resembled a gun on a tripod before a computerized snowmaking pumping system was installed at Appalachian Ski Mountain in 1993. The Blowing Rock Ski Slope opened on March 3, 1962. Ironically, the opening was delayed due to an abundance of snow, which slowed construction.

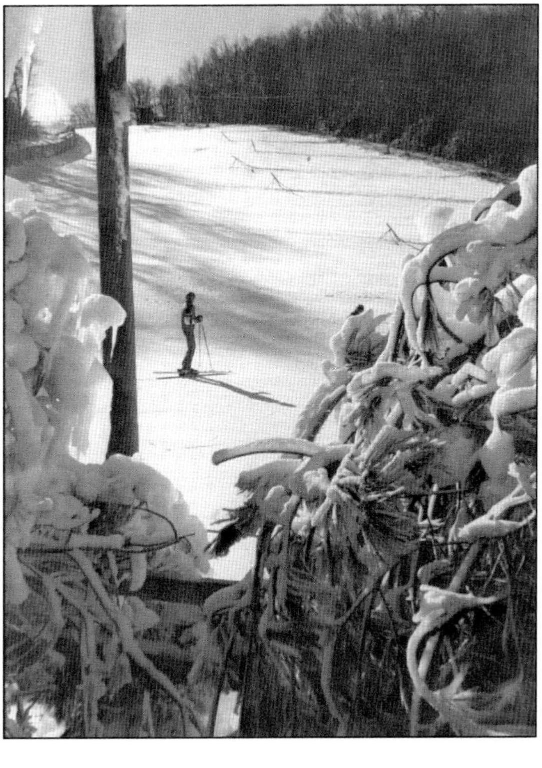

A solitary skier is pictured here among the positioned snow guns; 500 hours of snowmaking has been the average production in recent years. The Blowing Rock Ski Lodge and the Hound Ears Ski Area made covers of magazines frequently, including the cover photograph of the North Carolina *State Magazine* in 1964. Attendance already topped 12,000 by its second year, 1963.

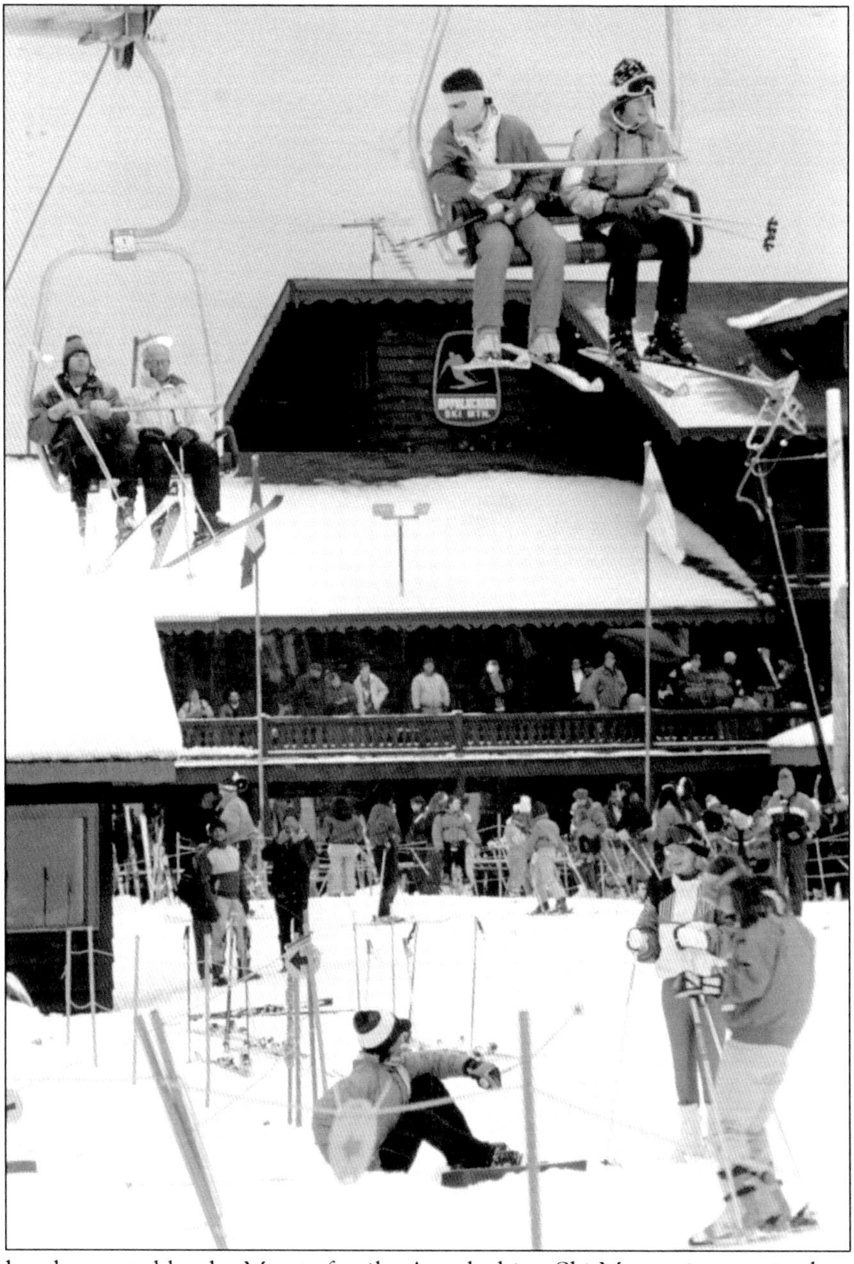

Owned and operated by the Moretz family, Appalachian Ski Mountain remains busy every winter weekend. The massive ski lodge completed in 1962 lends to the European old-world atmosphere, and past New Year's Eve events have included dancing and a torchlight parade. The venue features a dozen slopes and trails for skiing and snowboarding, six lifts, and an ice-skating rink. The French-Swiss Ski College on-site taught its one millionth lesson in 2005 and has given lessons to Green Berets, Navy Seals, West Point instructors, Marines, and Secret Service agents. The impact of the ski industry also broadened the retail offerings in Blowing Rock to clothing, equipment, and related merchandise. Appalachian State University's student population growth has also led to a steady supply of experienced and first-time skiers. Beech Mountain Resort and Sugar Mountain Resort provide additional ski mountains in the area.

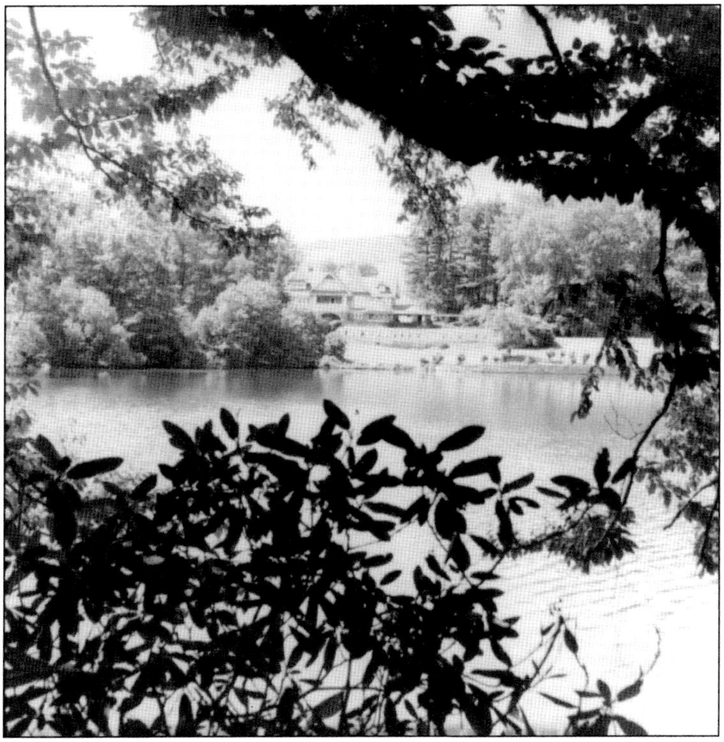

This early view of the property currently known as Chetola, said to mean "haven of rest" in the Cherokee language, showcases its landscape and natural setting. The location has become an attraction on its own with the annual festival of lights, polar plunge, wine festival, and symphony by the lake.

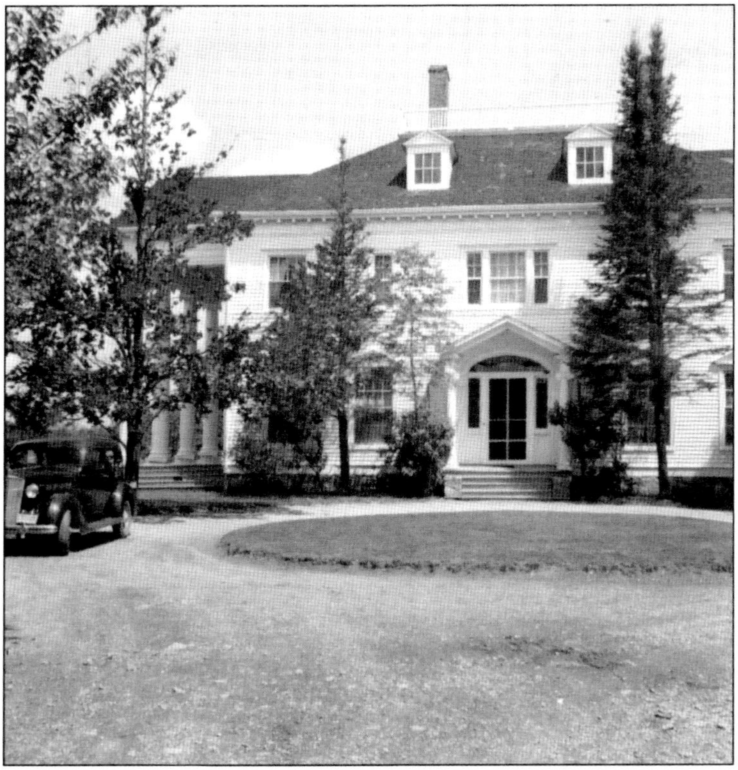

Construction of Westglow, home of famed artist and writer Elliott Daingerfield, began in 1916. The majestic Grecian columns were shipped from Italy by barge, and the elaborate construction was observed by local residents with awe. Now the internationally recognized Westglow Resort and Spa, the 42-acre estate is listed in the National Register of Historic Places.

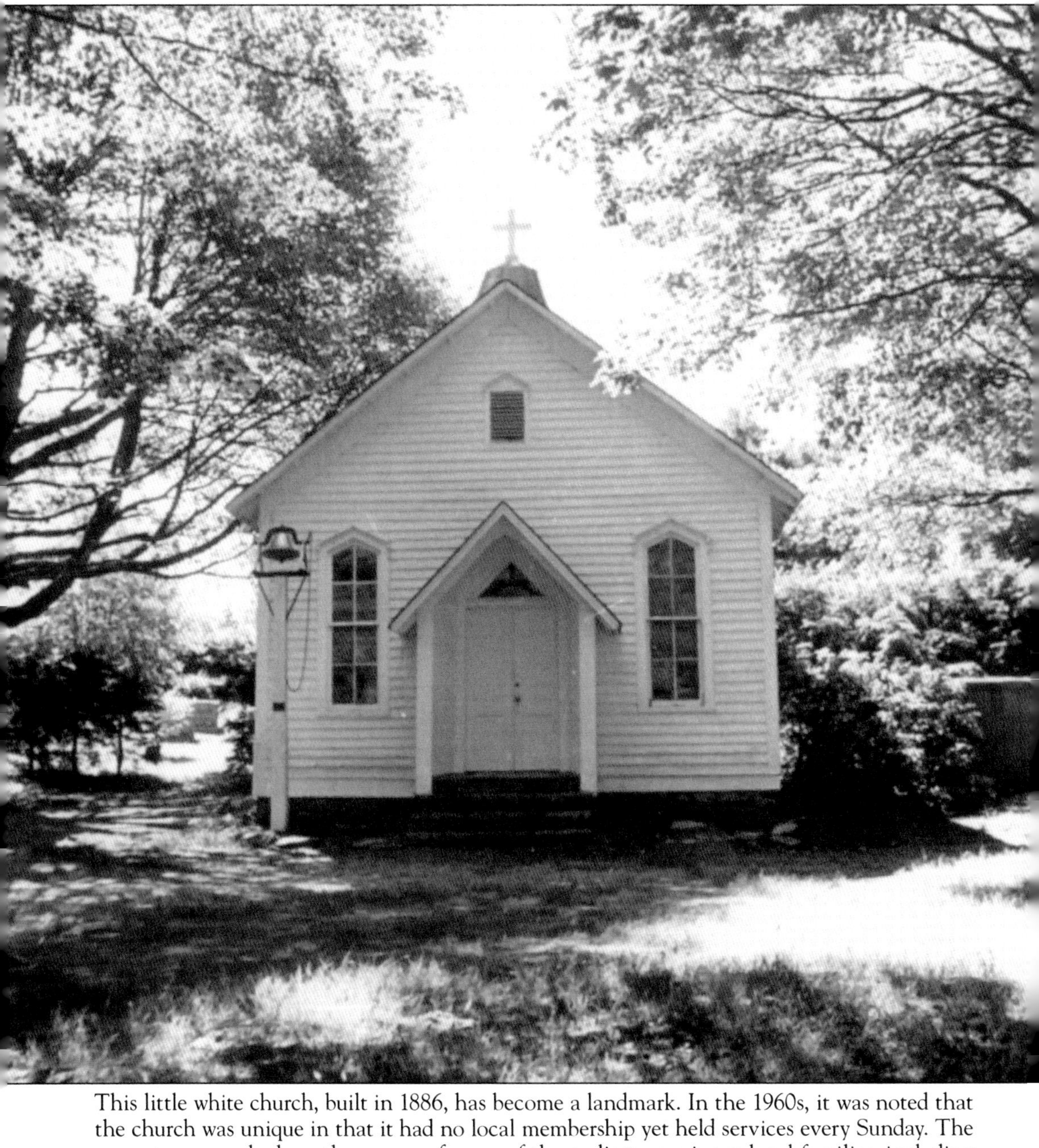

This little white church, built in 1886, has become a landmark. In the 1960s, it was noted that the church was unique in that it had no local membership yet held services every Sunday. The gravestones nearby bear the names of some of the earliest prominent local families, including Lentz, Holshouser, Greene, Robbins, Hayes, Coffey, and others. The structure is a simple weatherboarded frame building with a gable roof, stone foundation, pointed-arched windows with a four-over-four sash, double-leaf entrance, and a small three-sided reach apse. Awareness, education, and preservation of the architectural landscape of Blowing Rock through organizations such as the Blowing Rock Historical Society have increased its appreciation and visitation. Nearby is the Blowing Rock Conference Center, whose mission is to provide a special place where God's people can gather for community development, education, and spiritual growth. In a list of Blowing Rock attractions, it is easy to overlook the architecture and quiet spaces throughout the area.

Two

COMMERCE

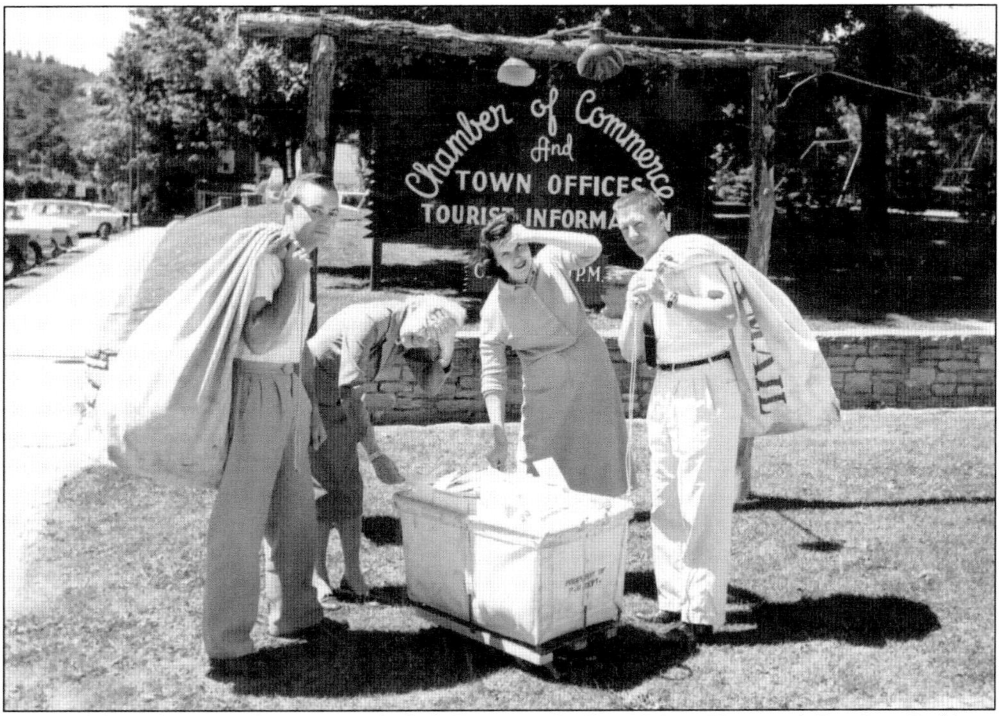

Pictured from left to right are postal clerk Everette Coffey, Helen Clear and Carolina Robbins of the chamber of commerce, and postmaster Harry Robbins. An influx of mail inquiring "What about this place called Blowing Rock?" was received in response to an article in *Parade* magazine in the late 1950s. The businesses of Blowing Rock cater to a mix of year-round and seasonal customers.

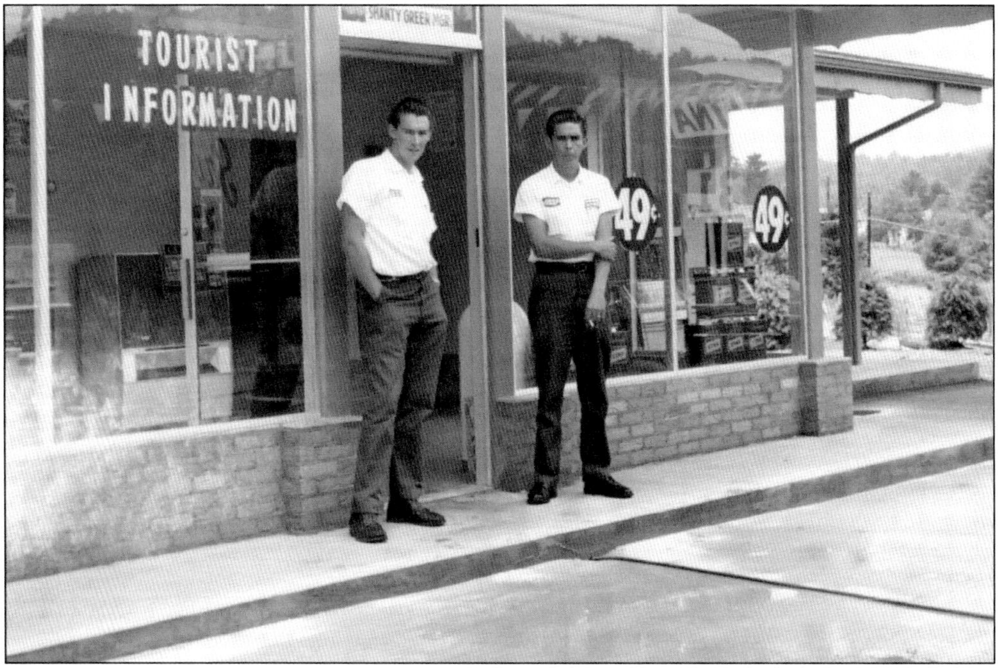

Brooks and Shanty Greer and other local businesses were outlets for tourist information in the mid-20th century. Editorials in the local paper in the late 1950s made comparisons to other mountain tourist destinations and asked, "Why not more people in Blowing Rock?" The chamber of commerce transitioned to the marketing theme "Holiday Highlands" at the time.

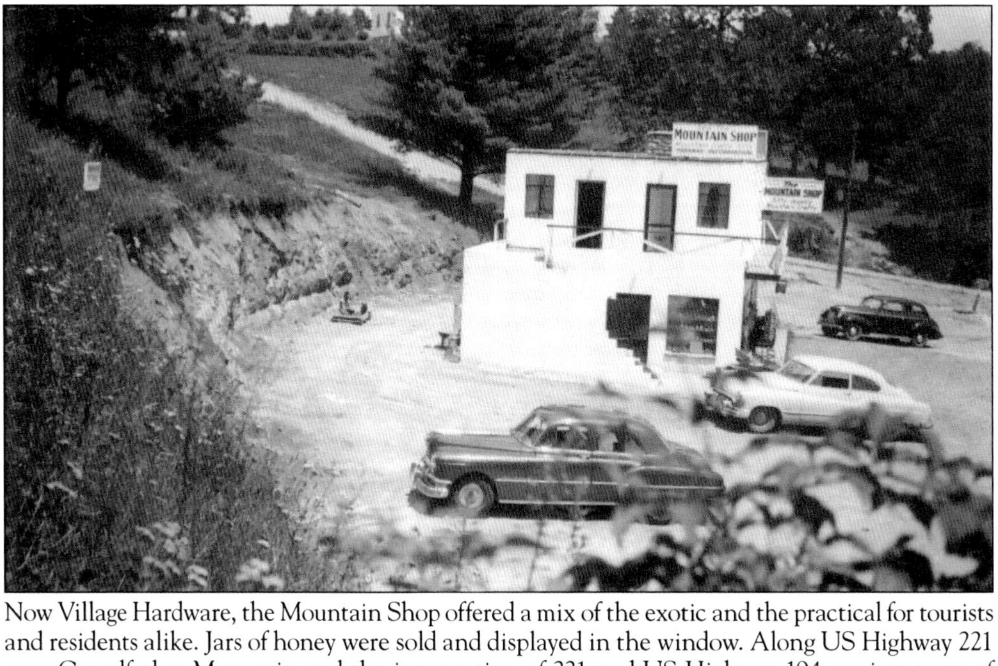

Now Village Hardware, the Mountain Shop offered a mix of the exotic and the practical for tourists and residents alike. Jars of honey were sold and displayed in the window. Along US Highway 221 near Grandfather Mountain and the intersection of 221 and US Highway 194 are just some of the many locations local honey is sold today in the High Country area.

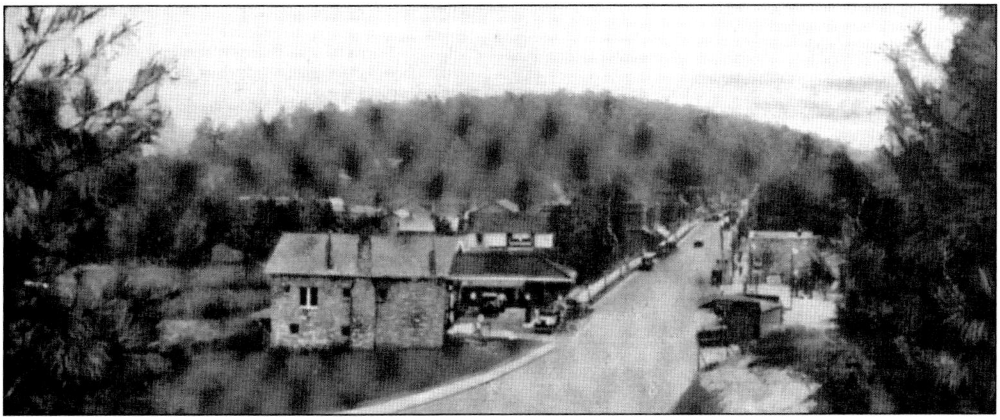

The first building approaching Main Street on the left was Lentz's Esso station, adjacent to the Greyhound and Queen City bus coach company structure (also known as Trailways and later Trexler's Hardware store). Stonemasons constructed the Esso station, and the shed-roofed frame addition originally served as a car wash. Across the street stands the Parkway Hotel, also one of the many former homes to the local post office.

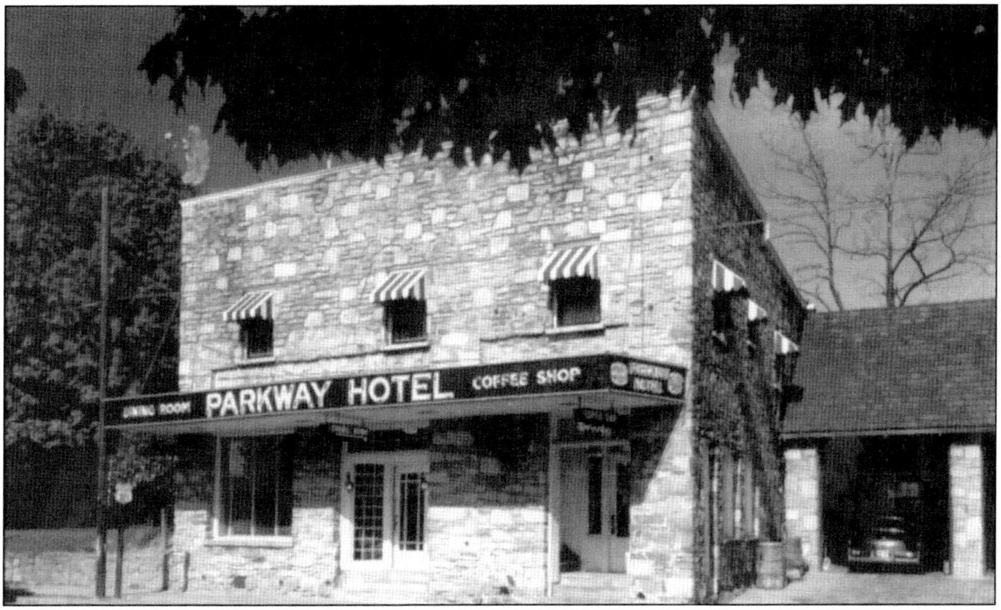

From a Parkway Hotel advertisement: "Rules for the guests in this house, Breakfast, when your rest's complete, Luncheon, anytime you choose, Dinner, when you like to eat, bedtime, when you want to snooze; clothes, wear anything you please, our jokes, you needn't laugh at these. P.S. If these rules are so strict, you cannot obey them, just write your own rules, and we'll gladly O.K. 'em."

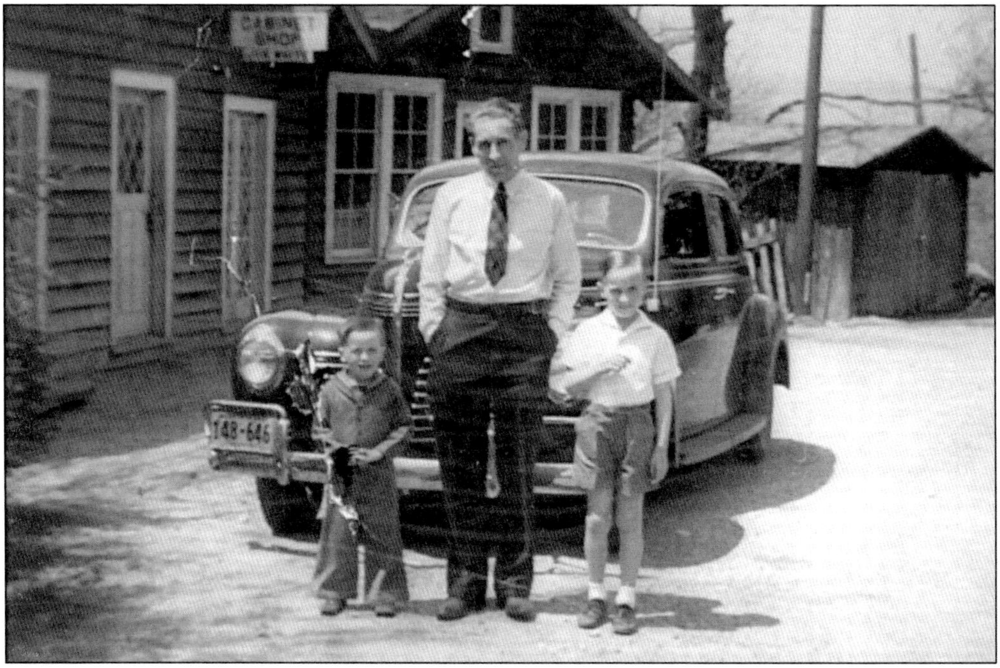

This photograph in front of White's Cabinet Shop contradicts the images of mountain people that were distributed during this time. Year-round residents typically appeared well dressed in front of their residences and businesses and took pride in these images. In shifting to a resort community with added customers, some businesses succeeded in remaining family owned and operated.

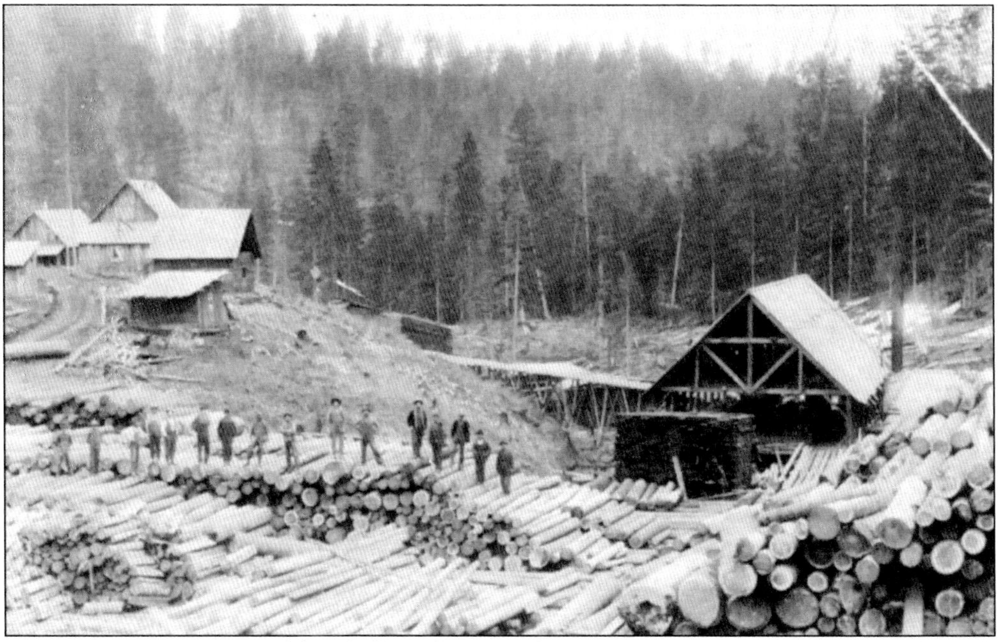

Places in Watauga County like Shulls Mill and Todd profited from lumbering in the early 20th century. The addition of railroad lines allowed these temporary operations, which were badly damaged in the 1940 flood and not rebuilt. Detailed interior woodwork in many residences may have been milled locally, but largely the mills shipped lumber to distant markets.

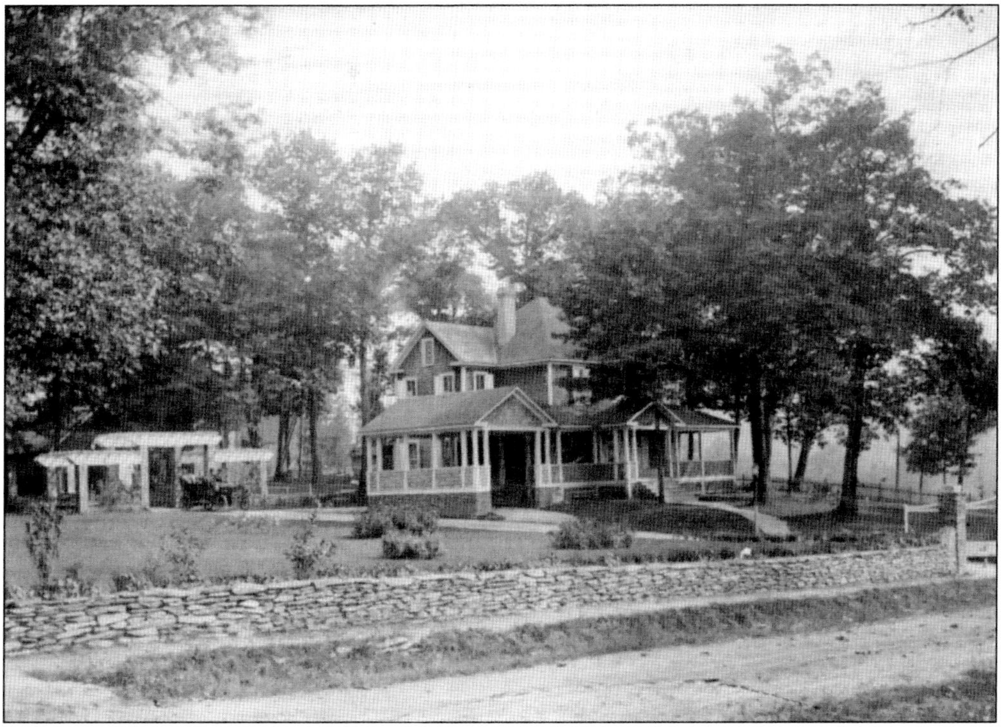

The A.W. Washburn House, now the Inn at Ragged Gardens, was built in 1900 on 11 acres, complete with riding trails. The house is demonstrative of the proximity of residences with downtown commercial buildings. The property, with its stone fences and vegetation, contributes to this blending of a unique cultural landscape. Craftsman bungalows and American Four Squares are architectural styles still found in town.

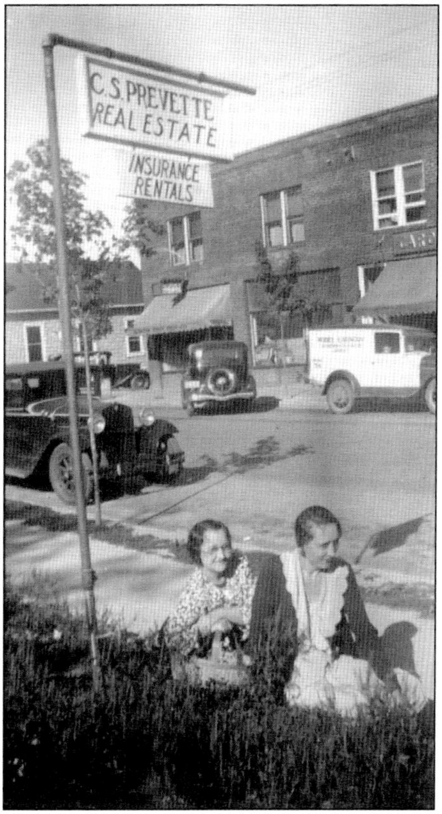

In addition to the insurance rental signage in front and the Blowing Rock Drug Company in back is the truck for Model Laundry, based in Lenoir. A decade after the fire of 1923, stone comprised the primary rebuilding material for downtown to reflect a natural setting. The town today continues this interaction of people and nature.

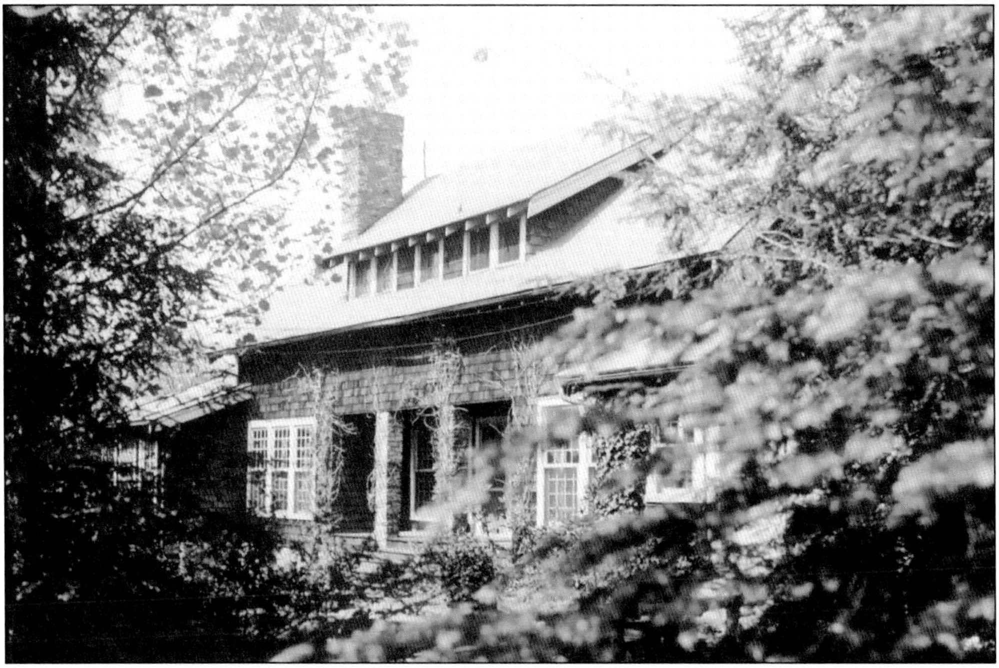

The Hob Nob Inn began as a teahouse "for conversation and refreshment." The most complete map and road information could also be found here, according to newspaper advertisements in 1938, and the property was later named the New Watauga Inn. Nearby Boone now features a Hob Nob Farm Cafe yet no accommodations locally named Watauga.

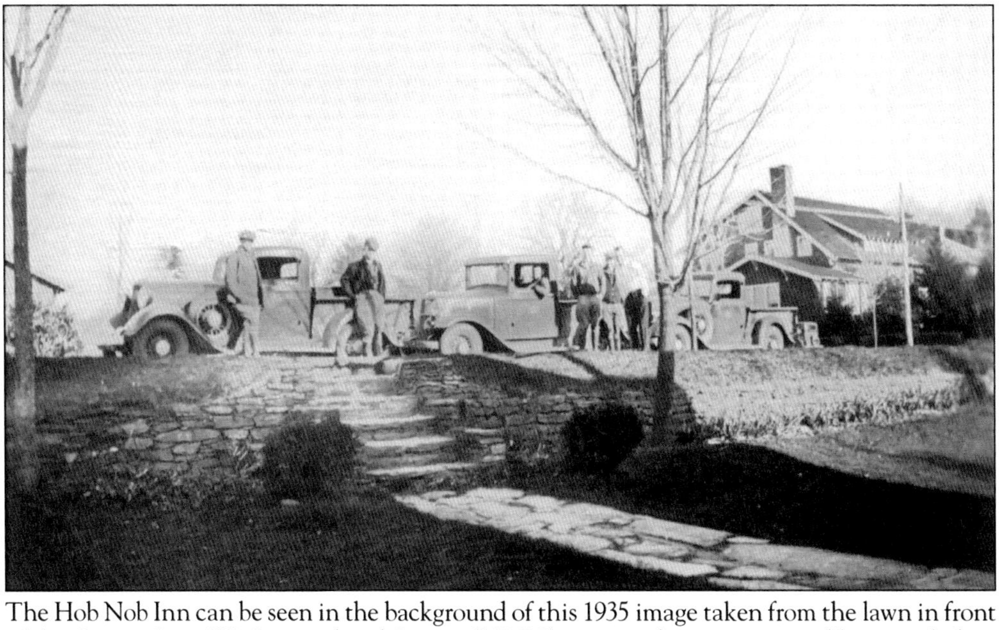

The Hob Nob Inn can be seen in the background of this 1935 image taken from the lawn in front of the Greene Inn. US Geographical Survey (USGS) topographers are pictured here, including Oulton "Red" Spalding. A Maine native, he conducted survey work in the mountains of Western North Carolina.

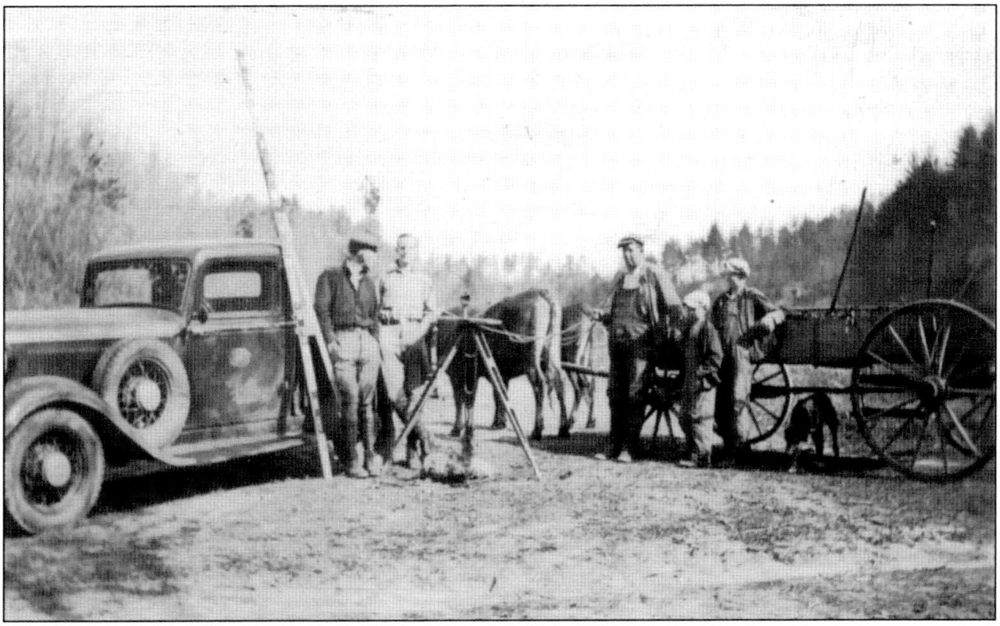

Red Spalding visits with a few "typical mountain farmers," as described in his journal. Between February and May 1935, he noted, "USGS Topo work in N Carolina, Rainbow Springs, Blowing Rock, mapping with the plan table—some of topo [elevation] 6,300 feet. Killed two rattlesnakes. Beautiful country in spring with dogwood, rhododendron, ivy, laurel, and peach trees."

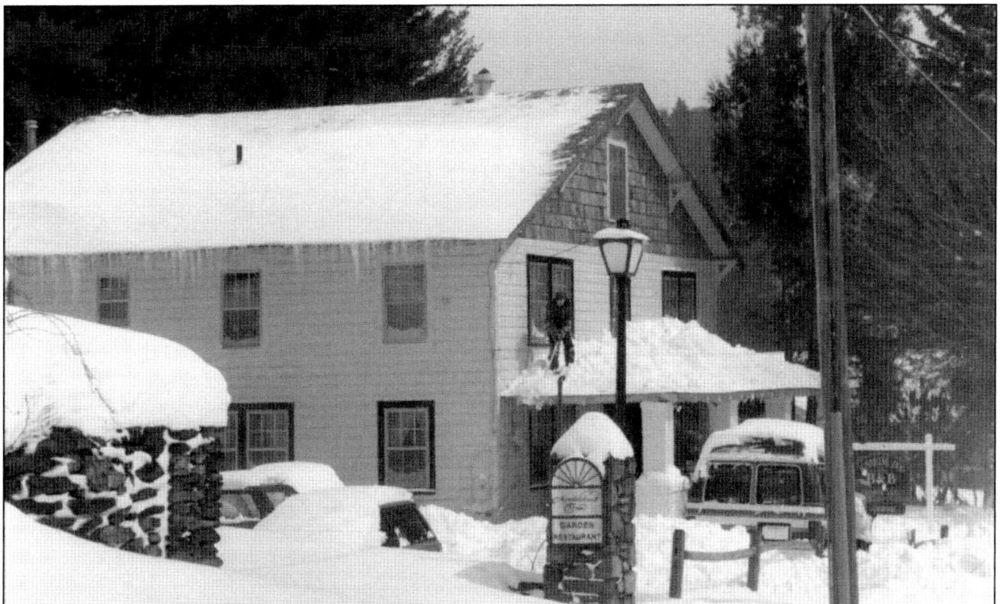

The parents of Jerry Burns, Jesse and Ethel, owned and operated the Sunshine Inn starting in 1929. The location on Sunset Drive serves as another example of blending vegetation and local materials such as stone walls with the overall appearance, even when these features are blanketed with snow. Recently known as Crippen's Country Inn and Restaurant, the property currently contains the New Public House and Hotel.

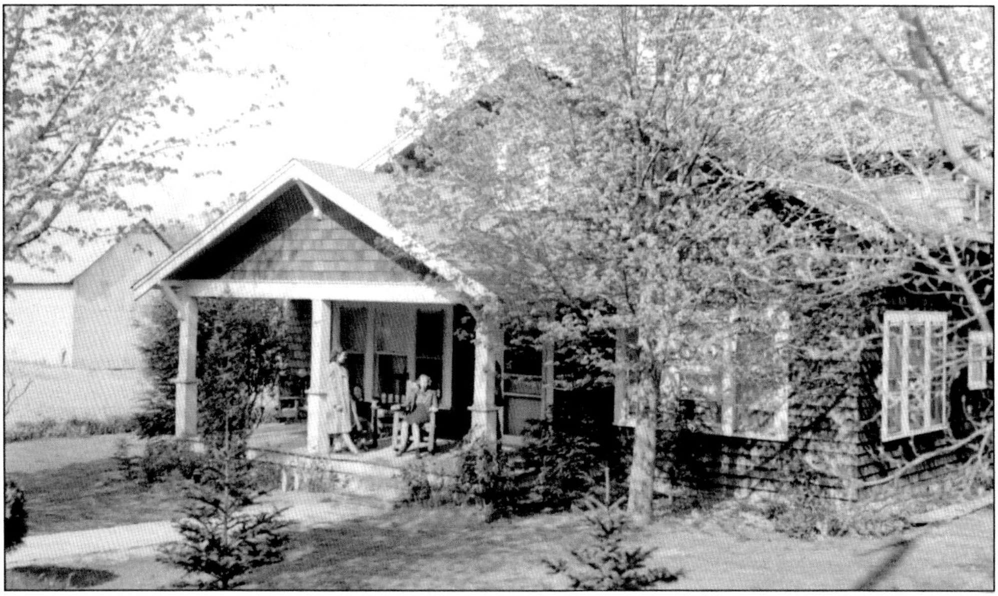

Under the supervision of "Granny" Greene, the Greene Inn served home-cooked meals each summer until the early 1960s. Greene converted her private residence, erected in 1923, to a boardinghouse for income during the Great Depression. It contained 11 rooms situated in a picturesque setting of native shrubs and trees.

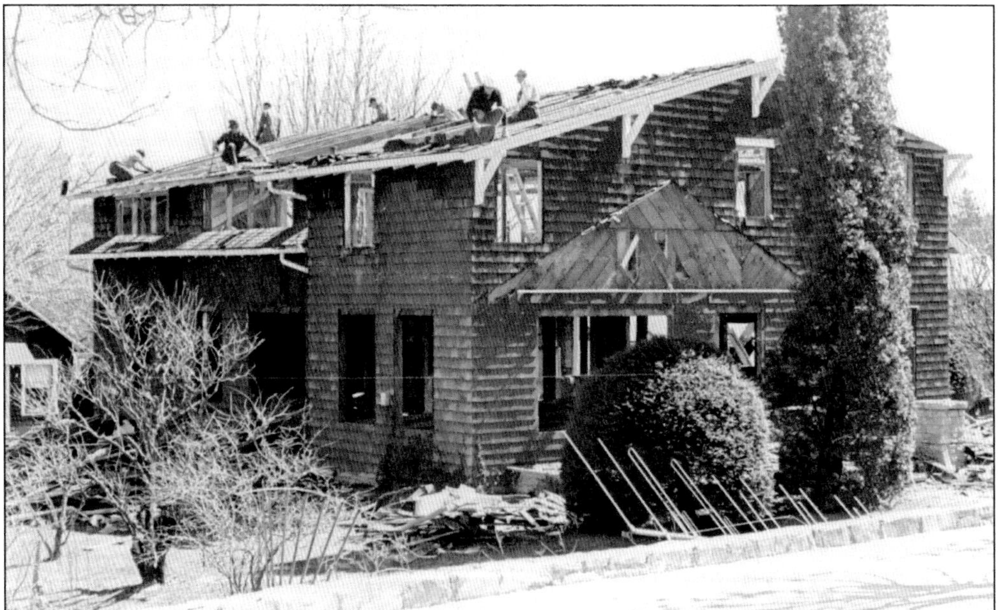

The Greene Inn was dismantled for the current First Citizens Bank parking lot. The local newspaper listed the accommodations used by summer residents. As this practice continued into the 1960s, it became clear that visitors were coming from more states than just the Carolinas, Georgia, and Florida. All reservations were also encouraged to go through the chamber of commerce to ensure availability and encourage more visitors.

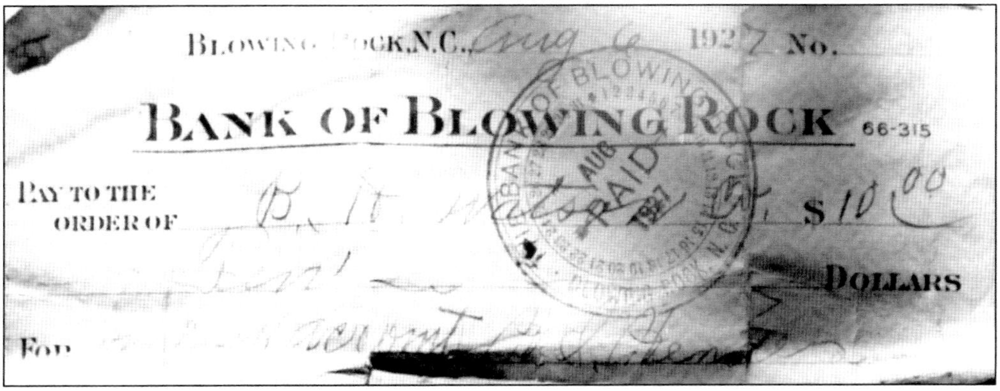

Built in 1904, the former Bank of Blowing Rock at the corner of Main Street and Sunset Drive currently serves as a realty office. This is believed to be the first bank established in Watauga County. It started with $5,000 in capital, $25,000 by 1934. Newspaper advertisements in the 1930s noted, "Your deposits in this bank have the protection afforded by Federal Deposit Insurance under the Banking Act of 1933."

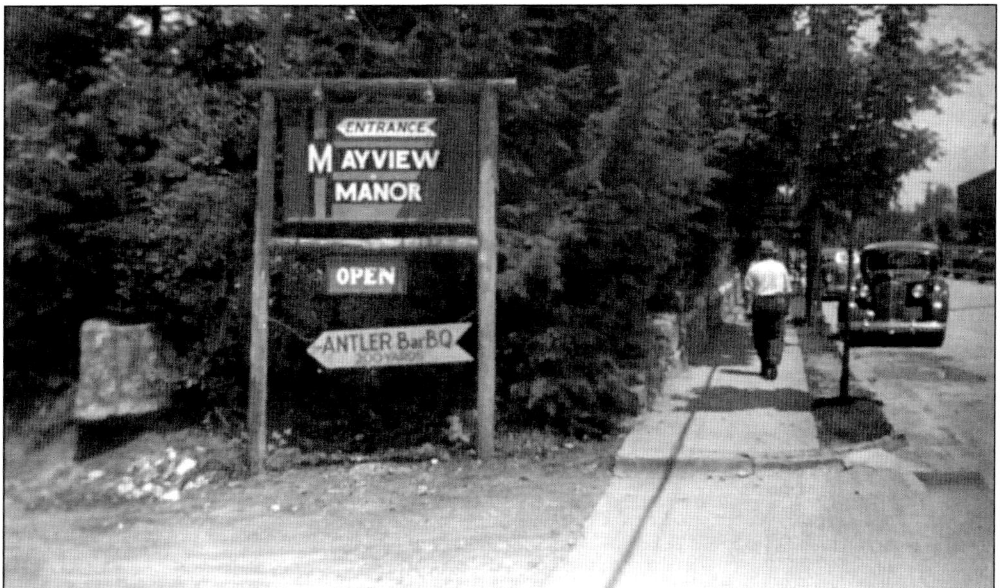

Walter Alexander of Charlotte opened Mayview Manor in 1922. The last guest checked out in 1966. The property was cleared in 1978 to make way for Mayview Manor Estates. Native rock made up all 16 of the manor's chimneys and a long rambling basement. At least seven presidents and scores of celebrities have stayed at Mayview. Signage on Main Street helped guests reach this destination.

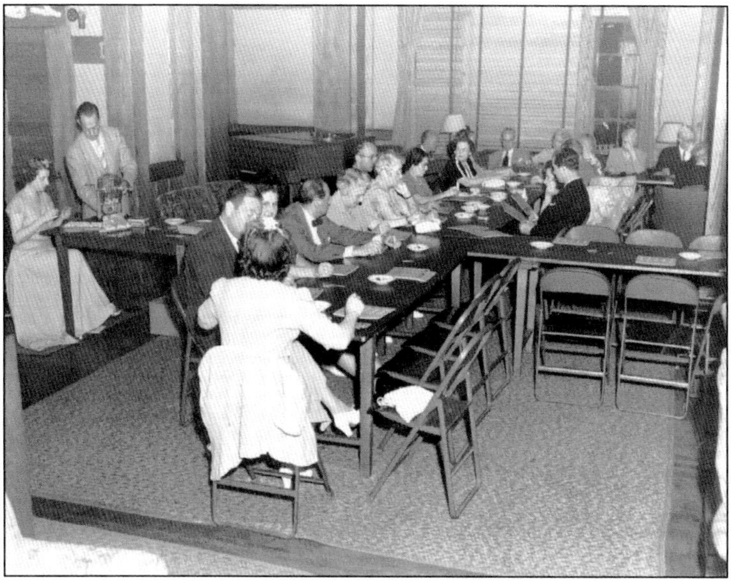

In the late 1950s, bingo took place every Monday at Mayview Manor in the Sky Room. Learning to play bridge was also a weekly event, in addition to regular competitions. General entertainment, formal and informal, could be found at the Green Park Inn and other smaller seasonal hotels. Even gambling existed briefly.

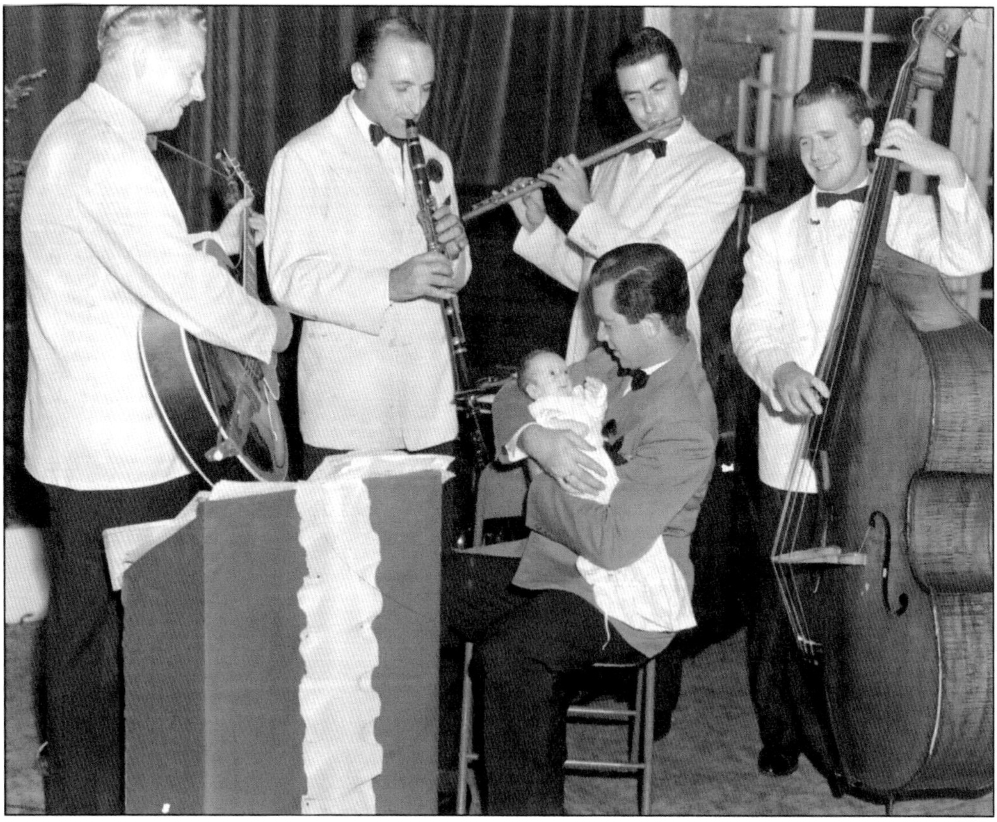

Rabbit Robbins was a popular entertainer locally, but big bands typically did not stay in fashion after World War II. Frank Stanley, Michael Marvin and his Indian Creek Club Orchestra, and other musicians were weekly attractions. Advertisements stated, and well-attended audiences confirmed, "You expect—and get only the best at Mayview Manor."

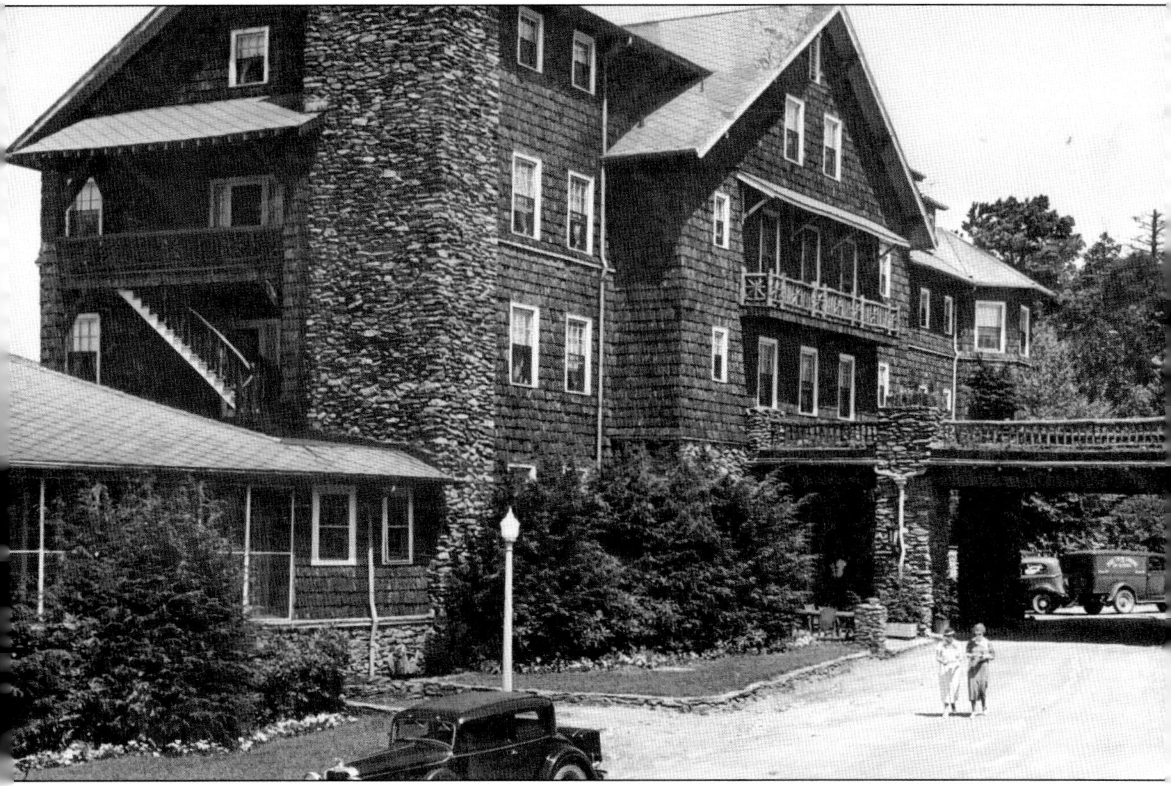

The 1930s population was similar to that of the 2010s: roughly 1,500 full-time residents and 8,000 seasonal ones. The town offers a cool climate, magnificent views, year-round activities, a safe environment, beautiful churches, an award-winning school, and the finest accommodations with superb restaurants and shopping. After the demolition of Mayview Manor in the late 1970s, a major preservation effort has massed to protect the proud heritage and maintain the community character of the town. In the 1930s, the hairdresser at the Mayview Manor, Minerva Bohren, noted her second location at Palm Beach in advertisements. Gi Gi was a clothing apparel specialist at Mayview Manor in the 1960s, with a primary location "off the mountain." Businesses at Mayview Manor relied on their seasonal guests visiting dentists, barbers, and beauticians who also opened seasonal practices in Blowing Rock.

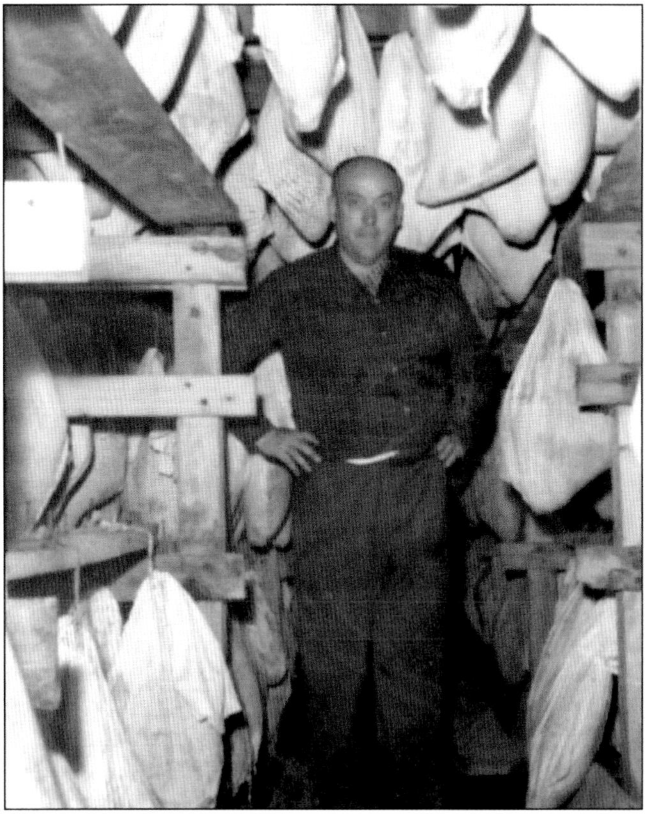

Here is Stewart Simmons in July 1965 at his ham house near Triplett, located in the Elk Valley near Blowing Rock. There are similar operations still successful within Watauga County. Prior to the local ordinance in 1896 requiring fencing of livestock, hogs foraged in and near downtown in the spring and summer before heading to Lenoir in the fall.

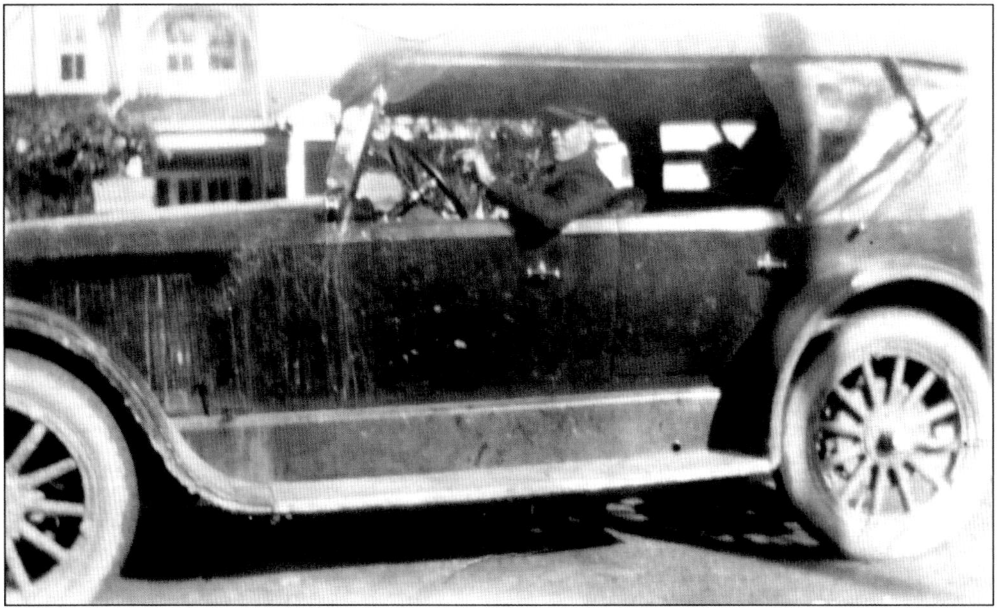

Once it became clear that automobiles were here to stay, a two-car taxi service between Boone and Blowing Rock opened in 1910, named the Auto Transfer Company. Taxi driver "Daddy" Jacques waits in front of the Hayes House. The move of the structure from Main Street to the corner of US-221 and Greene Street began at 4:30 a.m. on a Tuesday morning in May 1994.

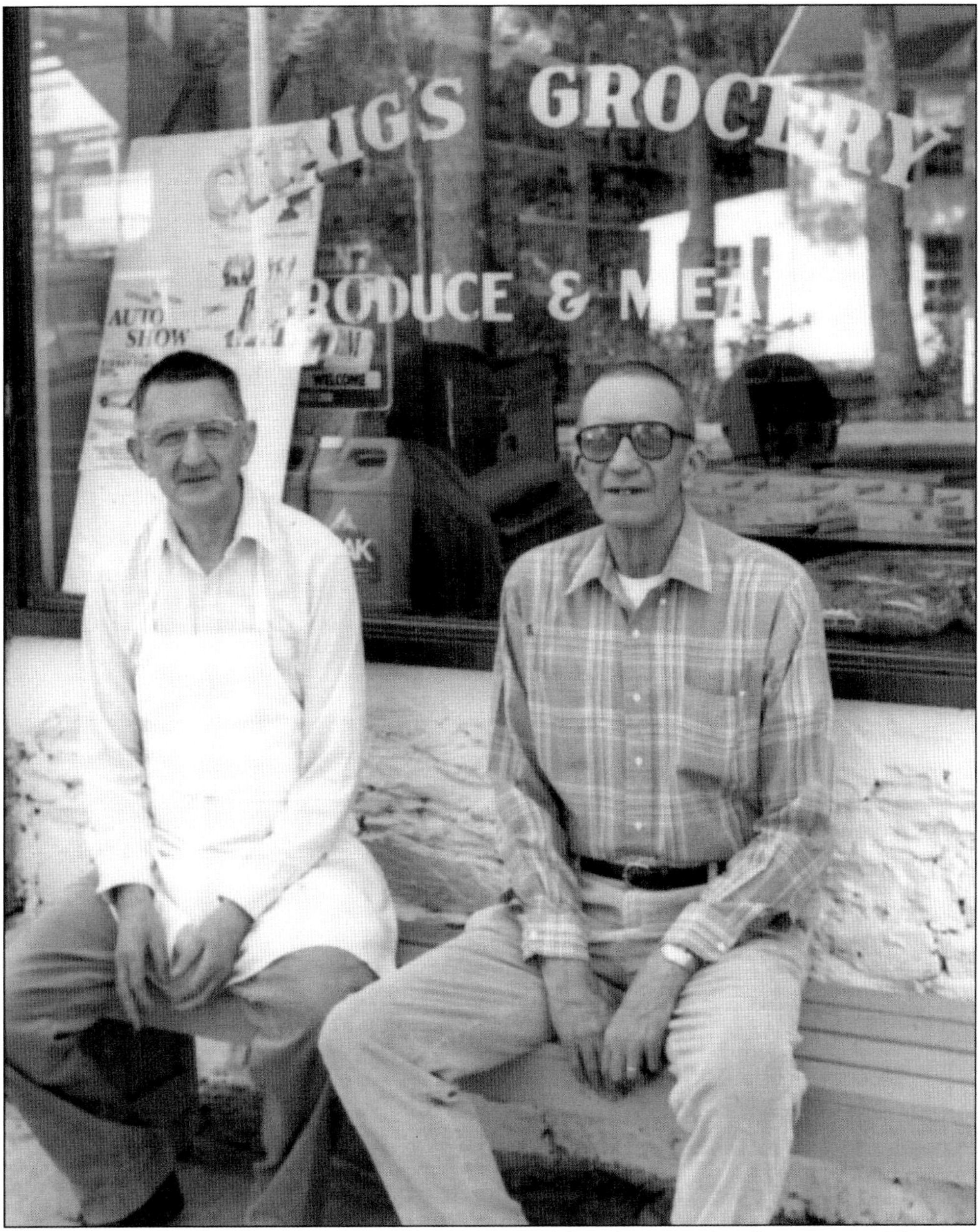

Allen Craig (left) and Perry Lentz (right) sit in front of their longtime local institution. The one-story building was constructed from stone from the Craig farm on Wonderland Road. Waldensian builders from Valdese executed the uncoursed stonework, in addition to several other buildings on Main Street. An advertisement from July 1959 reads, "Craig's Grocery, under new management, Allen Craig and Perry Lentz, specializing in Wester Beef, Mt. Lambs, and Country Hams." Jerry Burns reflected in the *Blowing Rocket*, "By the first snowfall you'd be hard pressed to find more than half a dozen cars on main street, and 5 of those belonged to merchants—Sonny Klutz (Sonny's Grill), Coman Storie (Storie's Soda Shop), Allen Craig or Perry Lentz (Craig's Grocery), pharmacist Larry Harris and Bob Hardin, who would leave his hardware to open the Village Shop in case anyone wanted anything from there."

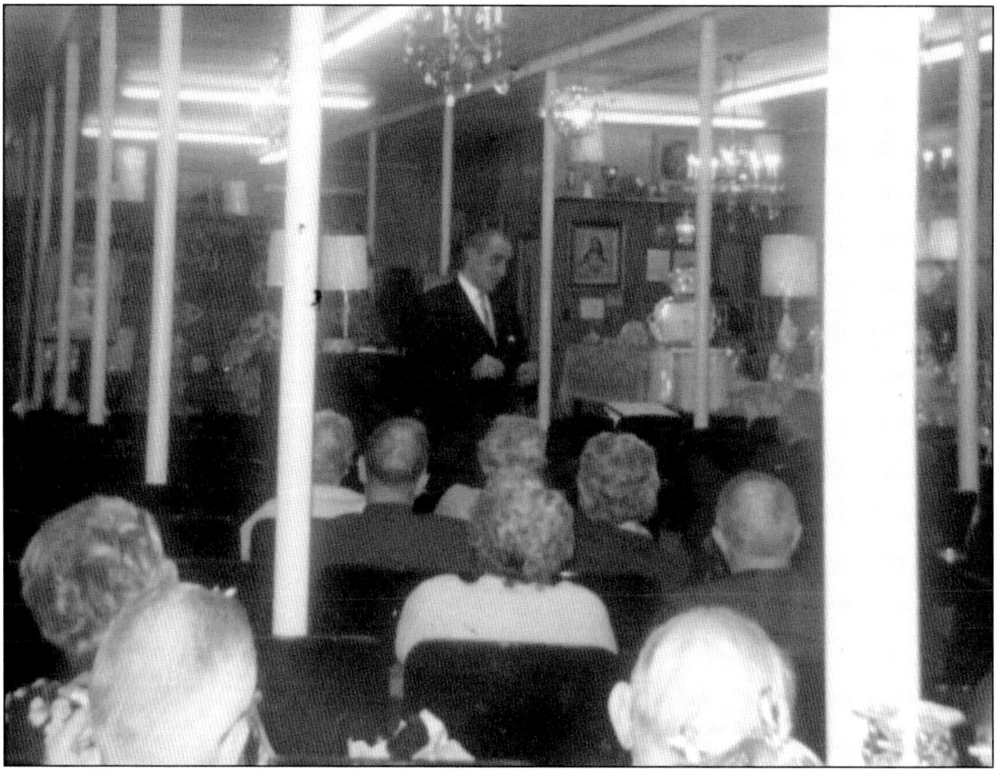

In 1949, the Blowing Rock Art Galleries started the beginning of auction houses downtown. "A visit to our galleries is a trip around the world." The gallery pictured here actually began when Elie S. Mattar started an auction house in Hot Springs, Arkansas. The opening weekend of sales in most years included 10 percent of all sales to local fundraisers.

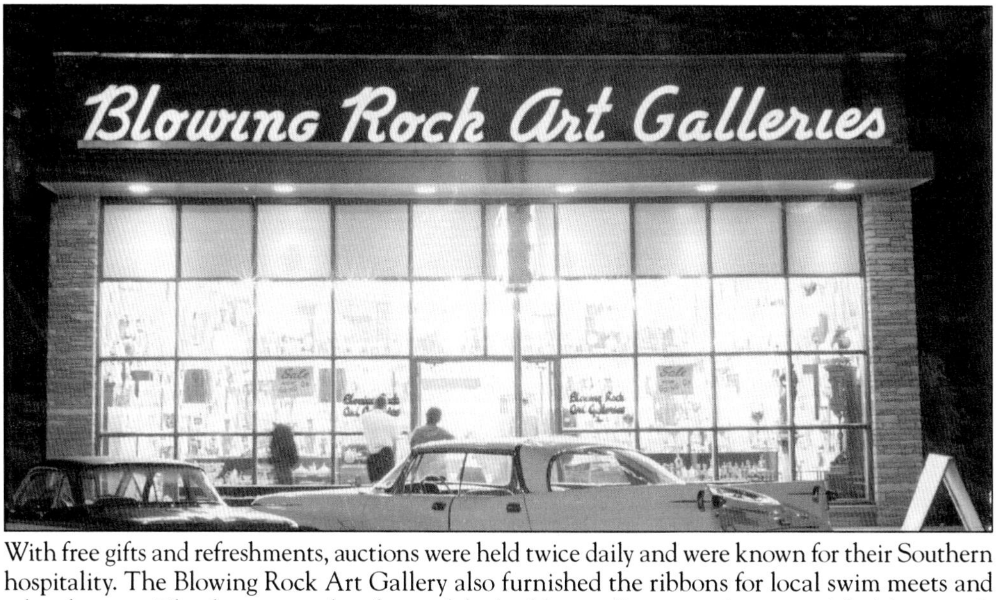

With free gifts and refreshments, auctions were held twice daily and were known for their Southern hospitality. The Blowing Rock Art Gallery also furnished the ribbons for local swim meets and related events. The distinctive glass front of the building still exists today in modified form, with Capel Rugs as the current occupant.

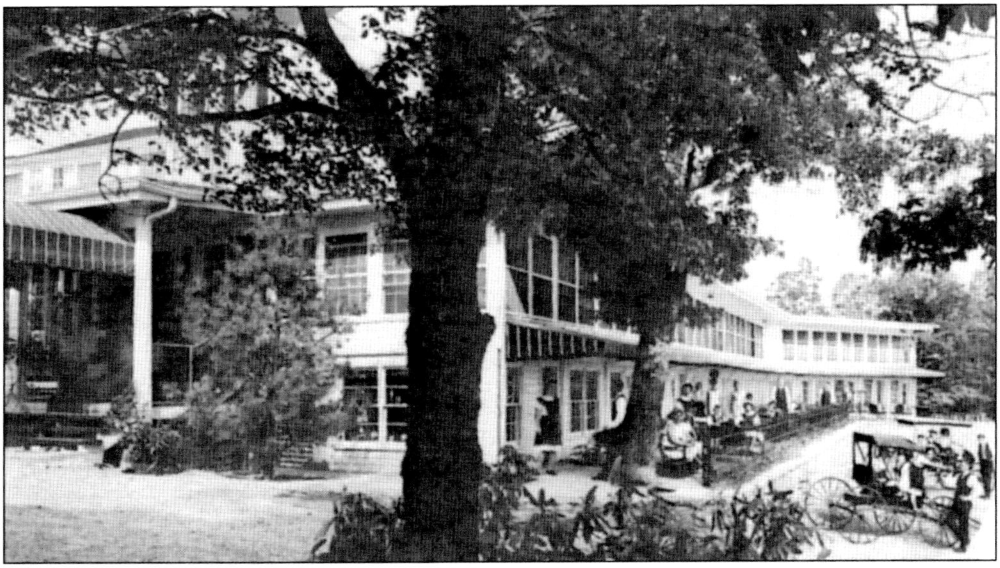

The Farm House Inn was previously the Skyland Inn and Stuart Hotel. The Village Grove contains the last remaining remnant of the Grove House on-site. The date of the above image (likely the 1970s) is deceptive, as the buggy was part of the nostalgic charm used by the Farm House Restaurant. After dinner, guests moved to the theater part of the inn for an hour-long musical performance by costumed singing waiters and waitresses.

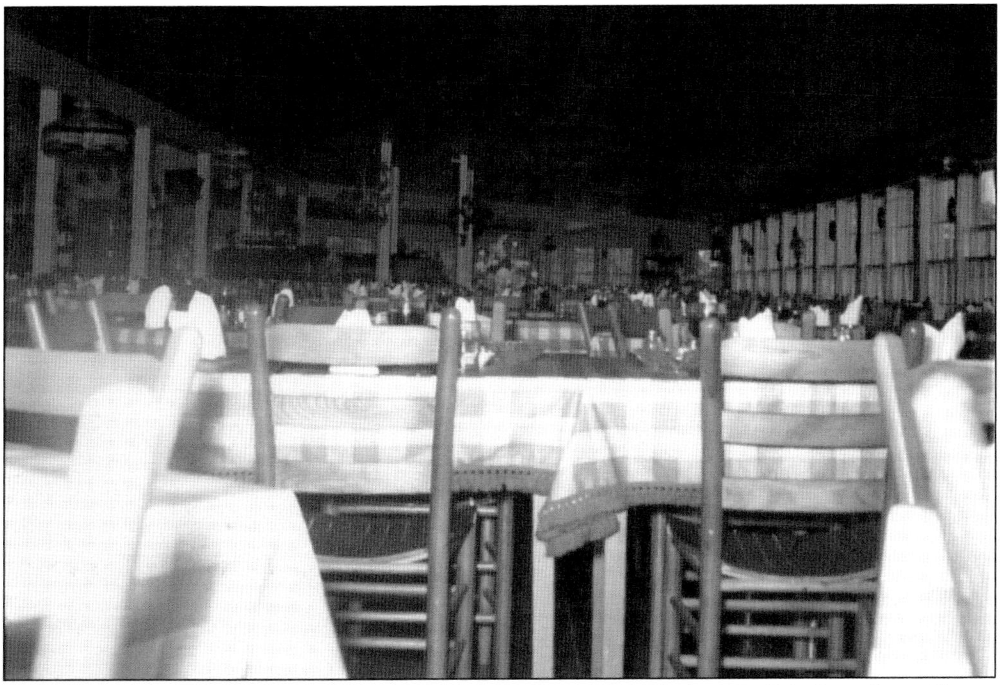

The following comes from a July 1962 advertisement: "E.J. Blackwell's Fabulous Farm House Lodge, with new dining facilities for over 500 guests. A breath-taking view overlooking John's River Gorge featuring singing waiters and waitresses for your pleasure; serving continuously 8 in the morning 'til 10 at night." The Farm House Restaurant sought musically talented college students to work as servers and serenade the guests.

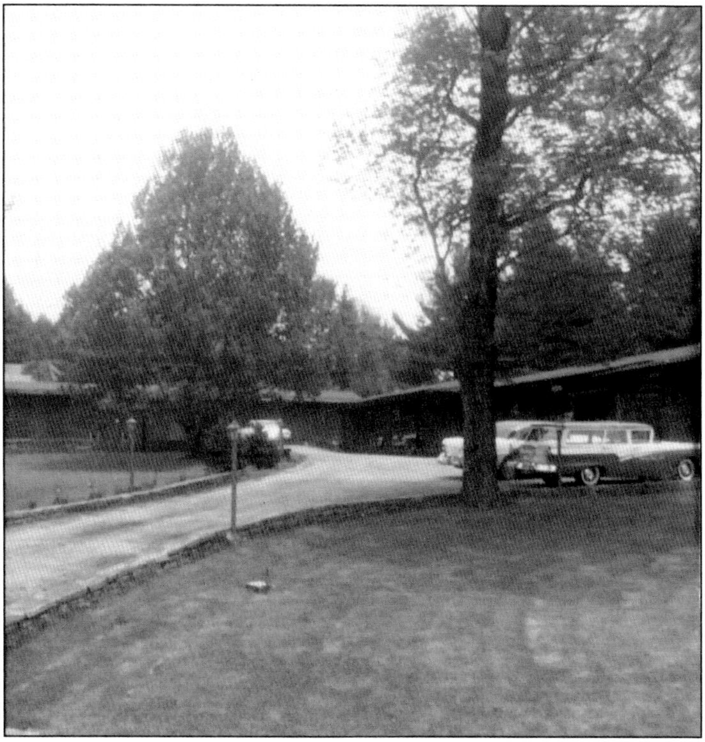

The Yonahlossee Motel, pictured in May 1962, is now known as the Blowing Rock Inn. The traditional 1950s format of parking in front of guest rooms was repeated at other local businesses. This specific location is easily within walking distance of downtown, and the luxury was highlighted by past advertising. This perhaps indicated traffic or rather the impression of traffic, which has a local history in and of itself.

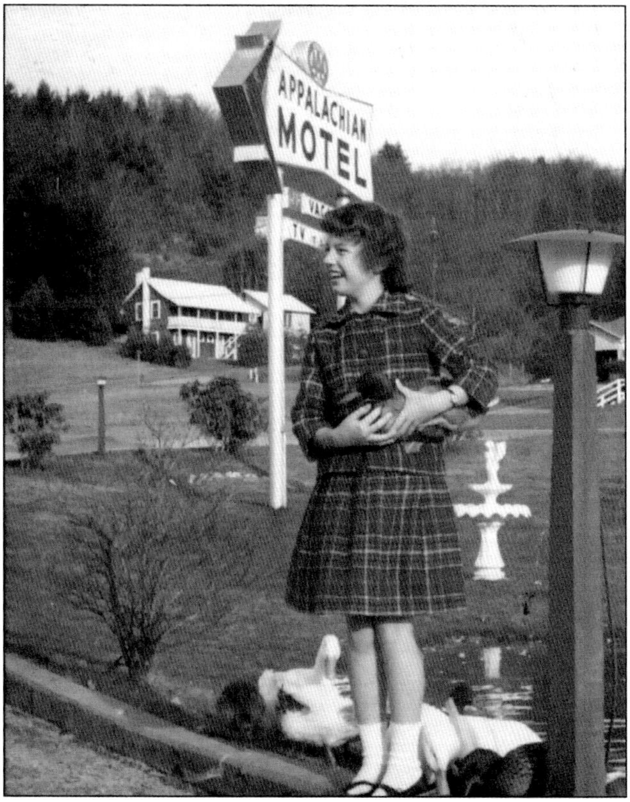

Joel Tyson owned the Appalachian Motel. His daughter Martha is pictured here holding a beautiful Canadian mallard in 1964. One of the most unusual sites around was feeding time; he once nursed back to health a duck injured on the nearby bypass, leaving only a slight limp. This property was built in 1951 and originally owned and operated by Grover C. Robbins Sr.

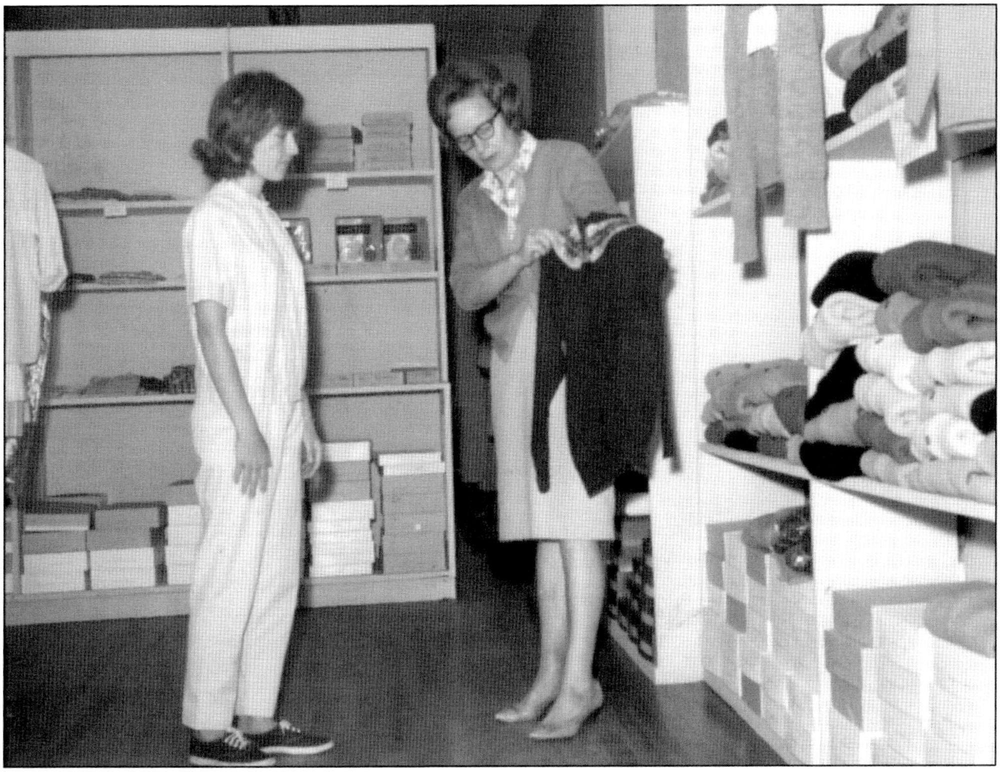

Jackie "Zubie" Taylor, owner and operator of Zubie's Ladies Shop on Main Street, shows one of her sweaters to Carolyn Stevens. Blowing Rock boasts a long history of fashion retail, beginning with showcases at the local resort hotels and continuing downtown and at the outlet mall. Historically, some stores advertised their seasonal Blowing Rock addresses while noting permanent operations in Charlotte, Miami, and other locations.

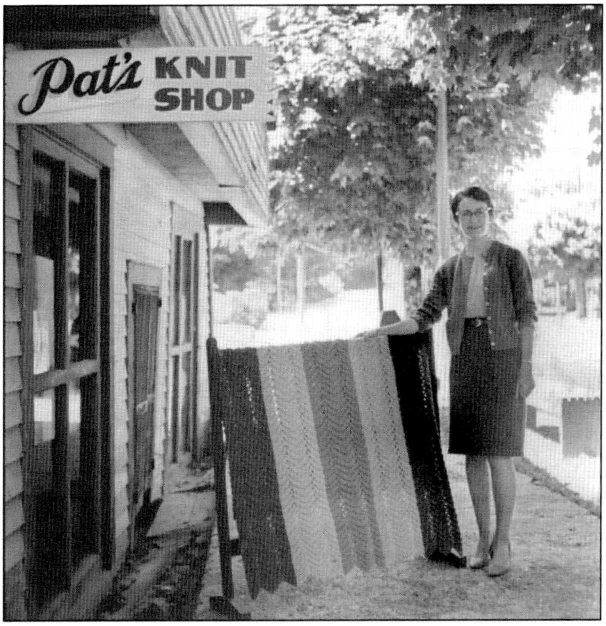

Pat Austin proudly displays her products in front of Pat's Knit Shop. The newspaper often highlighted the opening of local businesses, including the following in June 1968: "Mrs. Pat Simms comes to Blowing Rock from Los Angeles where she was a knitting instructor at Bullock's Department Store. Instruction and sales, located in the Lena Reeves' Woman's Exchange building on Main Street."

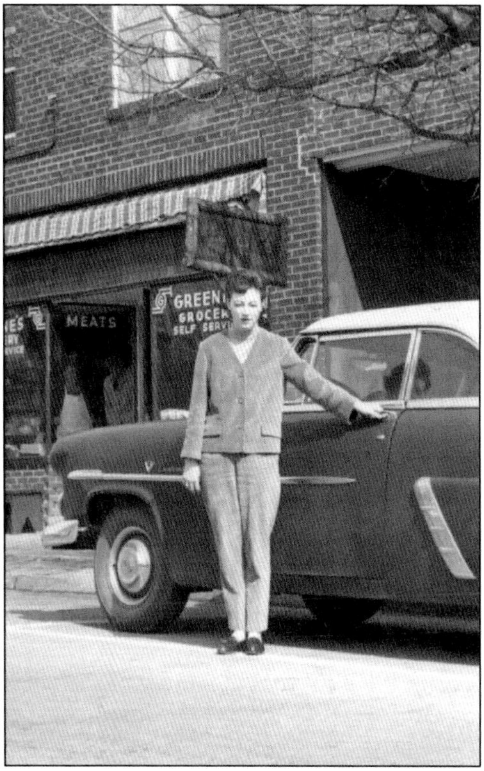

Martha Buxton Hough stands beside the 1952 Ford she won in a contest on WBTV. She submitted a card to the Sunday afternoon movie in a drawing for the car, awarded by the Courtesy Motor Company of Charlotte. Greene's Grocery and its storefront advertising with distinctive logo are in the background.

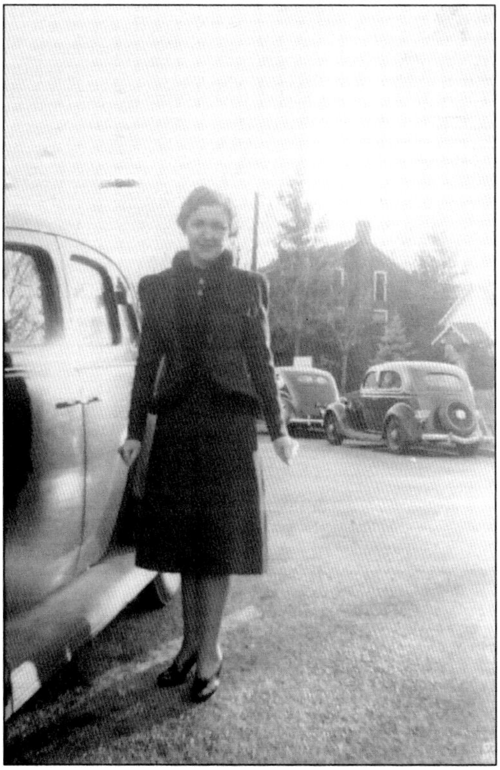

The background of this posed image includes the Martin House and the remaining cottage from the Watauga Hotel, now a museum of the Blowing Rock Historical Society. About 1870, H.C. Martin built a private residence that he expanded and opened as lodgings for summer tourists. Additions and alterations to the property have continued to allow retail shops and various uses, and the property now has six chimneys total.

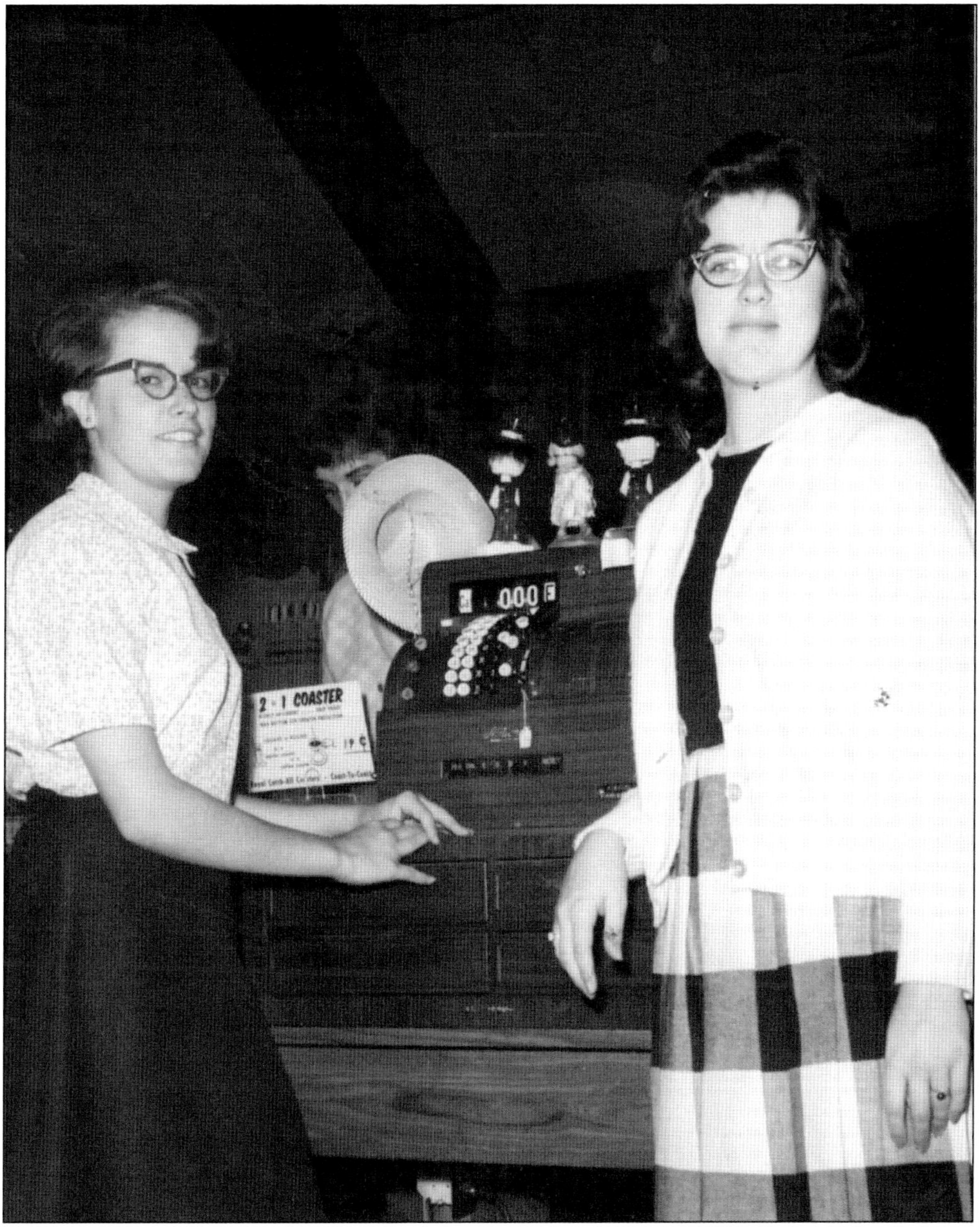

In the mid- to late 1960s, the *Blowing Rocket* ran segments titled Youth at Work on the employment of local high school students in the tourism industry. Here, Barbara Greene Harmon (right) and Imogene Fortune (left) work the gift shop cash register of the Blowing Rock attraction, where they were employed strictly in the summer and on weekends. The proximity of Appalachian State University students to Blowing Rock has also provided a ready labor force for attractions such as Tweetsie and the ski mountains, in addition to hotels, motels, and restaurants. An increase in enrollment of students from the metropolitan areas of North Carolina is certainly partially due to family vacations to Blowing Rock and the High Country area and students remembering their fond experiences. The mountains of Western North Carolina are now on equal footing with the Atlantic beaches in the minds of young people and their desired family vacations.

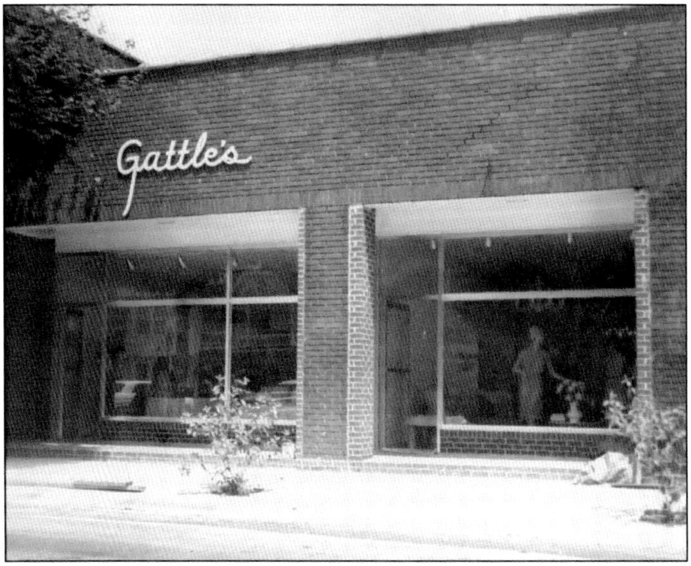

Later Christine's and Gattle's, Razook's was a staple of downtown Blowing Rock from 1921 to 1961. In addition to women's fashion, in the summer of 1941 Victor Razook sold British novelties to support the British War Relief Society. Razook's had a prominent retractable cloth awning, and many downtown buildings have begun again to utilize awnings, transom windows, and recessed entryways to enhance energy efficiency and appearance.

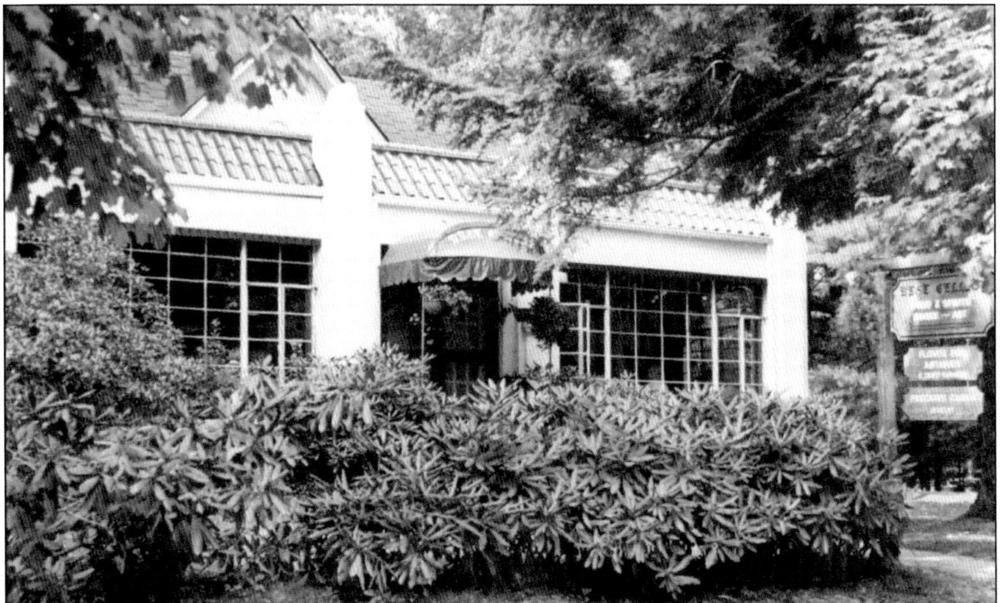

Presently known as the Town Tavern, this property has had over a dozen different occupants, including Montaldo's Dress Shop, Tijuana Flats, and Best Cellar, as noted in the image. A late 19th-century frame house lies underneath the building's Art Deco and Mission features, later added. Montaldo's also held showings of fall fashions in the ballroom of the Mayview Manor and its main store in Charlotte.

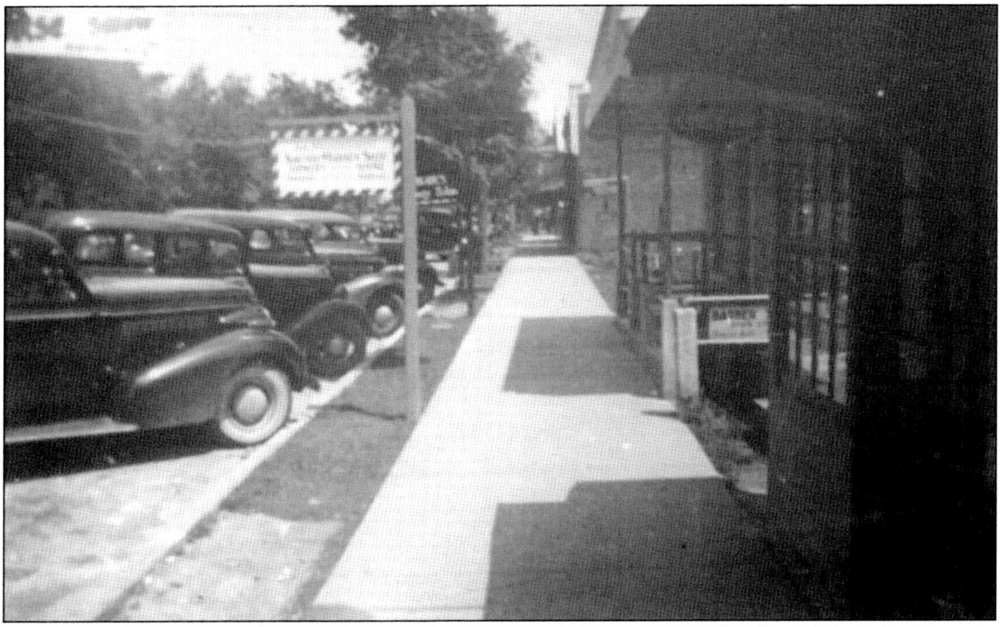

The horse show banner, beauty shop, and barbershop signage are highlights of this photograph. Like any downtown, signage is important in guiding potential customers to a purchase. In the immediate front corner of the image is the distinctive downtown facade of the current Six Pence Pub. Parking patterns have taken many variations downtown as well.

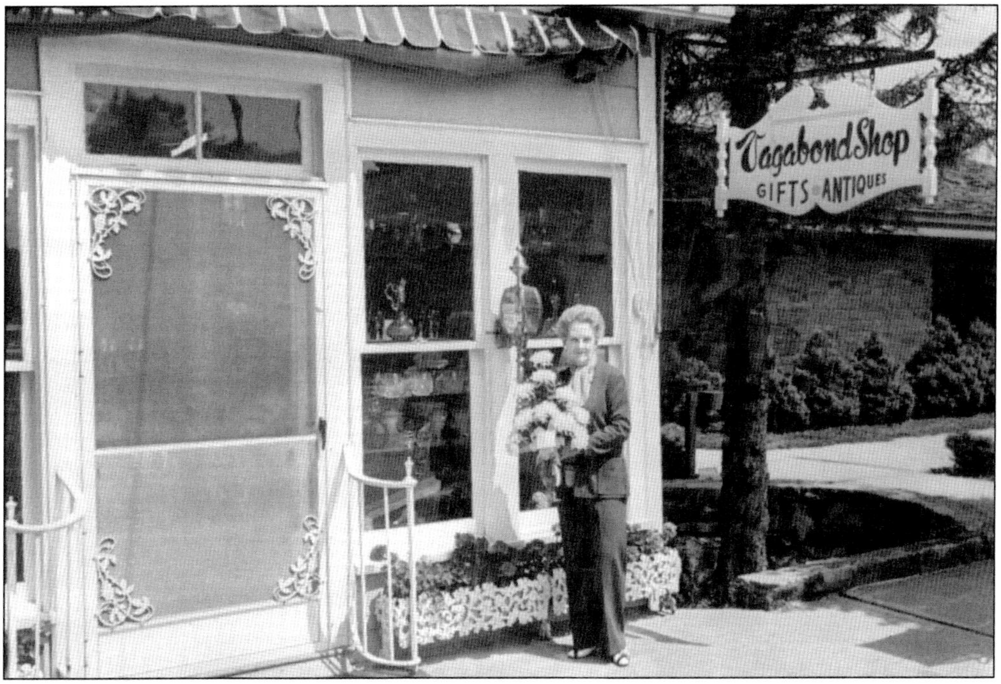

Virginia Wilson stands in front of her Vagabond shop, which once served as the local town hall. An early occupant of the structure was Henry Coffey, who had a barbershop here beginning in 1925. Like existing downtown buildings everywhere, occupants often change, and the structures remain functional for multiple adaptive reuses.

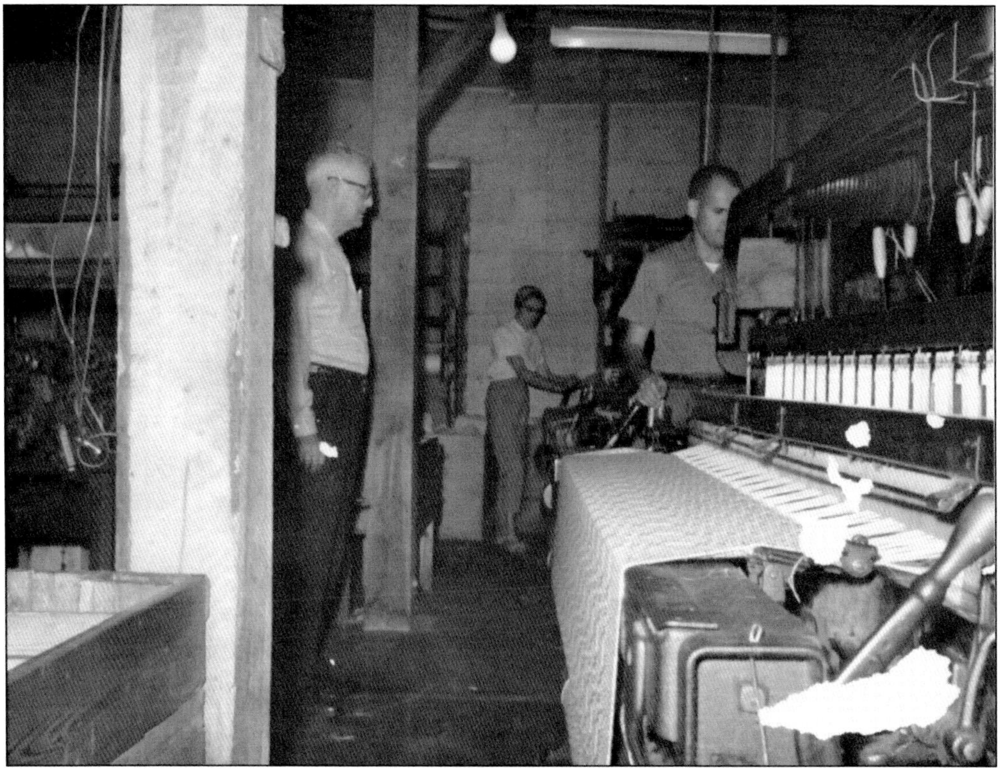

Goodwin Guild Weavers was located on the US-321 bypass next to the Appalachian Motel and the Chuck Wagon Restaurant. Goodwin can date its European lineage back to 1812, and many of their items sold at the Blowing Rock location are now quite valuable. Appalachian crafts, imports, and a combination of both have always found retail homes in Blowing Rock.

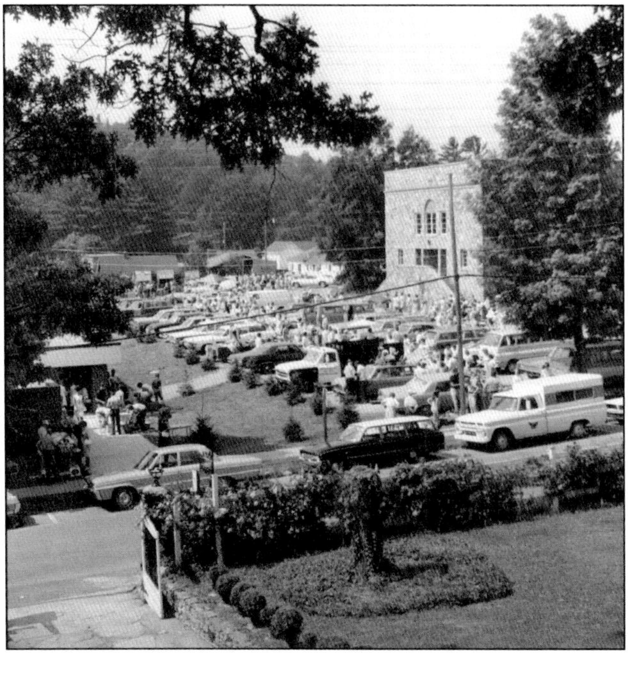

Texie Horton Barlow Russell's Flea Market was located at the school campus on Sunset Drive, between the auditorium and the gym. This image is from the 1971 flea market on Fourth of July weekend under the sponsorship of the local garden club; the estimated crowd was 10,000. In her memoirs, Russell claimed that the first ever flea market in the South took place at her home in Blowing Rock in 1962.

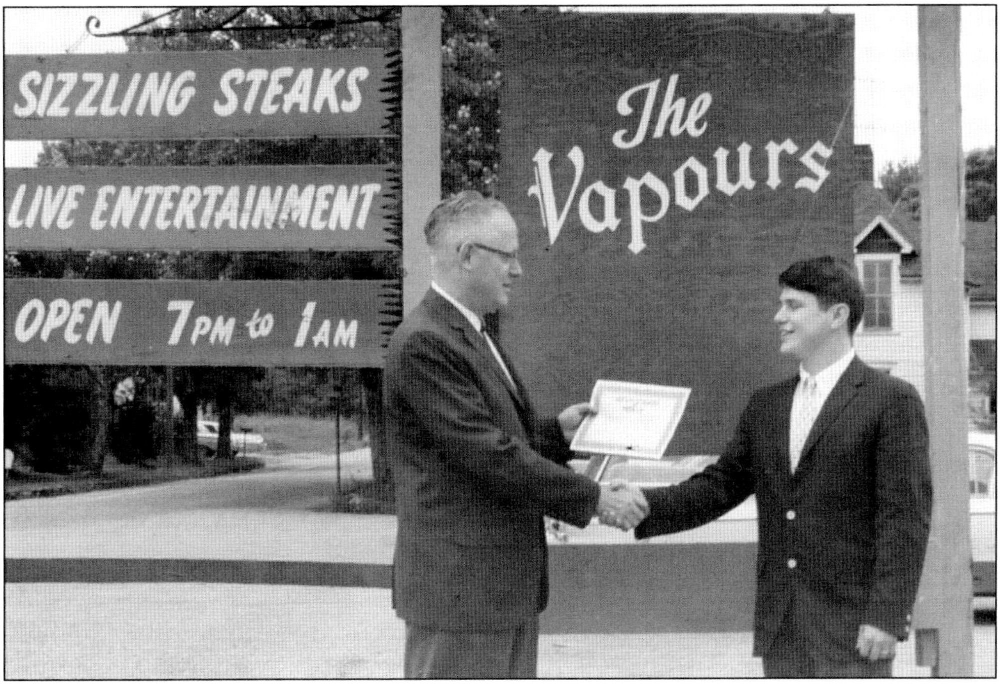

Mayor Robert B. Hardin presents John Day with a certificate of merit for providing Blowing Rock with wholesome entertainment in keeping with the high-quality environment of the area. Day was manager and part owner of the Vapours, a supper club that featured live folk music and jazz. This image appeared in the newspaper in July 1965; voters would approve a wine and beer referendum locally a month later.

P.B. Scott's, a local music hall that opened in 1976, greatly benefitted from the sale of alcohol, including to Appalachian State University students into the early 1980s. When Boone voted in 1986 to go wet, the attraction of Blowing Rock for students lessened. Regardless of legality, a July 1938 newspaper article indicated, "At the Bark the dance ends and the beer stops at 1:30; you'll see hundreds of students here from over Boone way."

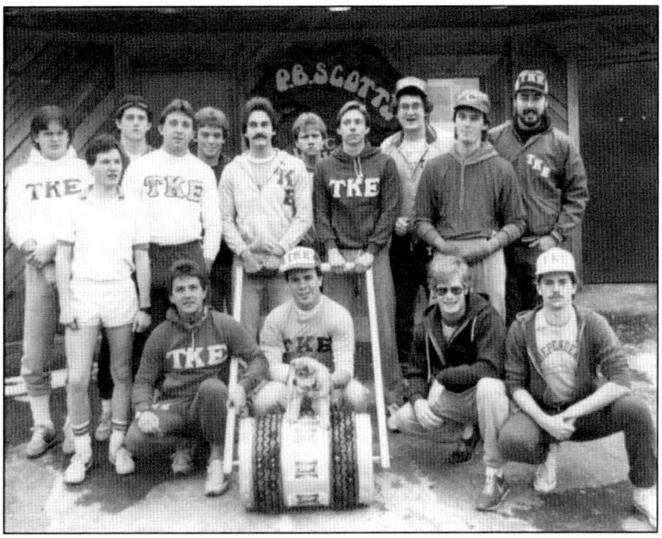

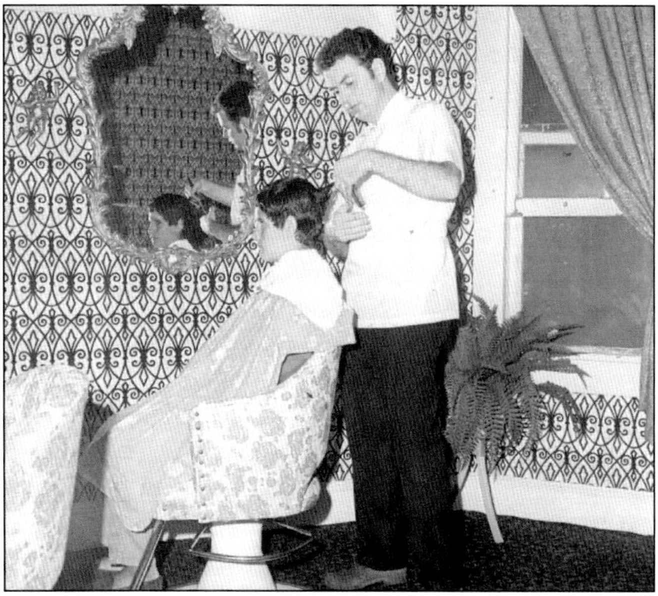

The 1888 Museum of the Blowing Rock Historical Society displays a barber pole. Coffey's Barber Shop was located under the Village Pharmacy/Rexall Drug Store on Main Street, which also included Ed Folette as barber. Joe Montesanti opened his shop on Main Street in 1938 for the summers; his primary barbershop was in Pinehurst, North Carolina. In this photograph, James Lombardo attends to a client.

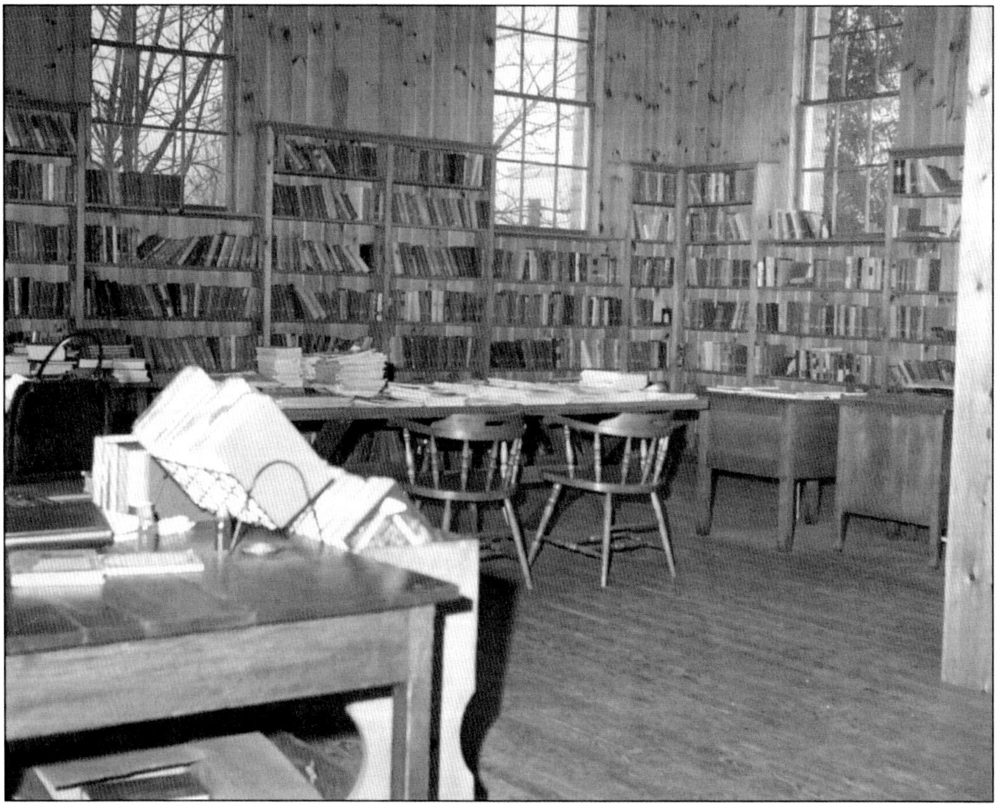

The community library interior from the 1960s is not unlike that of today. The Havermann Yarn Shop located in the community library, and dances often took place here. The history of the Community Club and the library are rooted together, and the collection went from 300 items in 1937 to 13,000 by 1969. Mary Carter founded the first public library, the Mission House Lend-a Hand Library.

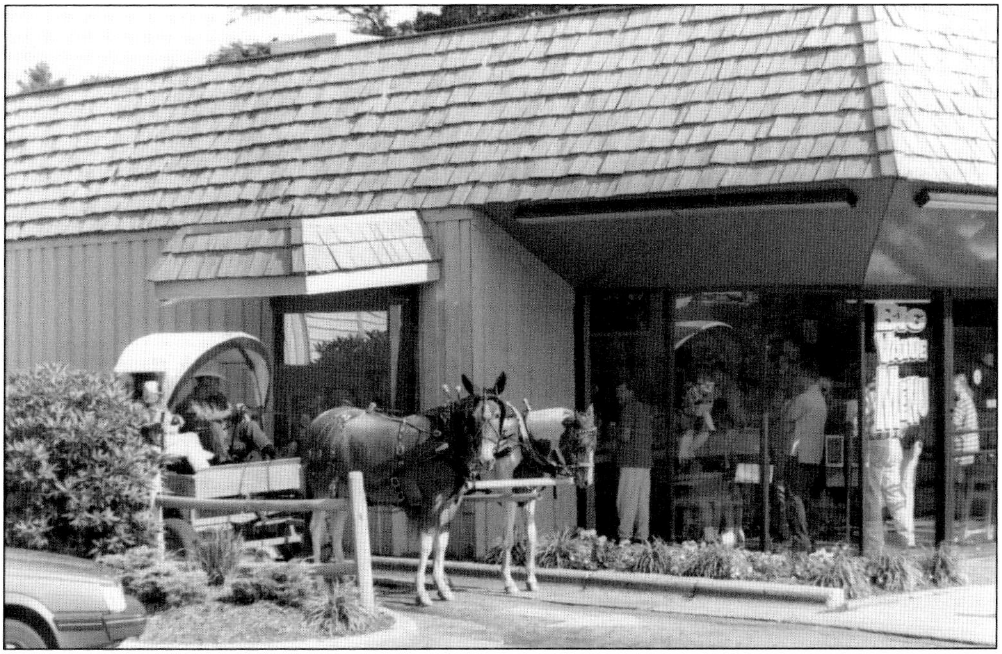

It is possible this interaction took place at the local Hardee's after the annual Fourth of July parade. The restaurant became the United Community Bank, and fast-food chain restaurants have been few in Blowing Rock. Only one chain grocery store, Food Lion, has been in town for the past 30 years.

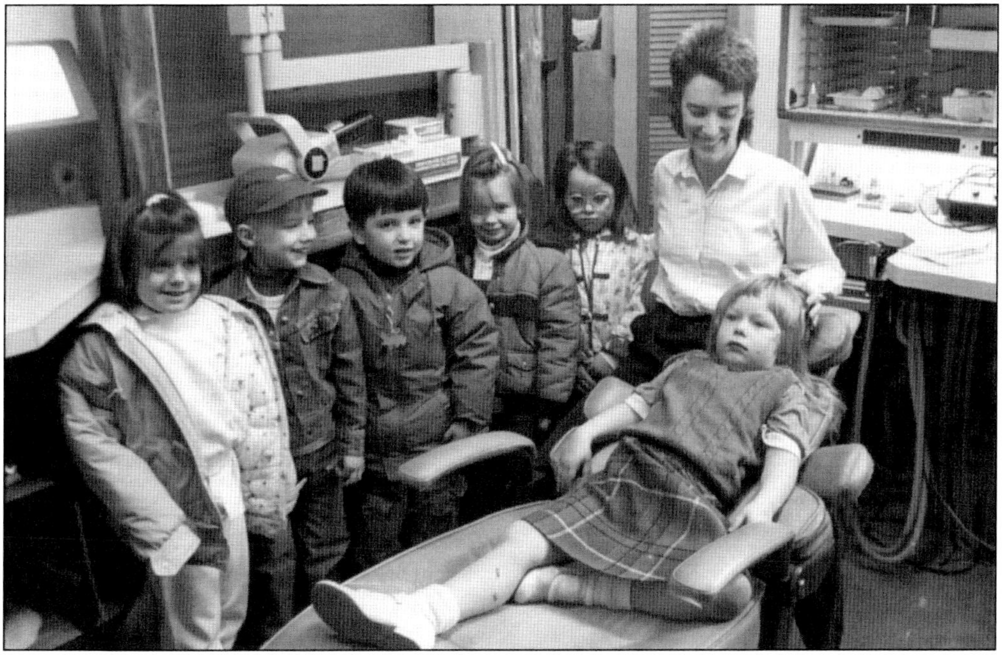

Contrary to popular stereotypes, dentistry is not foreign to the Appalachian region. Victoria Post gives a young girl a checkup, with onlookers. In the summer of 1933, the services of Dr. Sidney G. Main as dentist were highlighted, among other services that summer residents perhaps put off during the year and could take care of on vacation. Dr. Main had his primary office in Florida.

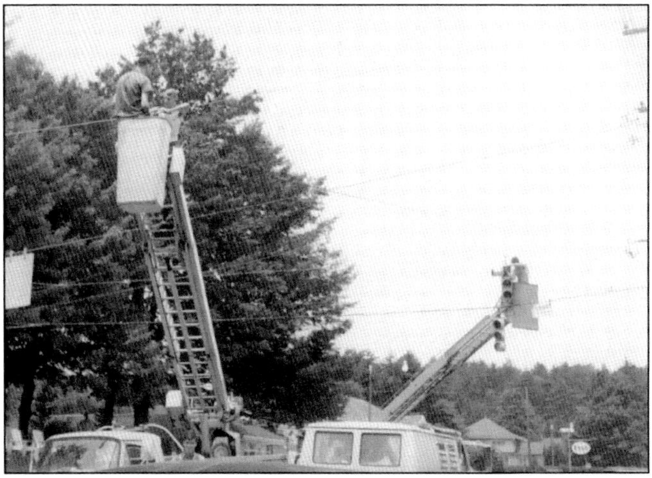

In 1960, the traffic light was removed from the intersection of Main Street and Sunset Drive by the state highway department, presenting a very dangerous situation. After local concern, it returned a year later. This 1968 image shows the lights raised higher for easier viewing and to permit larger trucks to pass through.

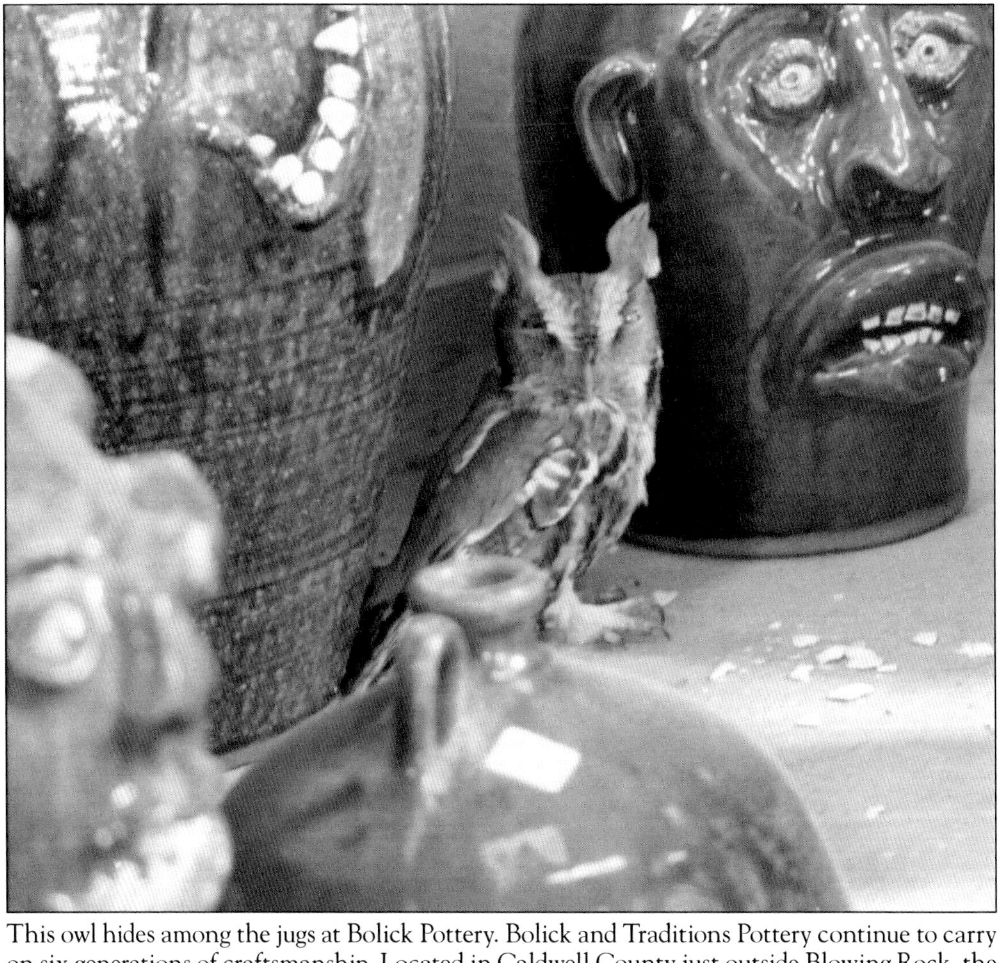

This owl hides among the jugs at Bolick Pottery. Bolick and Traditions Pottery continue to carry on six generations of craftsmanship. Located in Caldwell County just outside Blowing Rock, the annual heritage and wood kiln opening day is always the last Saturday in June. Deer are sometimes found on mornings feeding on the church lawns off Main Street, but for the most part wildlife and commerce remain separate.

Three

COMMUNITY

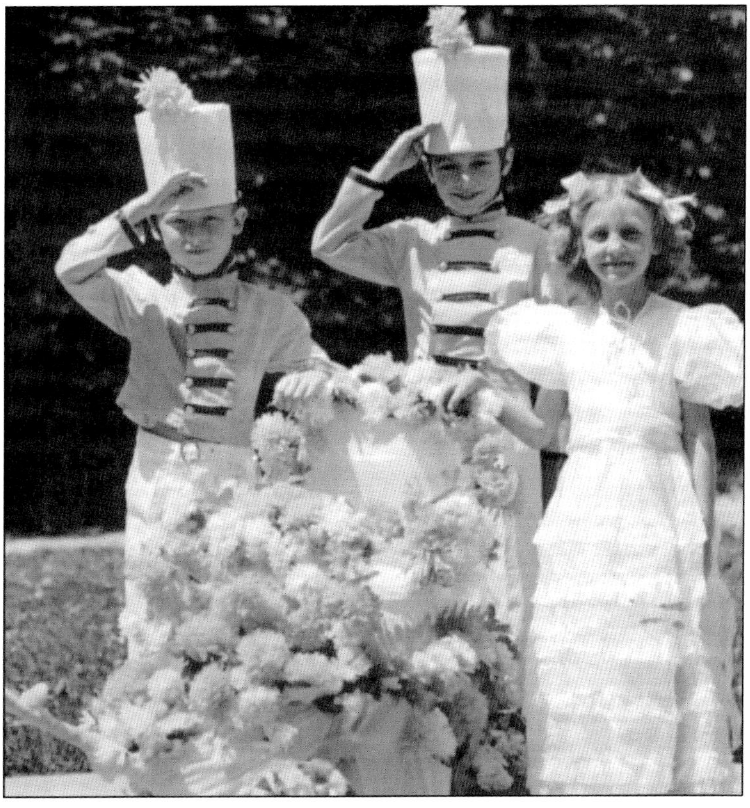

In May 1947, the second grade students at Blowing Rock School held a special chapel program to celebrate the arrival of spring in the mountains. Three of Mabel Henson Hollars's students pose here, ready to parade their wagon decorated with flowers across the auditorium stage. Pictured here from left to right are Jerry Burns, Thomas Buxton, and Nancy Trivette Wood.

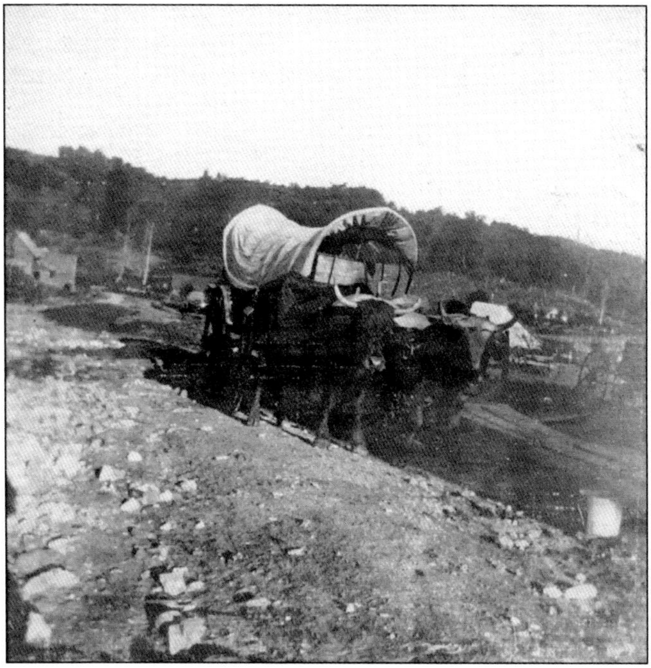

Oxen pull south out of downtown in 1888. While goods and supplies appear here, other early wagon photographs clearly show families, including children, going to and from Blowing Rock. The Lenoir-Blowing Rock Turnpike was essential for increasing visitation and town growth, and animals proved a necessity for transportation to the mountains.

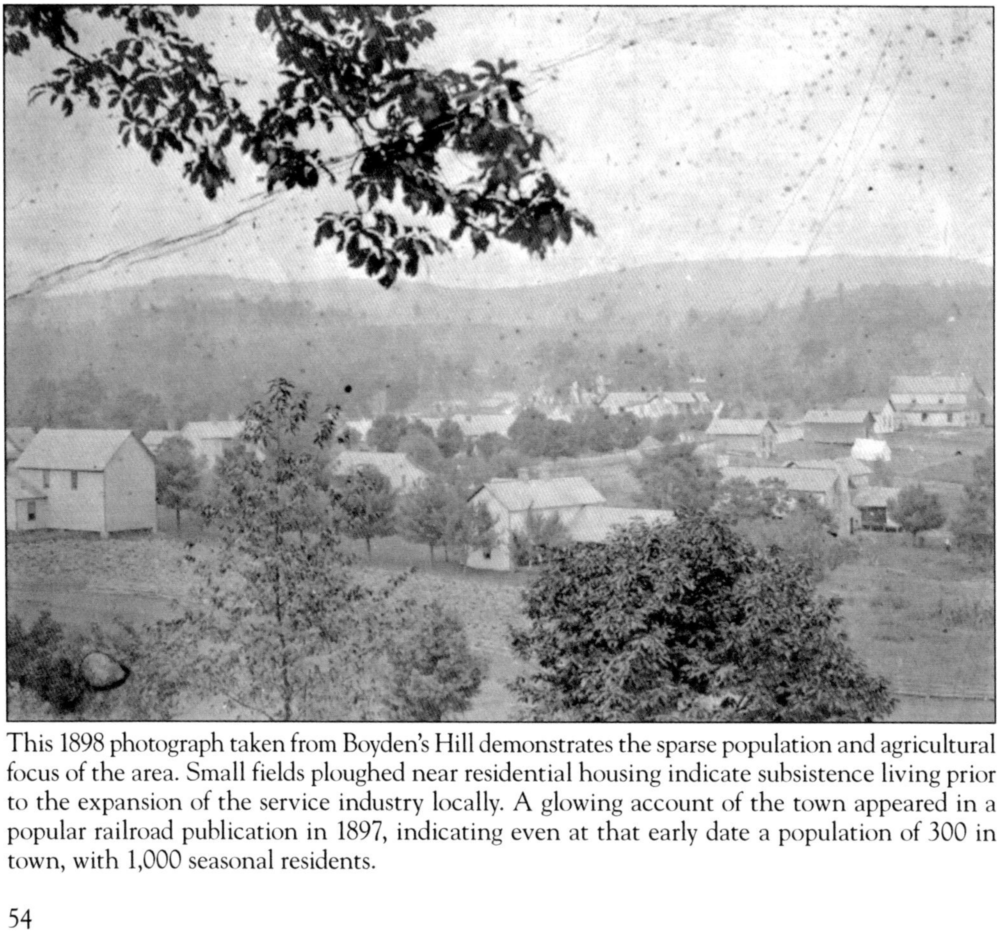

This 1898 photograph taken from Boyden's Hill demonstrates the sparse population and agricultural focus of the area. Small fields ploughed near residential housing indicate subsistence living prior to the expansion of the service industry locally. A glowing account of the town appeared in a popular railroad publication in 1897, indicating even at that early date a population of 300 in town, with 1,000 seasonal residents.

Rev. William Savage, pictured here at the water well, was the local Episcopal minister from 1902 to 1917. He also organized the Randall Memorial Workshop, where artisans worked on traditional crafts. He eventually moved to Jefferson, North Carolina, where he collected arrowheads and worked in his garden. The workshop building is now home to the Village Café and listed in the National Register of Historic Places.

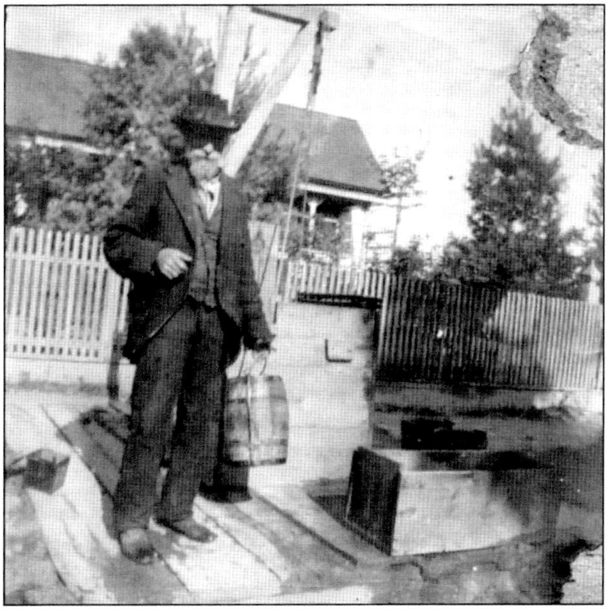

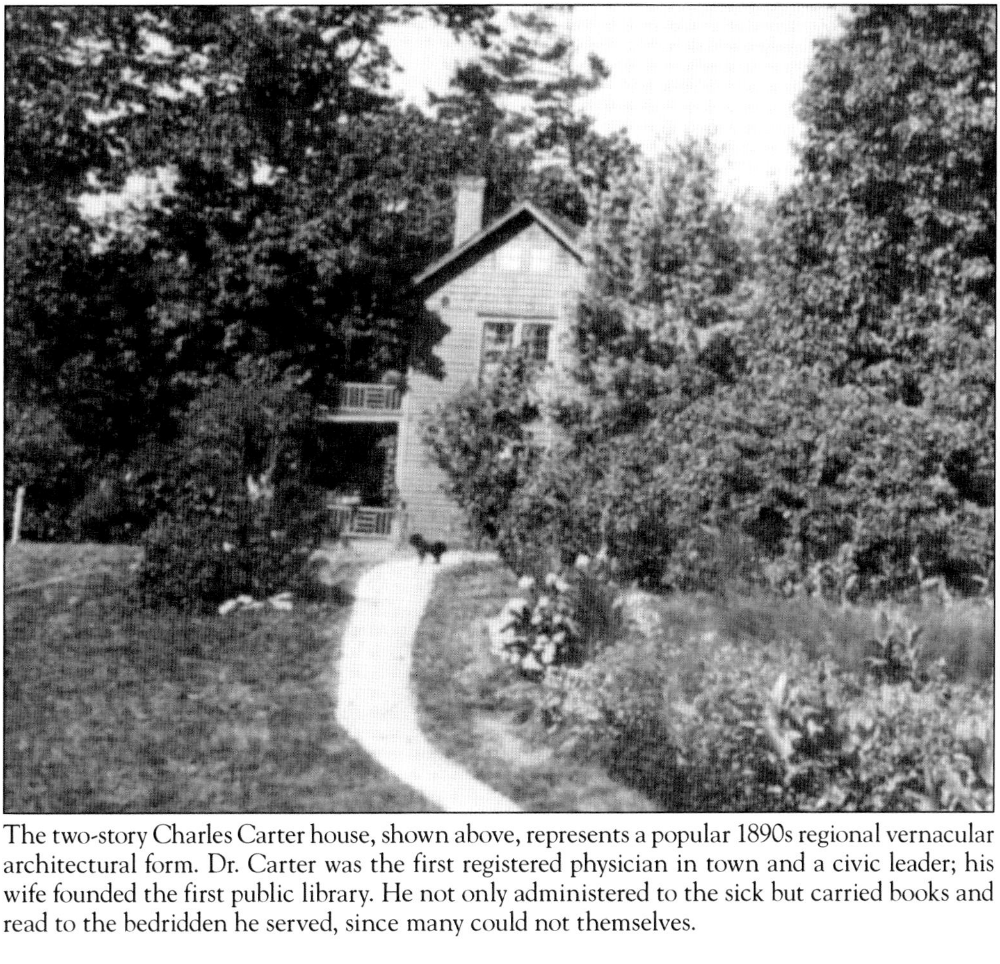

The two-story Charles Carter house, shown above, represents a popular 1890s regional vernacular architectural form. Dr. Carter was the first registered physician in town and a civic leader; his wife founded the first public library. He not only administered to the sick but carried books and read to the bedridden he served, since many could not themselves.

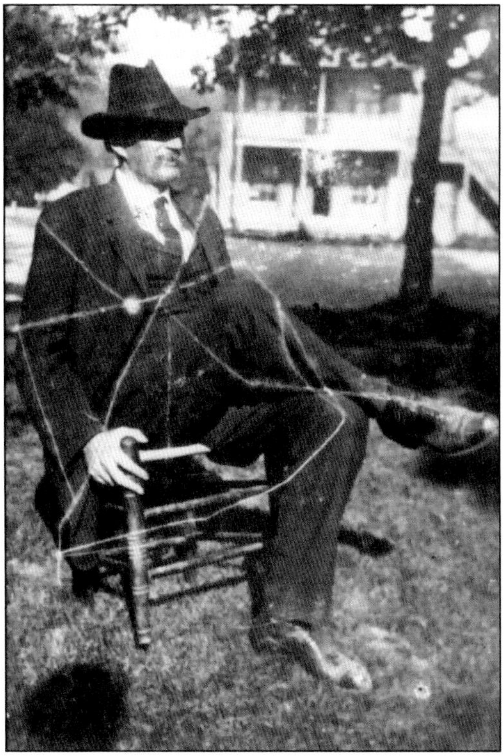

Dr. Calvin J. Parlier moved from Boone to Blowing Rock to establish a medical practice in 1899. Elected mayor two years later, he also helped establish the Bank of Blowing Rock. Dr. Parlier traveled throughout the county on horseback to provide medical services until poor health in 1914 forced his retirement and involvement in civic affairs.

This photograph shows the Holshouser house in 1915. Family members pictured here are, from left to right, Eunice, Katie, Peck, Howard, Jane (grandmother), William, Mary, Eugene, Ethel, Bill, and Laura Clampitt Holshouser. Operators of the Holshouser general store on Main Street, their descendants still live in the area. The bicycle in the image is displayed prominently, and recreational cycling in Blowing Rock continues, along the Blue Ridge Parkway and area roads.

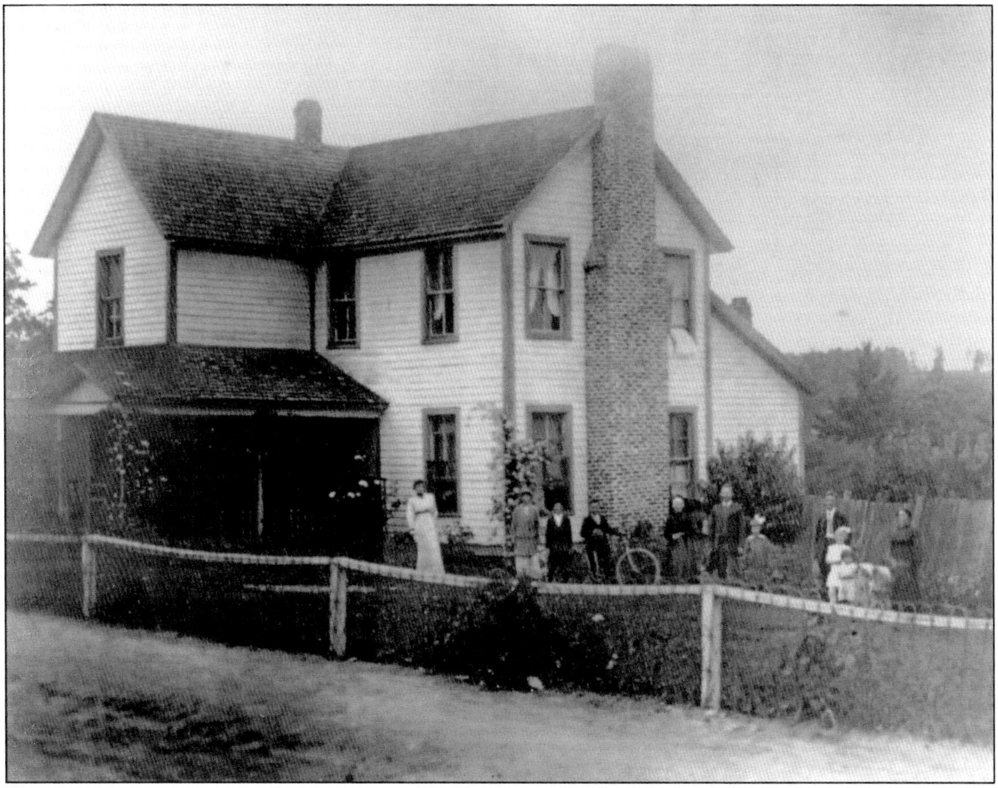

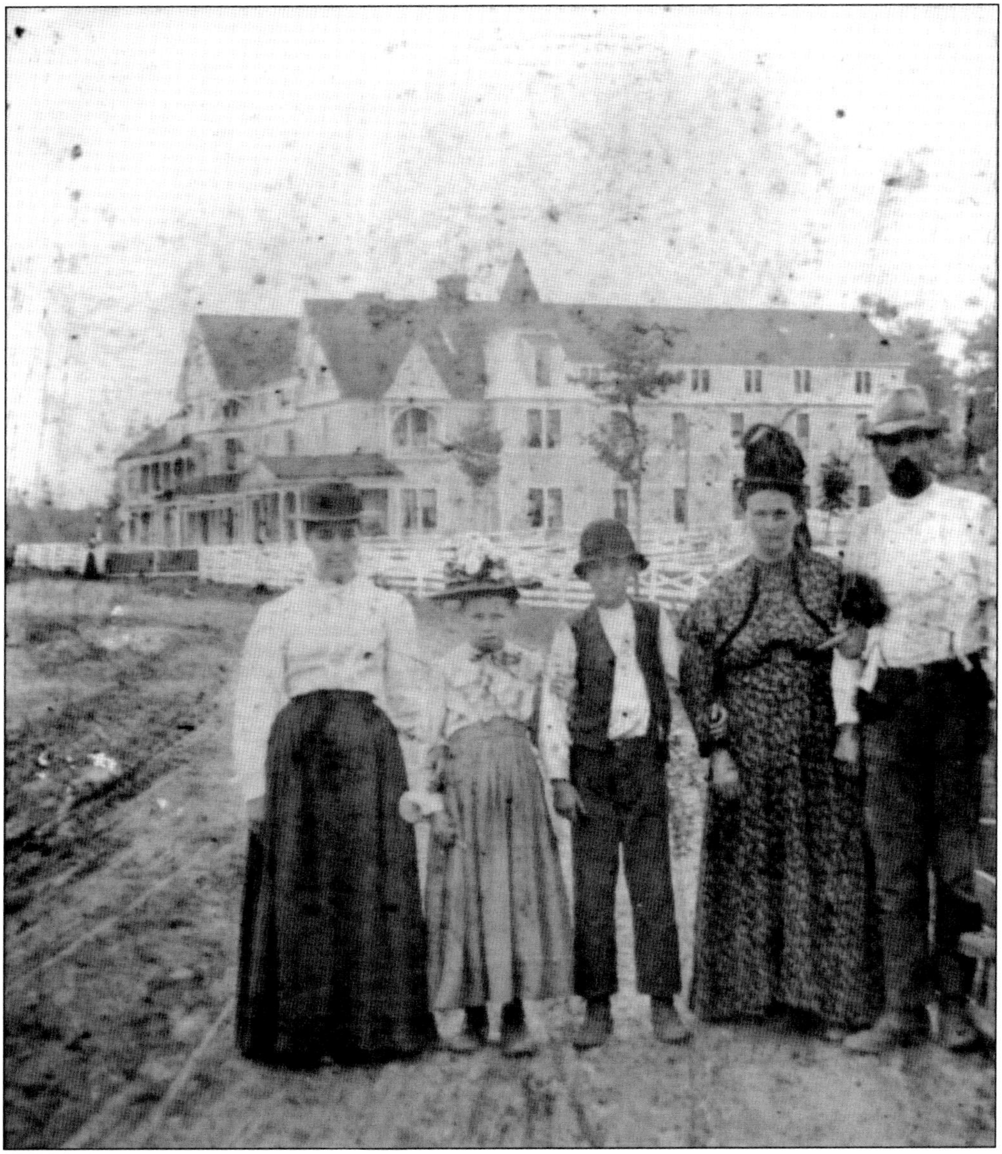

The Green Park Inn opened for business in 1891; this image dates to shortly after its completion. Its three-story frame and original Queen Anne style were later enlarged and modernized in the Colonial Revival style, and there have been subsequent alterations and additions. Set close to the road, the structure is a welcome sight coming up the elevated landscape of what is now Highway 321 from Lenoir. The hotel had bowling alleys, dancing, tennis, croquet, fishing, horseback riding, and a casino, among other amenities. The legendary grand dame of the High Country is part of the Historic Hotels of America and the main component of the larger Green Park Historic District listed on the National Register of Historic Places. Past guests of the hotel include John D. Rockefeller, Herbert Hoover, Annie Oakley, Calvin Coolidge, Eleanor Roosevelt, and Margaret Mitchell.

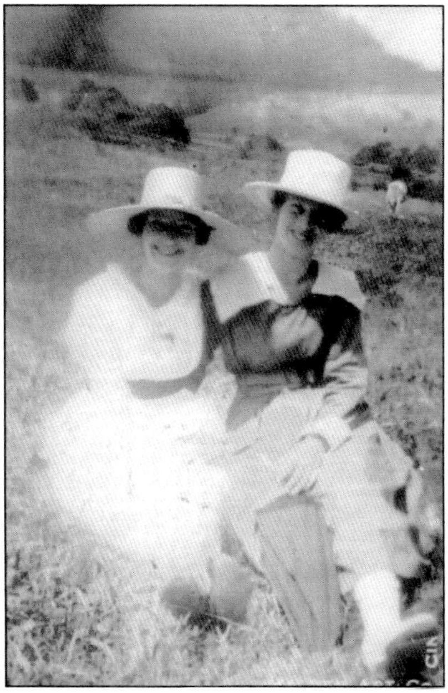

Lillian Hayes Isenhour (left) and Katherine Noel (right) were teachers at the Sandy Flat School. Sandy Flat was the first public school in Blowing Rock. Sandy Flat, Silver Lake, and Blowing Rock Village's school districts combined in 1927 into a new brick facility. A majority of this building was torn down in 1966. The current elementary school dates from 1957, with several expansions and improvements.

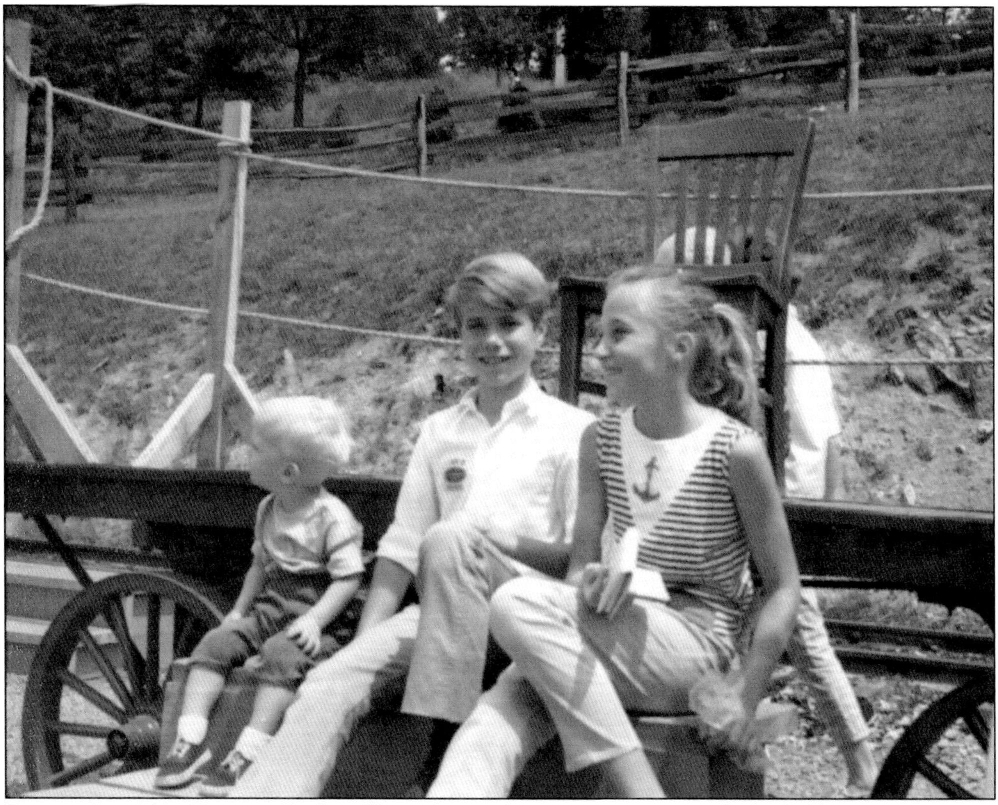

During the 1960s, Tweetsie Railroad brought in television stars, particularly child actors, to attract additional visitors. Pictured in the middle is Jon Provost, known for his role as Timmy Martin on *Lassie*. Jay North of *Dennis the Menace* and Butch Patrick from *The Munsters* were among other notable celebrities to visit Blowing Rock during the decade.

Edgar Hart, owner and proprietor of Hart's Motor Court on Chestnut Drive, collects old mop and broom handles and converts them into walking sticks for local residents. Hart makes a level surface on the bottom of the stick and inserts a large nail that will penetrate the ice and snow, preventing slipping. He estimated that he made 500 to 600 sticks over the years.

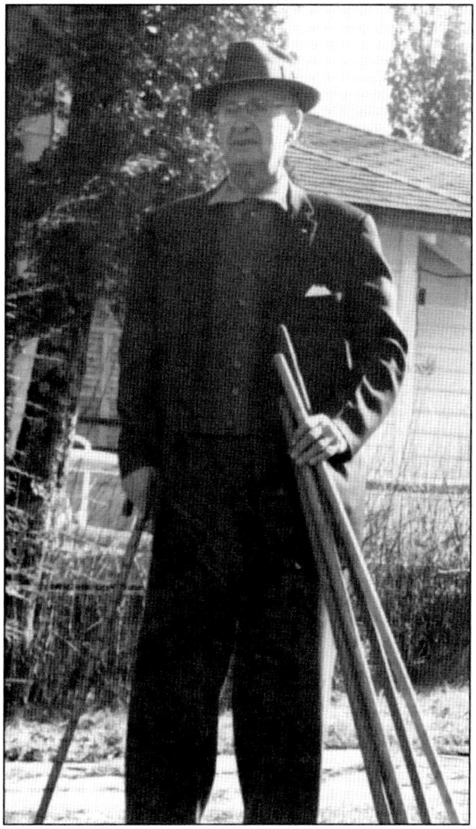

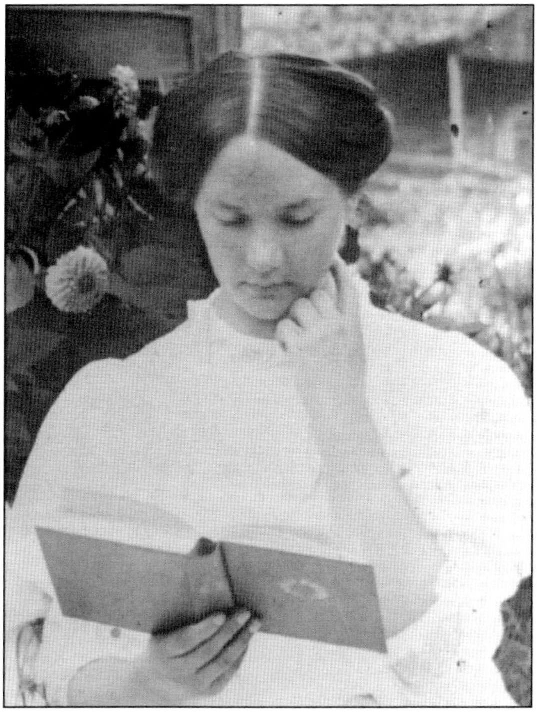

Laura Lee Wooten holds a hymnal. Many churches provided activities for teenagers in the 1950s and 1960s, including dances, hay rides, and a party where all were asked to dress as their favorite comic-strip characters, always with chaperones. Churches competed with other less-wholesome entertainment options locally and strove to keep young persons in town.

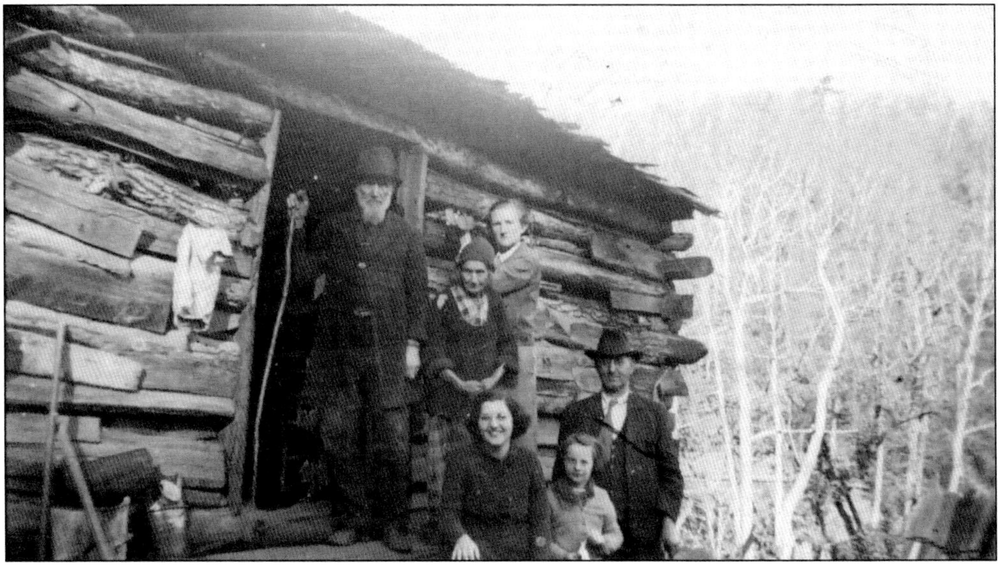

Pictured from left to right are Pinky and Jane Baldwin, Ellen and Suzanne Coffey, and George and Blaine Sudderth. Pinky told tall tales until his death in 1938; he came up the mountain from his cabin off the Yonahlossee Road every day carrying his knapsack over his shoulder. The case of his brother William Baldwin, involving alleged bootlegging, murder, and a private grudge, went all the way to the state supreme court.

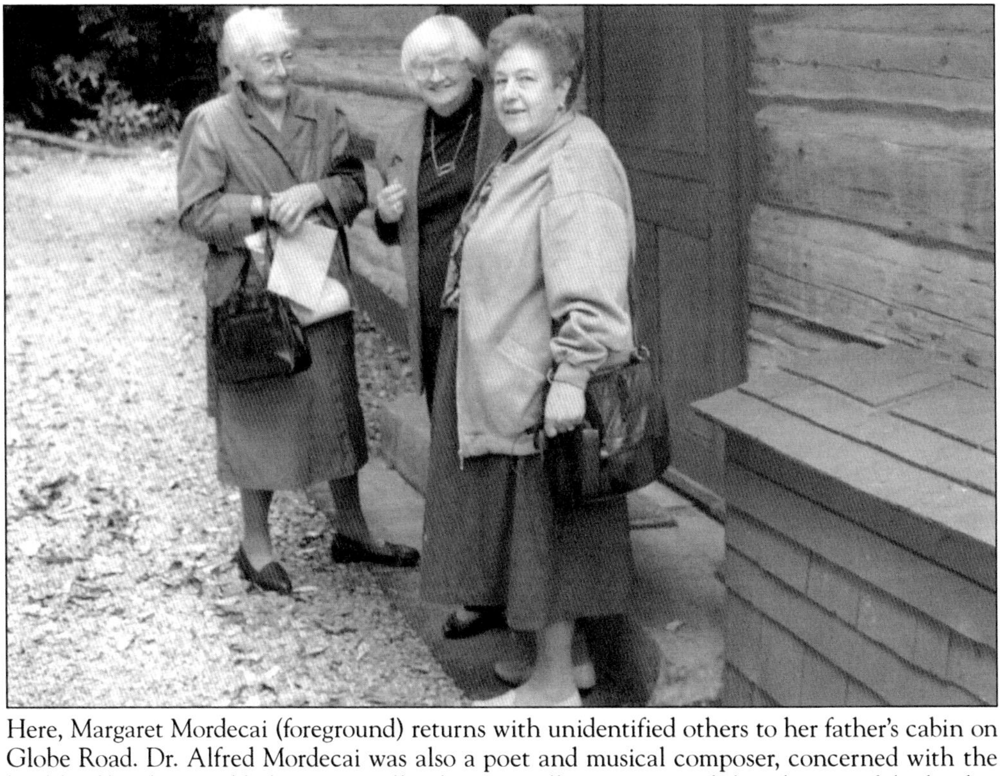

Here, Margaret Mordecai (foreground) returns with unidentified others to her father's cabin on Globe Road. Dr. Alfred Mordecai was also a poet and musical composer, concerned with the health of local natural habitats, as well as human wellness. He noted that the rise of the lumber industry in the region threatened social values in addition to habitat.

Elliott Daingerfield built his first studio, Edgewood Cottage, in 1890. Soon after it was completed, his wife, Roberta, died in childbirth, bringing tragedy to his life and art. Edgewood Cottage was unique as a boxed house in Watauga County; he used it as a summer residence, working studio, and a future teaching center for his summer art school. Boxed construction used sawn planks as both structure and enclosure.

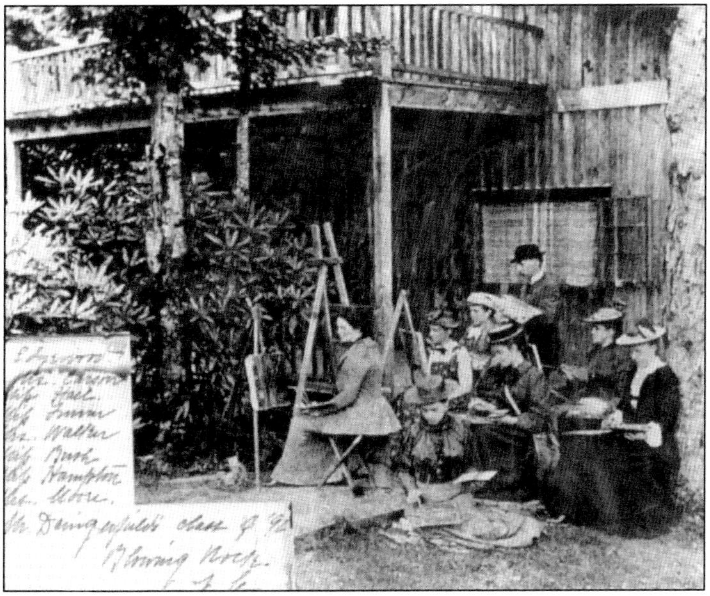

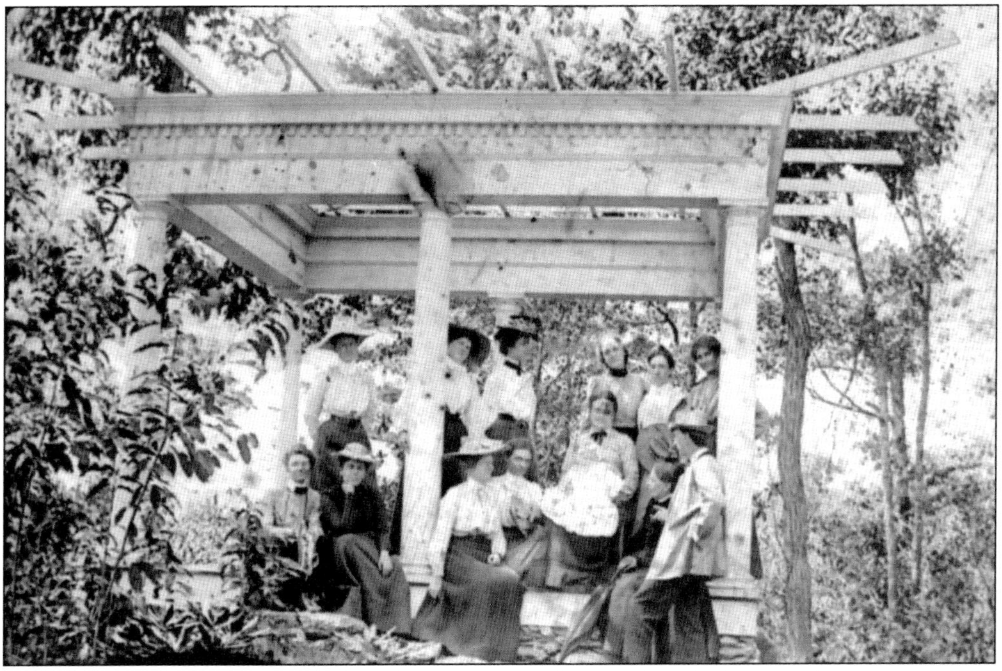

The painting ladies were a local staple, often seen, discussed, and photographed. Daingerfield founded the Permanent Art School of Blowing Rock, catering courses and programs to the types of young women he regularly taught in New York and Philadelphia. By the early 2000s, Edgewood Cottage had become severely deteriorated. Efforts by the town and the Blowing Rock Historical Society led to its reconstruction.

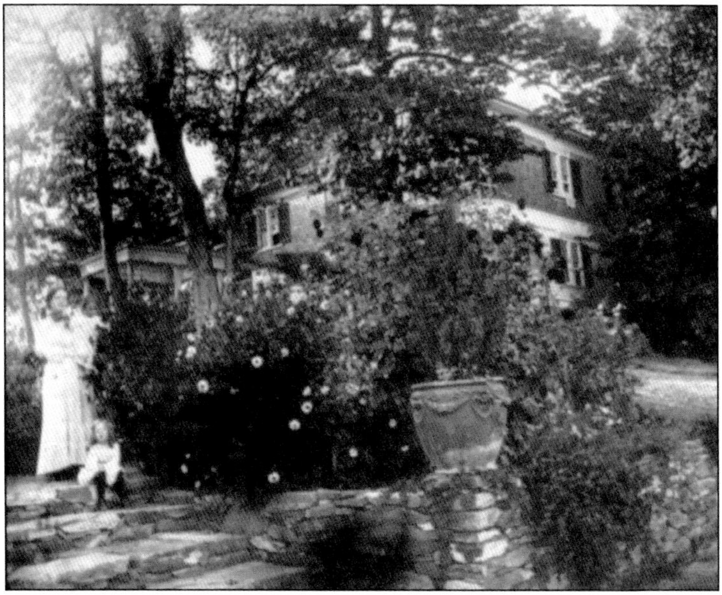

Anna Grainger Daingerfield is pictured here at Windwood with her youngest daughter Gwendolyn and her older daughter Marjorie (on the steps) in 1902, two years after Windwood's construction on Morningside Drive. The porch and grape arbor were an important part of this site and its inspiration. Anna Daingerfield became a major subject in his art, including his noted Madonna paintings.

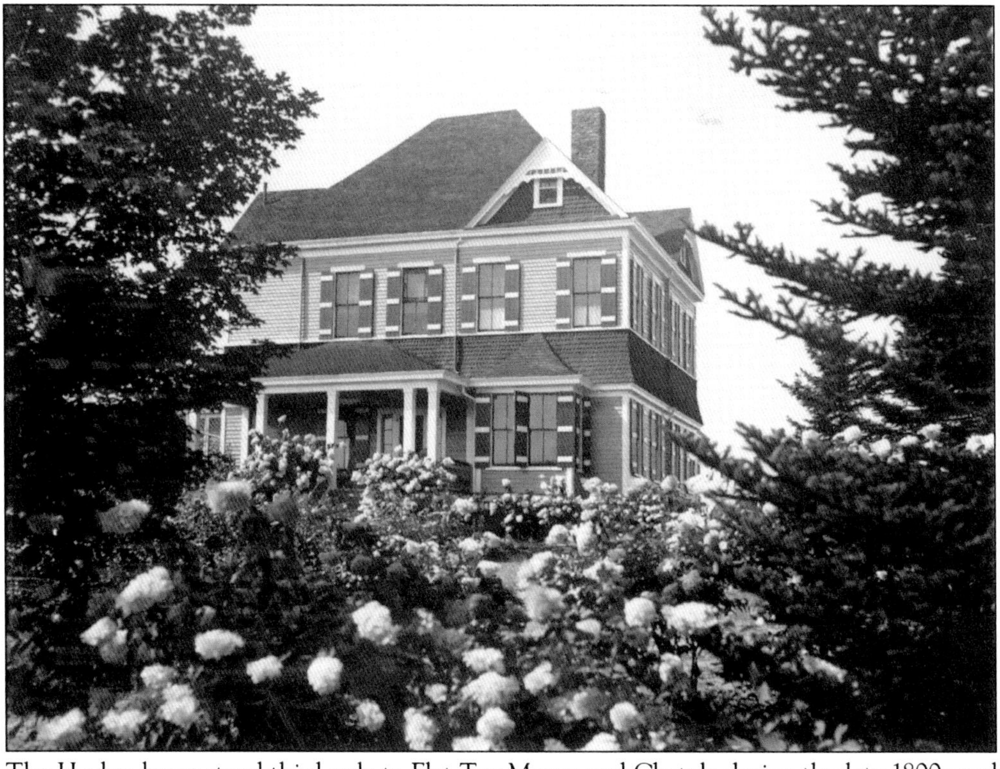

The Hughes home stood third only to Flat Top Manor and Chetola during the late 1800s and early 1900s in the scale of grand residential construction. All three properties made a point of cultivating the vegetation around them, including rhododendron. The Hughes had no children, and their imposing home was torn down in 1979 to make room for the new facilities of the Blowing Rock Assembly Grounds.

This still operation was likely located in the Shulls Mill area. Moonshining continued despite North Carolina legislating Prohibition in 1909, before the nation followed. A June 1933 local newspaper article expressed realistically, "Every public dance in the state for many years has been abundantly illuminated with good, and bad, corn liquor. So have most of the private dances."

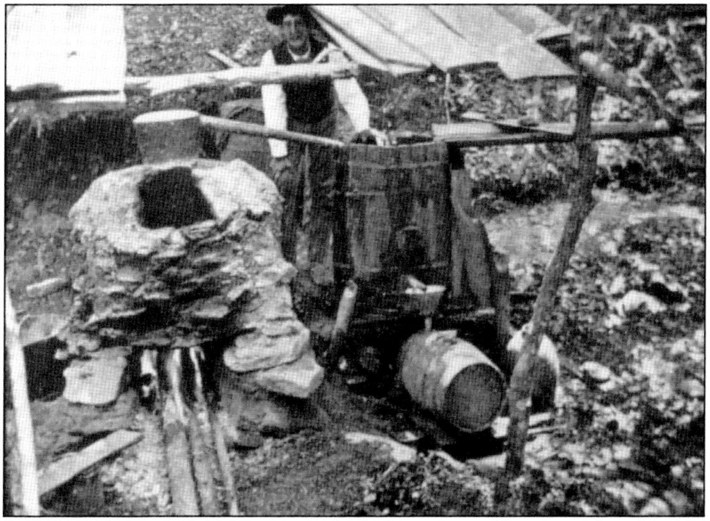

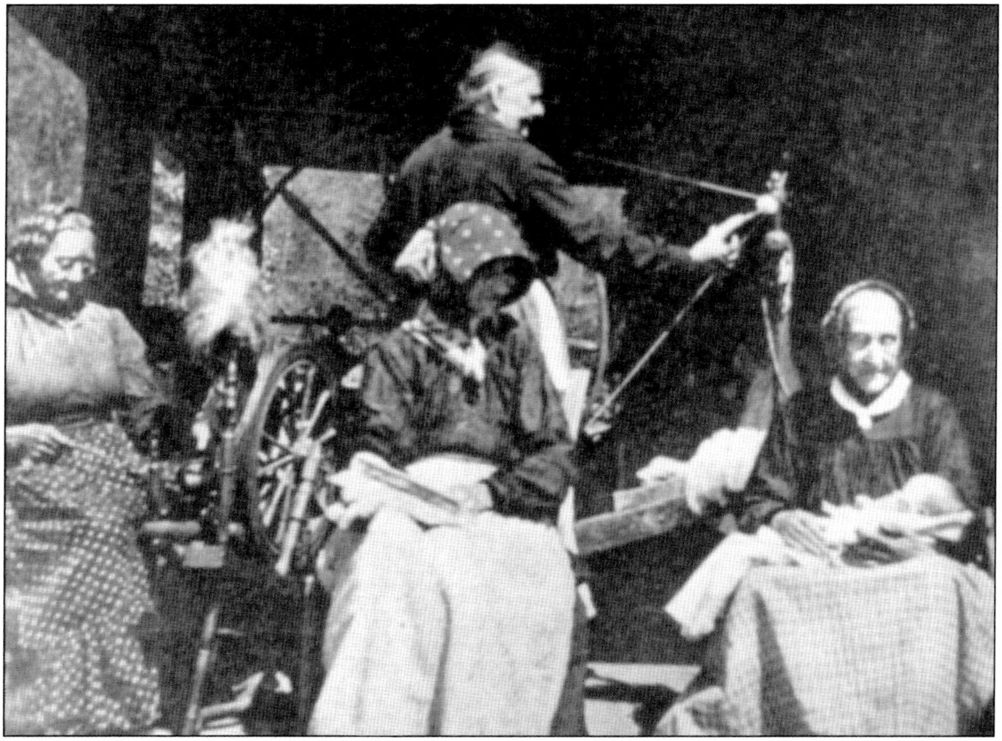

Shulls Mill had a population of 25 in the 1910 census. After the Whiting Lumber Company located here, it boasted 1,000 total residents by 1917. This helped bring a train depot for the new railroad spur, a barbershop, movie theater, hospital, and housing for workers. Shipping goods from here to Blowing Rock became more cost effective than sending them up the mountain from Lenoir.

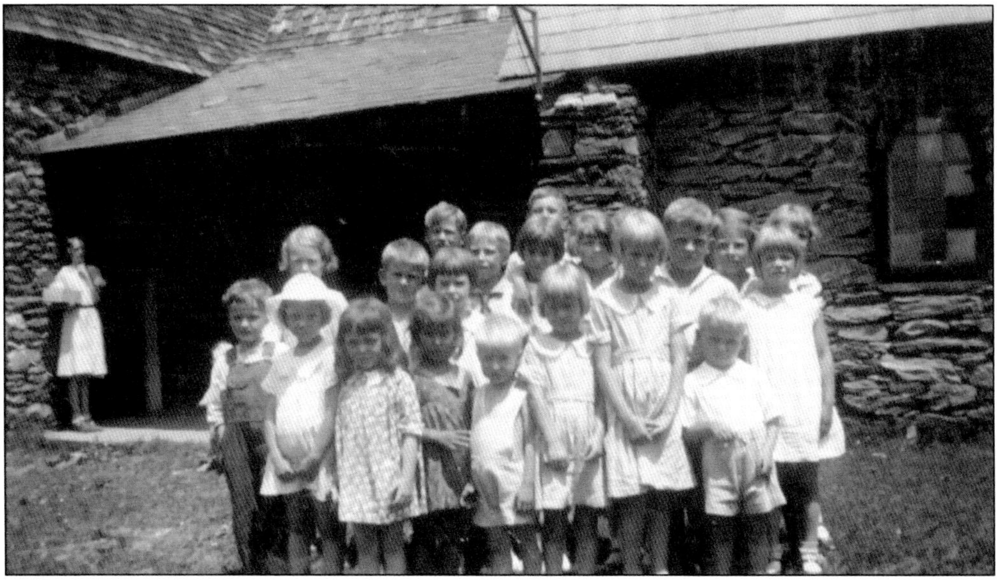

St. Mary's Sunday School was well attended in the 1930s, as were the programs led by Annie Cannon at Rumple Presbyterian across the street. After World War II, when the area faced a severe teacher shortage, poor pupil-teacher ratios, and dilapidated buildings, the inventive programs of churches fulfilled a strong role in education of youth. St. Mary's Parish Hall opened Saturday nights as a teen recreation center.

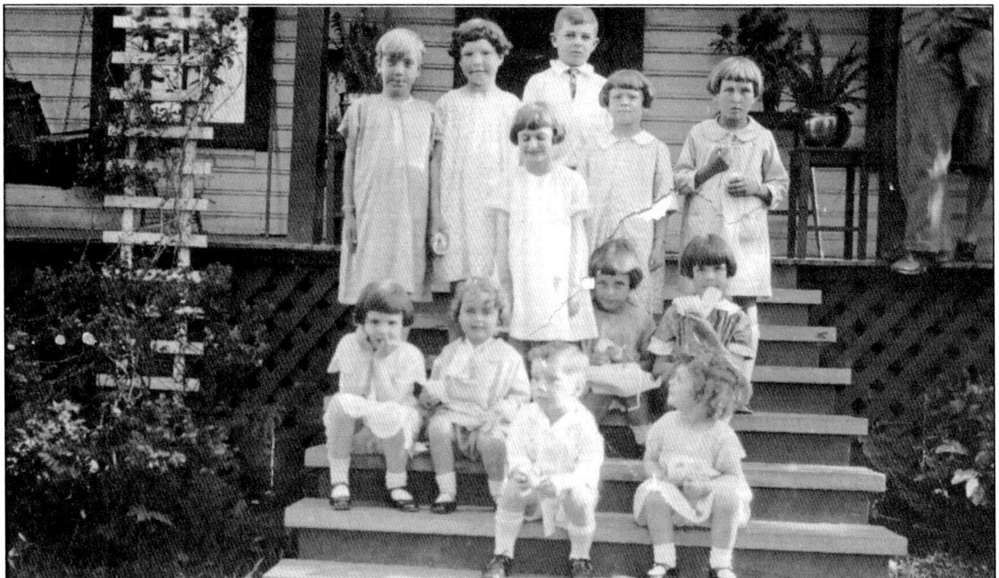

In summer 1938, a kindergarten called Happy Mornings for Little People opened with limited enrollment, moderate prices, and terms set on application. Dorothy Upton supervised this play group for children ages three to seven. The newspaper described in detail the activities weekly for the children. Known as the Playhouse, there currently is a Children's Playhouse located in Boone.

This 1930 class photograph shows the Blowing Rock fifth grade. An interesting note in a 1933 newspaper article stated that 28 children and adults had their tonsils removed at the tonsillectomy clinic at the schoolhouse. One child, after one whiff of ether, made his escape but was quickly recaptured. Certain days of the year also had local doctors providing physical assessments of students.

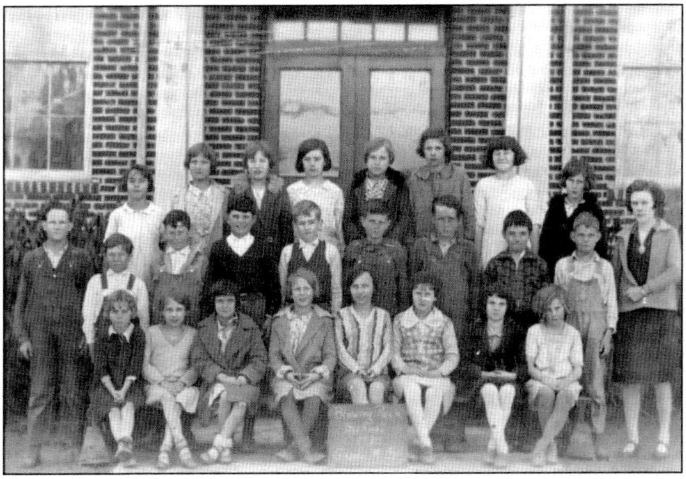

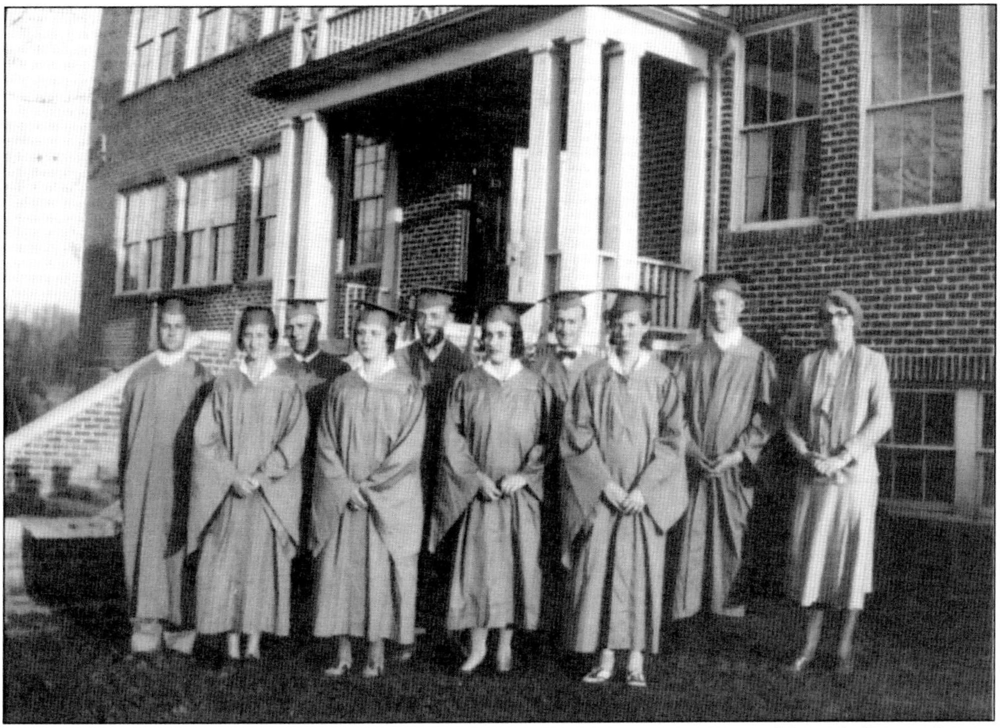

Above is the 1932 graduating class of Blowing Rock High School. Pictured from left to right are (first row) Mande Powell Kaufman, Edith Walker, Edith White, and Elizabeth Walters Bolick; (second row) Edward Coffey, Joe Bolick, Archie Sims, Omer Coffey, Sidney Cannon, and Mrs. Gene Story (class sponsor). After construction, the primary grades were located on the ground floor, the middle floor mostly had middle school students, and high school students occupied the top level.

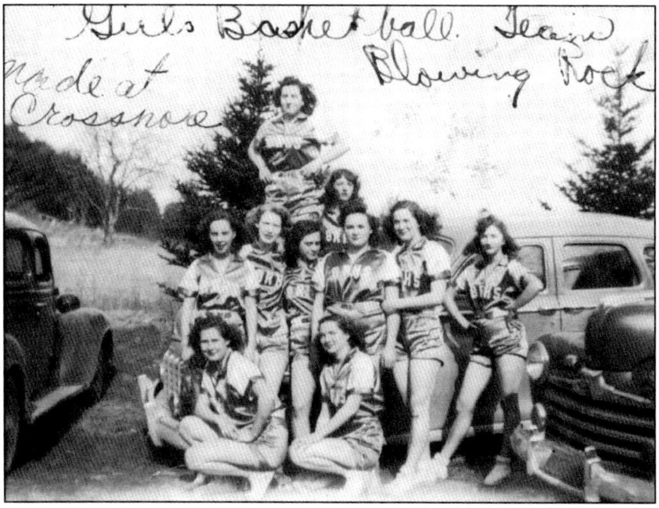

These uniforms match those worn by the Blowing Rock women's basketball team in the late 1940s, depicted here celebrating a win against Crossnore. By 1961, conference opponents included Collettsville, Piney Creek, Virginia Carolina, Cove Creek, Appalachian, Riverview, Lansing, Bethel, Cranberry, Newland, Kings Creek, Happy Valley, and Crossnore. Current opponents for the county high school team include many "off the mountain."

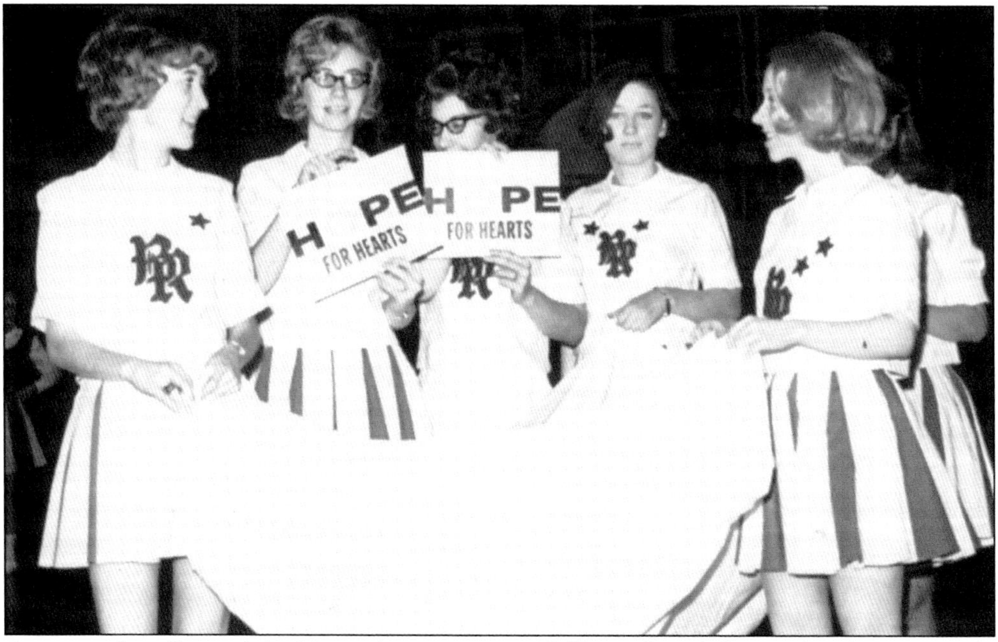

Assisting the efforts of the Heart Association in 1965 are, from left to right, Ginger Smith, Linda Rainey, Nancy Hyler, Dianna Church, and Susie Greene. Much like the majority of acts in the school talent contest, in the fall of 1964, many cheers were Beatles-themed. The on-court entertainment offered by the cheerleaders would later include unusual chants and accompanying costumes, sometimes also with musical instruments.

The Rhythm Band of Mrs. Council Cook is pictured at the Blowing Rock School around 1946. The auditorium also held a presentation titled *Heaven Bound* by an all African American cast from Cleveland County that year. *An Ideal Husband* and *The Importance of Being Earnest* by Oscar Wilde did not make it past the first rehearsal attempts in the summers of 1932 and 1933.

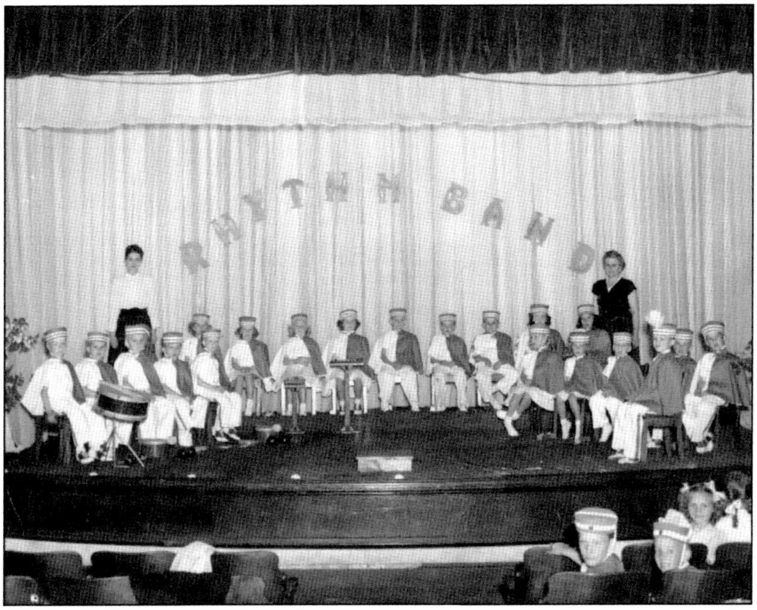

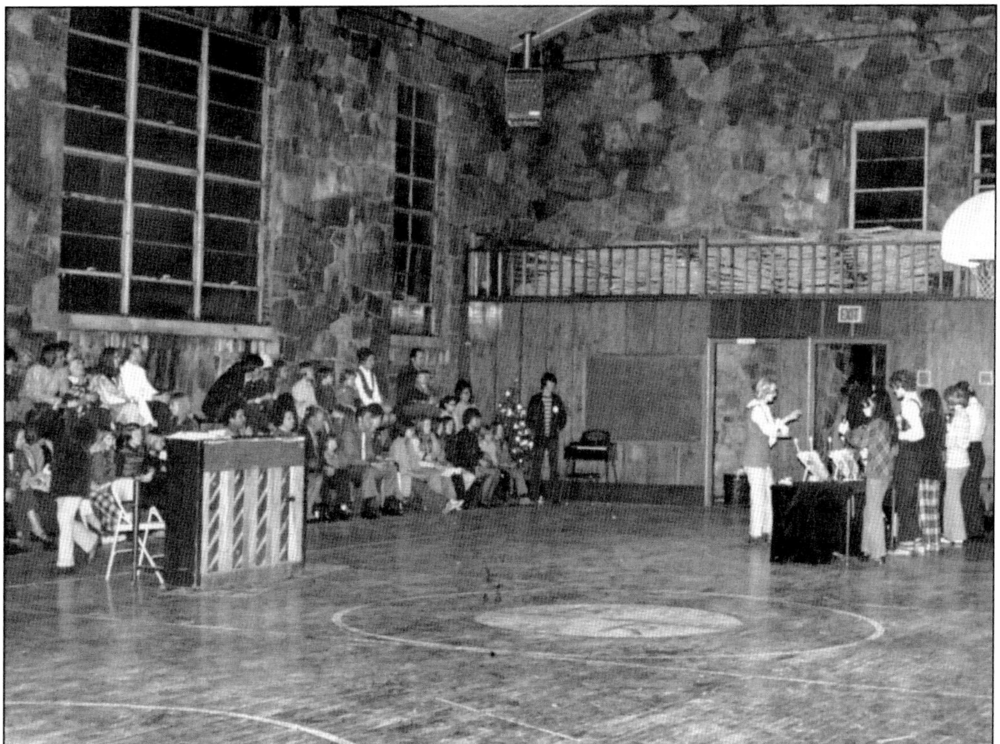

By the 1970s, the large rock gymnasium built by the Works Progress Administration (WPA) was in poor condition, with a leaky roof, sagging varnished hardwood floor, and other problems that made playing basketball dangerous and inconvenient at times. Blowing Rock teams still did well, and other community uses included a hand bell performance, seen here.

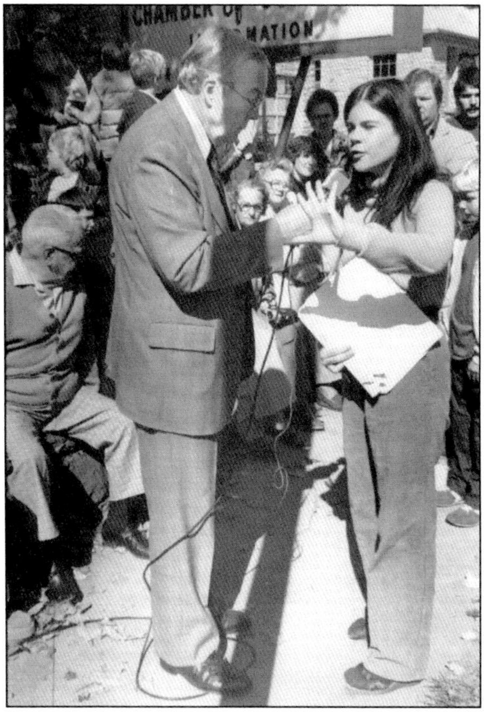

In October 1980, Doug Mayes, broadcasting legend, speaks with residents of Blowing Rock for the *On the Square* segment that visited small towns in the WBTV coverage area. Schoolchildren were also on hand in front of the chamber of commerce and in awe of the television helicopter that landed in the nearby bank parking lot.

Since 1920, Grandfather Home Day at Rumple Memorial Presbyterian Church has attracted an overflowing crowd and raised funds for the mountain orphanage at Banner Elk. In August 1961, events with Metropolitan Opera Stars raised roughly $27,000. In the 1980s and 1990s, music for the annual Grandfather Home Day was provided by the Farmhouse Singers under the direction of Shirley Blackwell.

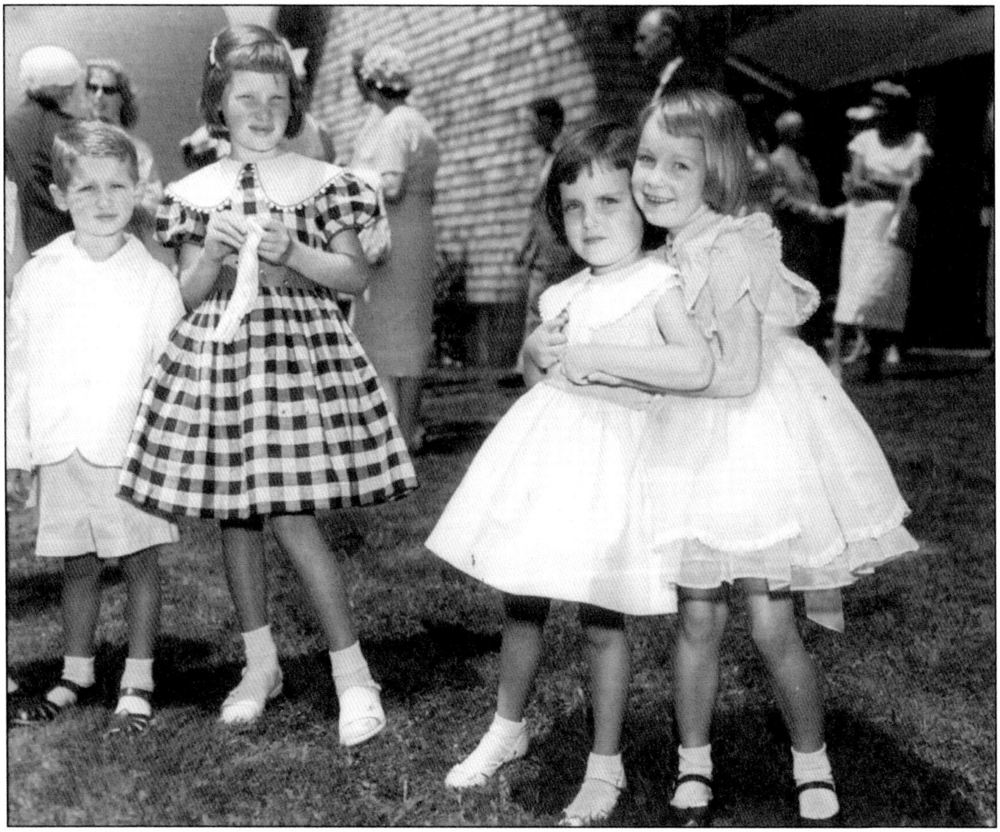

A 1948 fund drive led to the incorporation of the Blowing Rock Negro Community Church a year later. Members of the new board of trustees are, from left to right, Dr. Walter K. Keys, Rhonda Horton, John Douglas Smith, Mrs. Henry Wilson, Lynn Brown, Annie Brown, Will Tomlin, and Fred Jenkins. Local fundraising replaced a damaged roof after the 1960 winter, with the Broyhill family providing furniture.

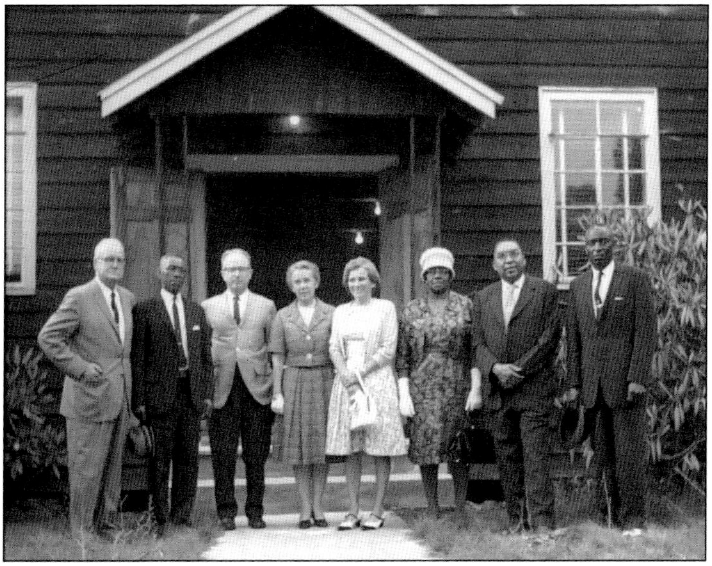

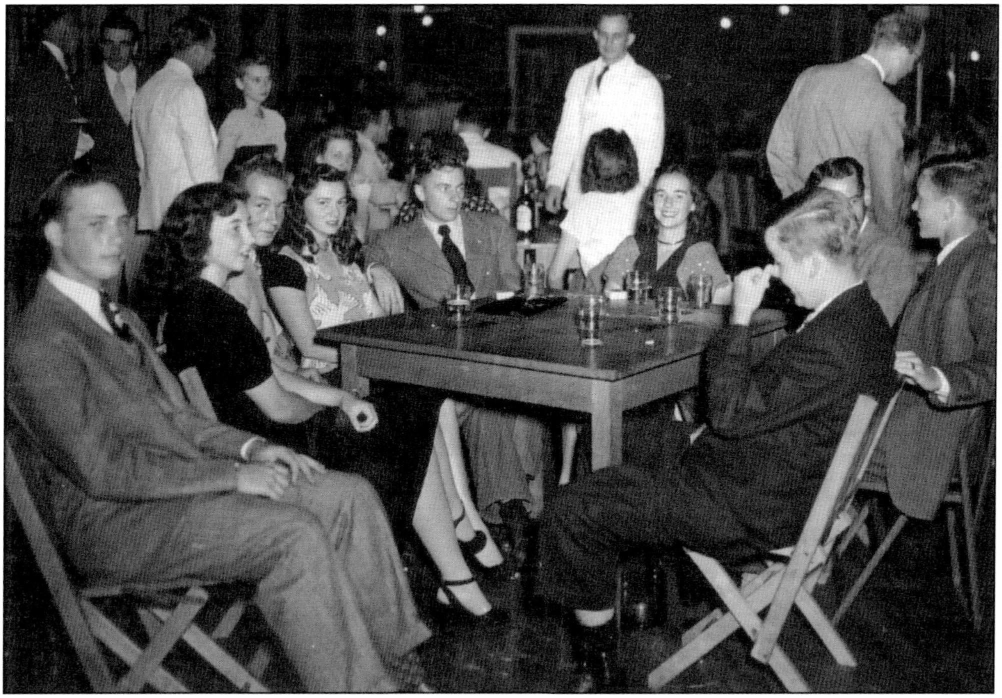

Ann Cannon Reynolds, June Bug Tate, H. Coffey, and David Bowers are some of youth found in this photograph taken at the country club's ballroom. Roughly 60 summer residents of Blowing Rock convened in 1939 for the organization of a private country club. The existing golf course was known as the Green Park Norwood Golf Course.

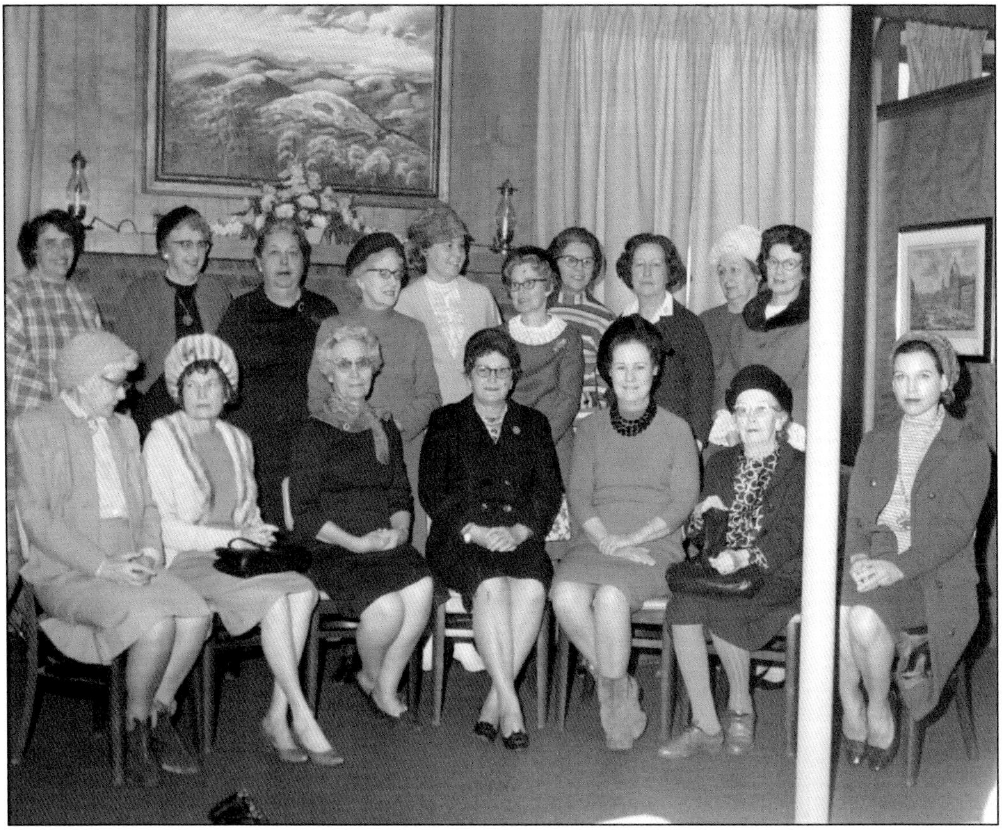

The above photograph created the unanswered question as to whether the image is of the garden club or Community Club. The exact same photograph is found in the collection of the Blowing Rock Historical Society as well as in the Blowing Rock newspaper in different years, with completely different names listed. Some of the charities supported in the 1930s by the local community club included the Well Babies' Clinic, wildflower protection, the horse show, and the library.

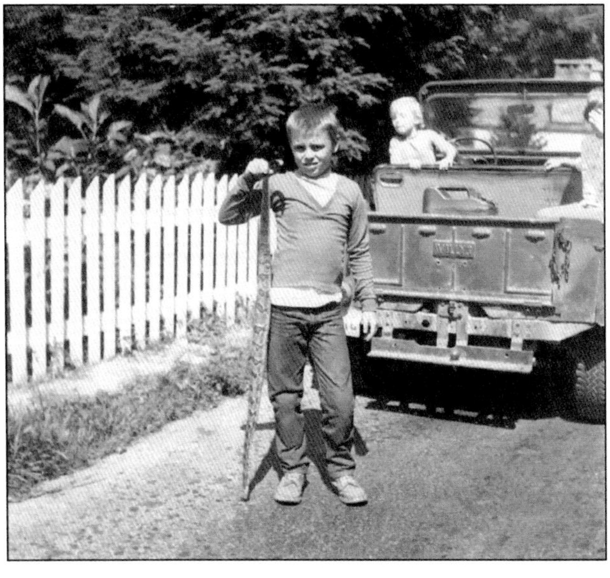

Historically and currently, the fear of venomous snakes in the region greatly eclipses the actual danger. Blowing Rock, like many Appalachian communities, may have sponsored contests for killing snakes in the past. Odd local rumors continue to persist (despite the efforts of the state wildlife resources commission to dispel them) of rattlesnakes being dropped from helicopters. The commission further states that usually the harmless king snake is mistaken for the copperhead.

Four

The Horse Show

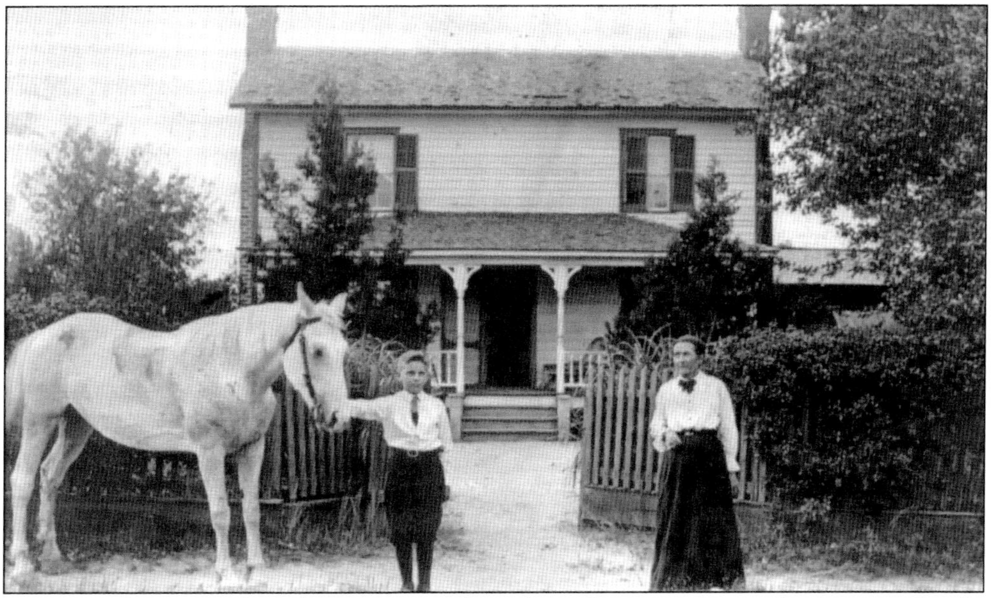

Horses in Blowing Rock and communities throughout America were a valued commodity for transportation and agricultural purposes. Taking care of the family horse was a task passed on to younger members. Before Lloyd Tate created the Blowing Rock Charity Horse Show in 1923, it is believed there was a prior horse race from Green Park to Blowing Rock and back on Green Hill Road for the amusement of hotel guests.

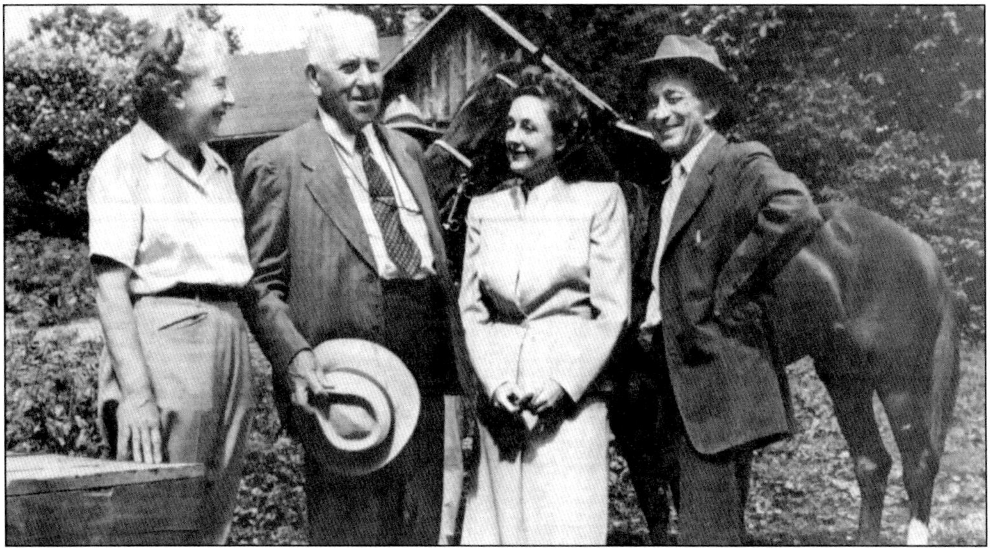

Dedicated horse show leaders include, from left to right, Annie Cannon, Luther Snyder, Elizabeth Coker, and Lloyd Tate. The oldest continuous annual outdoor horse show in America celebrates its 93rd anniversary in 2016. The show has grown from a weekend affair with a handful of show horses in 1923 to three weeks of a massive field of participants, generating more than $6 million for the local economy.

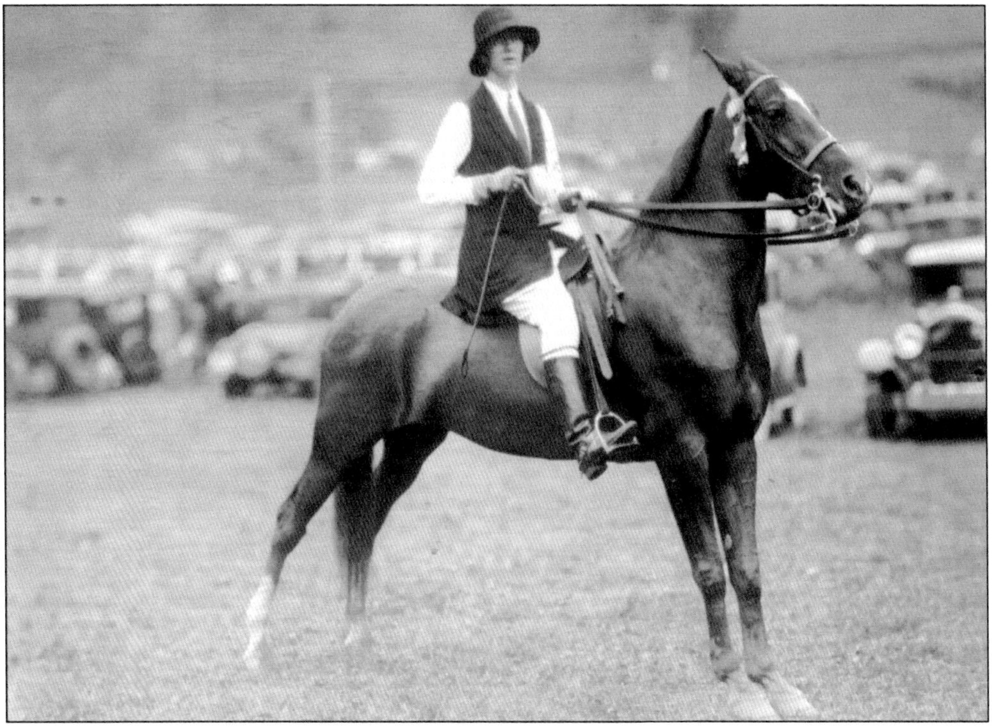

This image from the horse show dates to the 1930s, and the rider is identified as Virginia Jones of Charlotte, holding a trophy and riders crop. Female riding etiquette at the time included the proper hat, vest, tie, and especially pants. In the early 1930s, women abandoned the sidesaddle in droves in favor of riding astride, a growing sign of liberation.

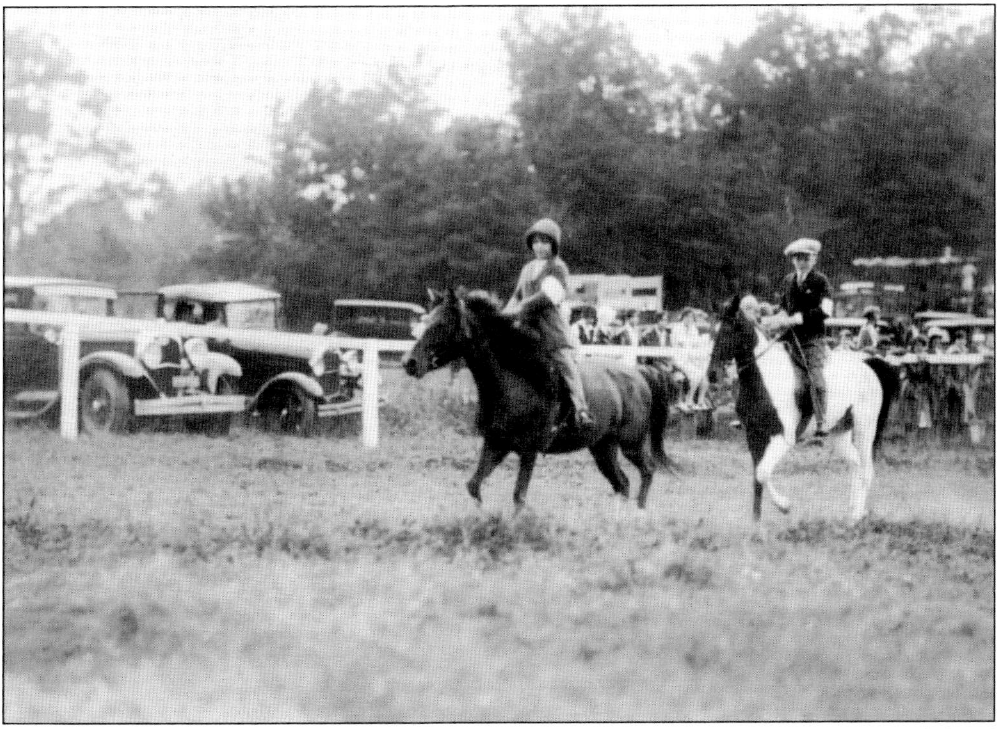

Another image from the 1930s shows youth riding horses. Spectators sit atop wood benches behind a fence with automobiles nearby and a refreshment stand in back. The horse show has never been just about horses and riders; it also supports many local organizations, including the Blowing Rock Rotary Club, Blue Ridge Parkway Foundation, and Horse Helpers of the High Country.

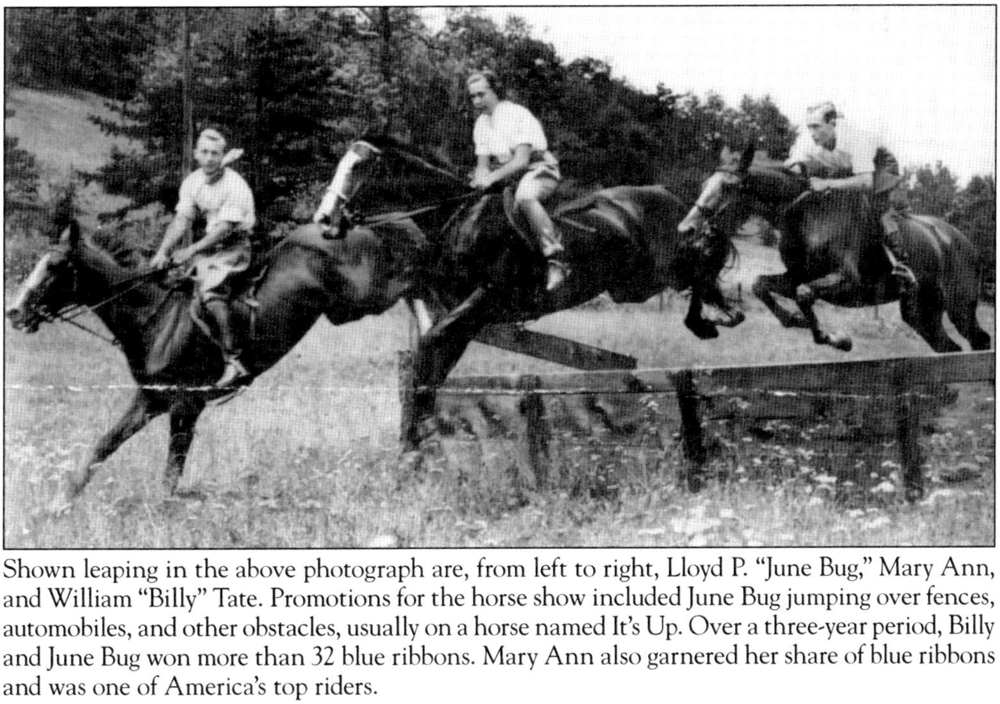

Shown leaping in the above photograph are, from left to right, Lloyd P. "June Bug," Mary Ann, and William "Billy" Tate. Promotions for the horse show included June Bug jumping over fences, automobiles, and other obstacles, usually on a horse named It's Up. Over a three-year period, Billy and June Bug won more than 32 blue ribbons. Mary Ann also garnered her share of blue ribbons and was one of America's top riders.

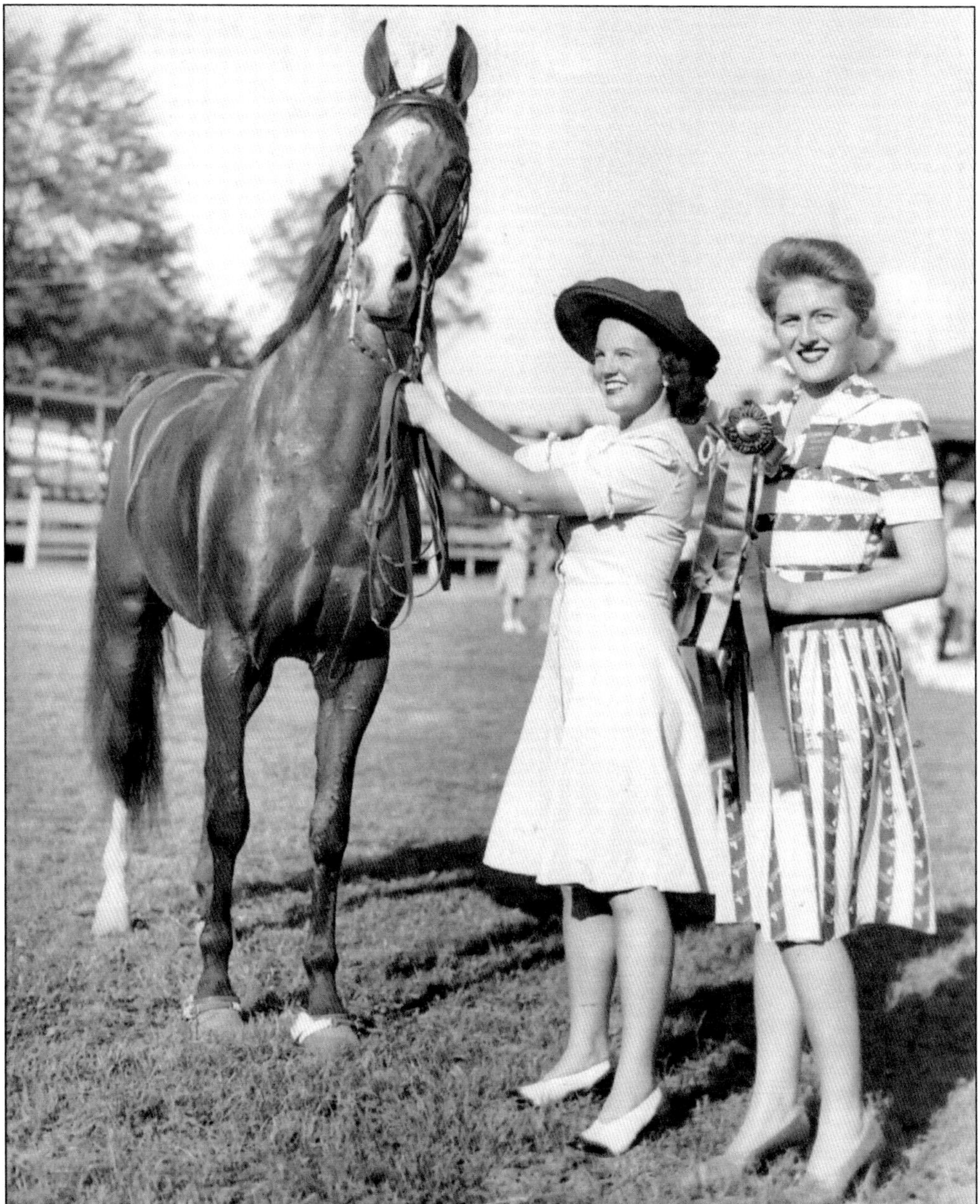

Unidentified women with blue ribbons stand with a horse named Ellawee in the above image. The following memory comes from a *Blowing Rocket* article that featured horse show reflections. Claire Boyce came to the mountains in 1923 for the first horse show and until at least 2004. In between those 81 years she exhibited, managed, or was a spectator at every show. "I remember coming from our stables in Greensboro to one of the first horse shows in Blowing Rock in the 1920s. We had 12 horses we wanted to show. We rigged up two horses to a wagon, pulled two behind the wagon, both my brothers and I rode a horse while leading another, and we had a fella that worked for our stables, and he rode a horse and led another. We had to ride our horses or walk all the way. It took us three days to get up that mountain. But it was all worth it, just to be in Blowing Rock and be in the Horse Show there."

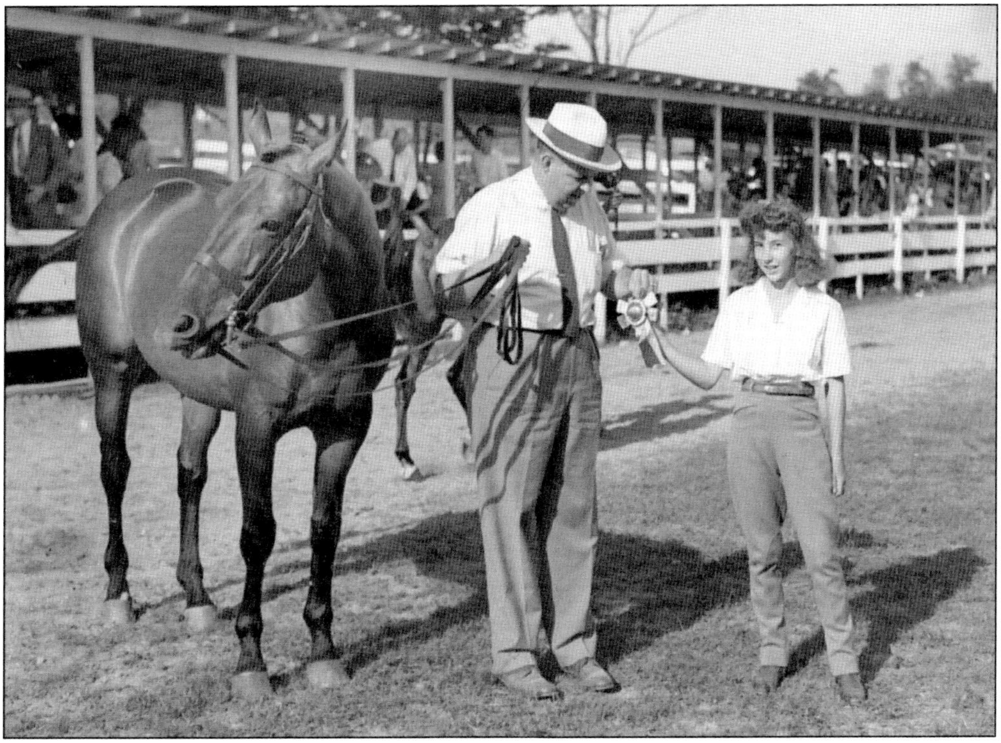

In the above photograph, Anne Cannon receives a blue ribbon at the 1942 horse show. In 1933, the children's class included June Bug Tate, and those in attendance included Gov. John Christopher Blucher Ehringhaus and Matilda Ehringhaus. This advertisement ran in a June 1932 newspaper: "The ranch riding school, Savannah, GA. Operating the Green Park Stables, Horses for Hire, Riding Instruction, Children's Classes a Specialty."

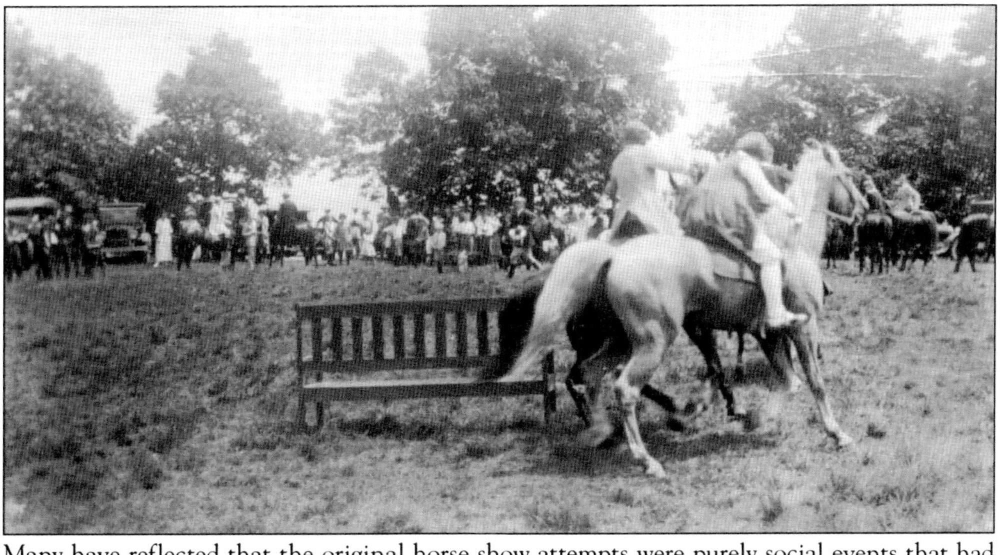

Many have reflected that the original horse show attempts were purely social events that had none of the show's current professionalism. There were several unusual events like the balloon race, potato race, doughnut race, and musical chairs race. The doughnuts were strung from a rope across the track while the riders ate them without touching them with their hands.

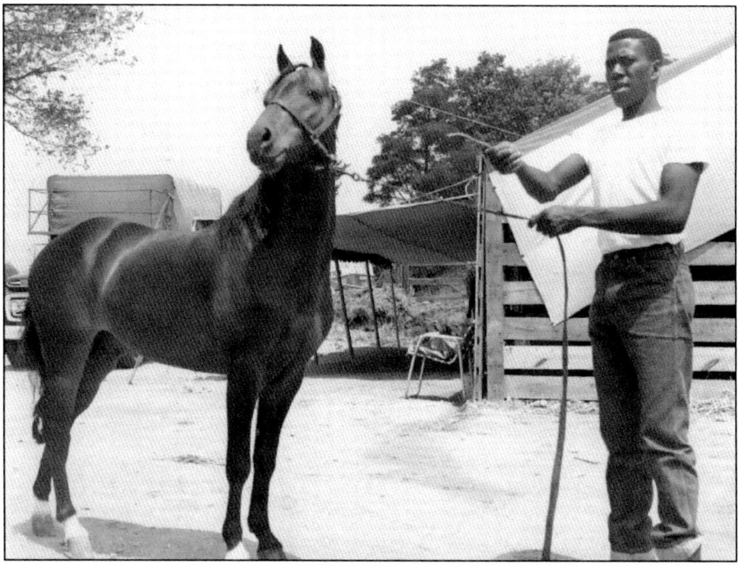

Pictured, groom Wallace Grey cleans and walks Cain, owned by Steven Miles, around the horse show grounds. Miles rode Cain in the 41st annual horse show, in 1964. In 1973, the 50th anniversary of the horse show was celebrated statewide by Gov. Jim Holshouser, who proclaimed the week in August Horse Show Week across the entire state.

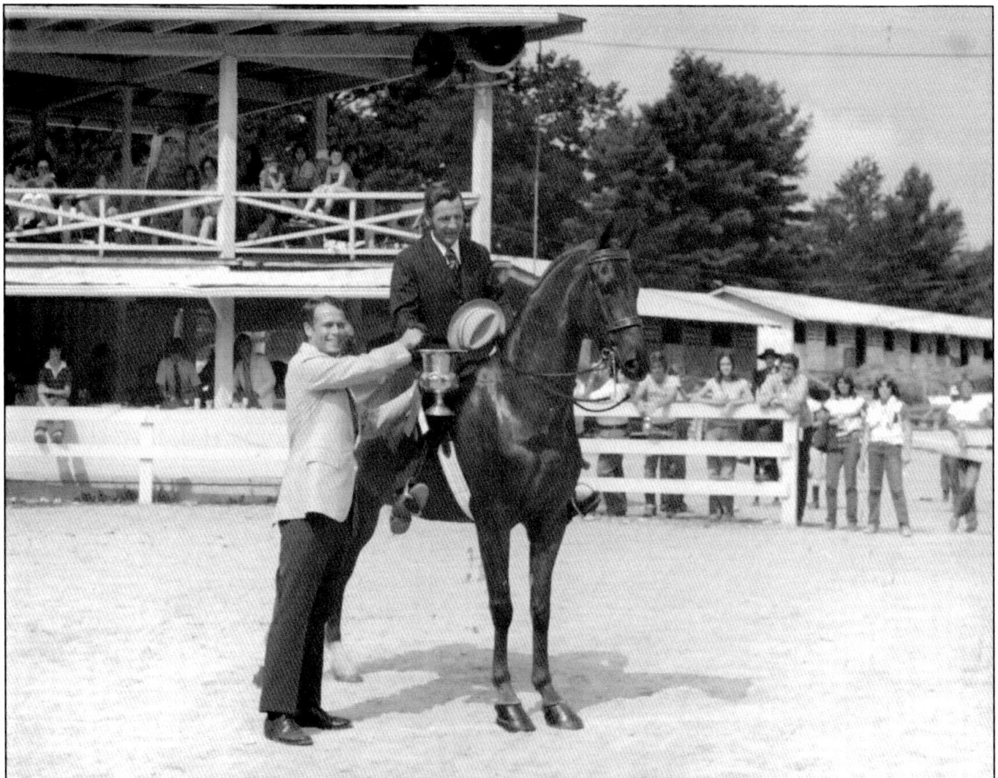

Senator Davis presents a trophy to John Tester with spectators and stables in the background. Stabling advertisements were constants in the newspapers, including those for the Green Park Inn and "C.A. Hendrix Stable located at Sudderth stables in the Village. Good five-gaited horses for rent. Old Bill Simmons will please you." Bill Simril, known as "Old Bill," was an African American man who trained two generations of aspiring horsemen locally.

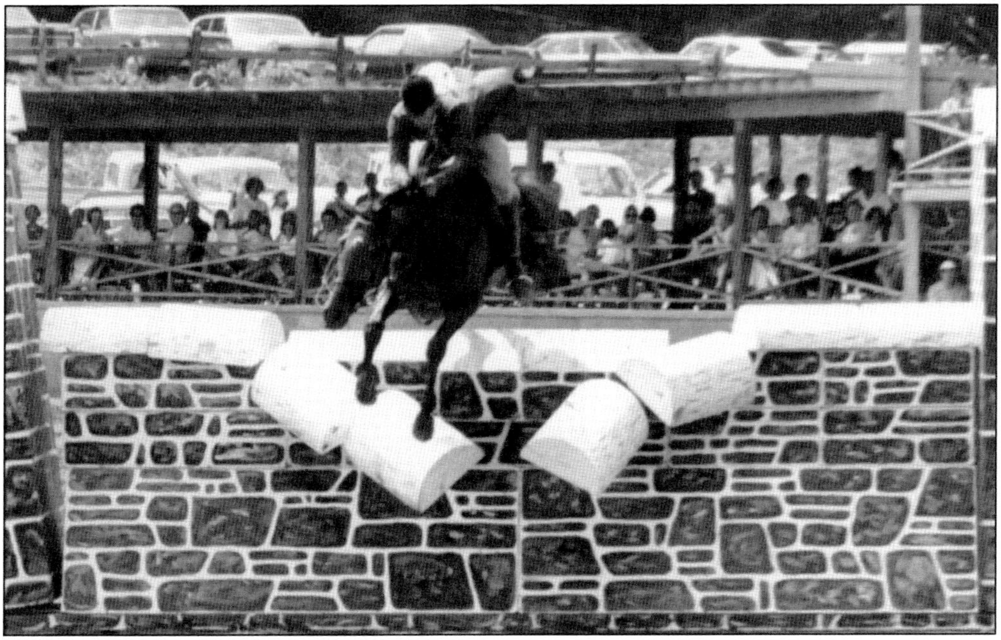

Horse and rider almost clear the wall with spectators and tiered parking in the background. The saddlebred division is in early June and the hunter and jumper division is in late July. The Linville Horse Show started in 1933. One in Hendersonville was typically the week before, which helped keep competitors locally in the area.

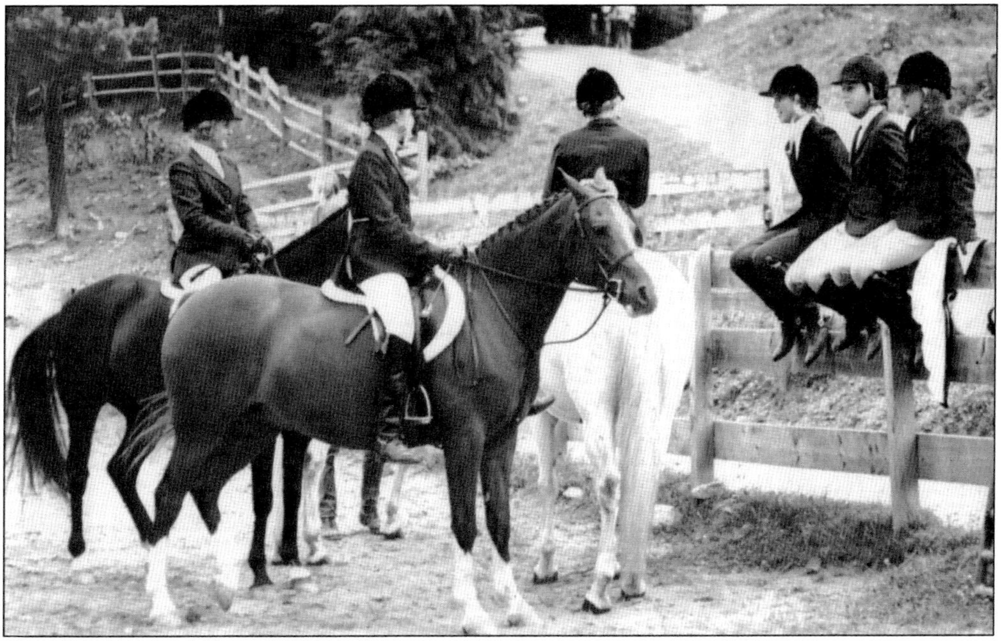

Camp Yonahlossee was one of the first summer camps for girls in the area, begun in 1922 under the direction of Dr. and Mrs. A.P. Kephart ("Kep" and "Keppie"). In 1941, the camp had 40 entries in the horse show, besides those riding in the drill team. The boys at Camp Catawba also attended the horse show, and many campers kept an interest in riding to view and compete in the annual event.

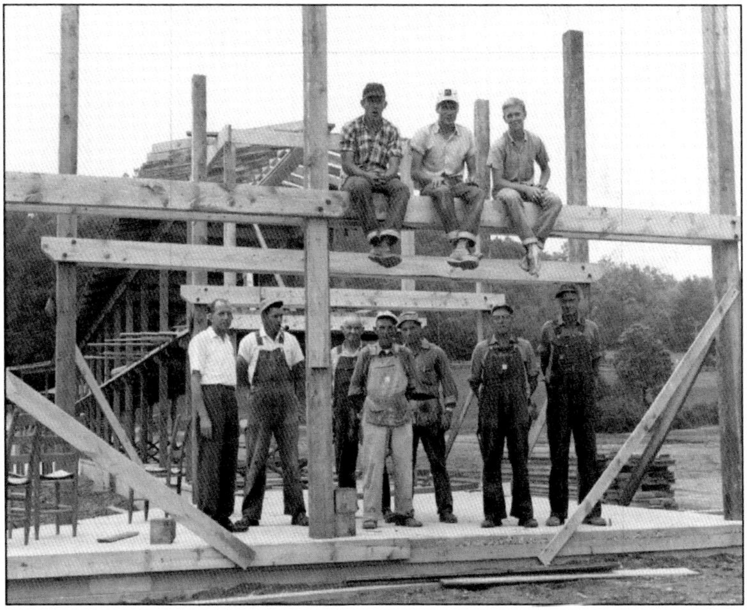

A new grandstand for the horse show was constructed in March 1966. Spectators could now enjoy upper-level viewing and still do today. Ticket costs for spectators remain reasonable, and box seats typically sell out each year. In 1964, the building of the second ring at the now officially named L.M. Tate Showgrounds began.

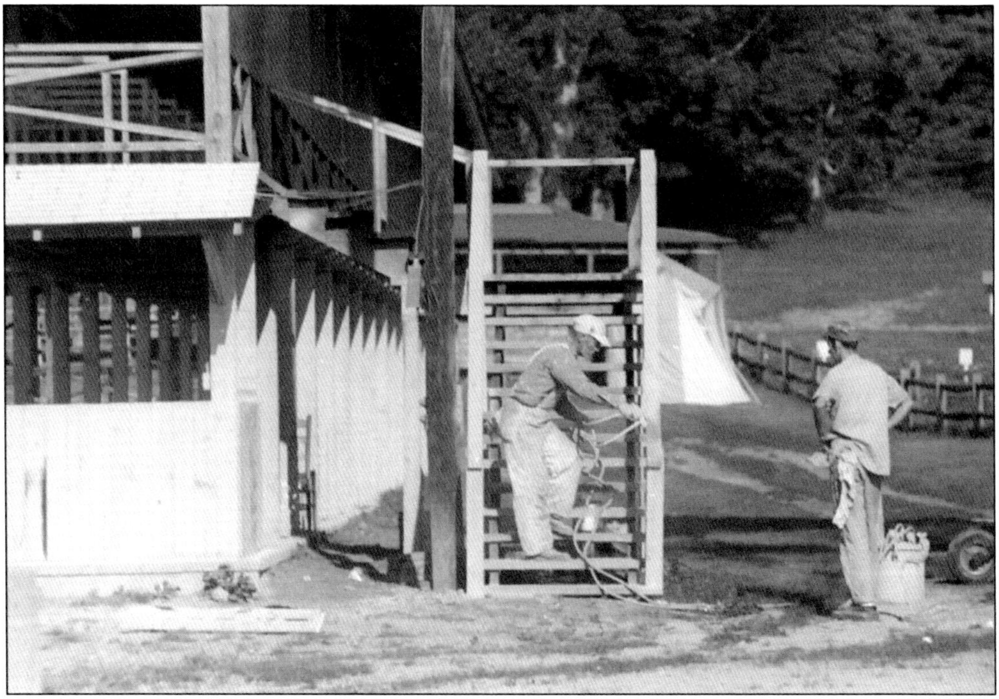

The 36th annual horse show in 1959 boasted over 1,000 new grandstand seats among substantial improvements to the overall grounds. Attendance was noted at over 5,000 in 1959 for the first time ever. In 1966, a $100,000 expansion was completed, including the larger stable barn, which housed dormitory space for grooms and offices for the show secretary and manager, plus large box stalls.

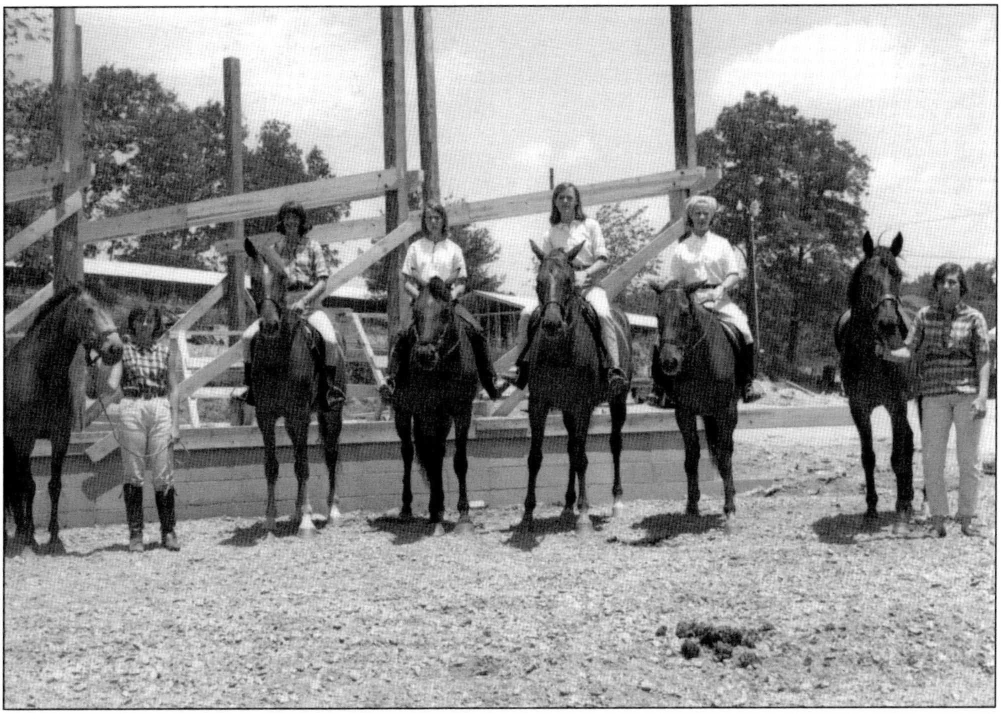

Lynn Darnell is among those posing with construction on the horse show grounds in the background. Several television and radio stations were on hand for coverage of the 1960 show, including WBTV. In 2012, the saddlebred division sold out for the first time. There were over 1,700 general-admission tickets sold over three weeks in 2012.

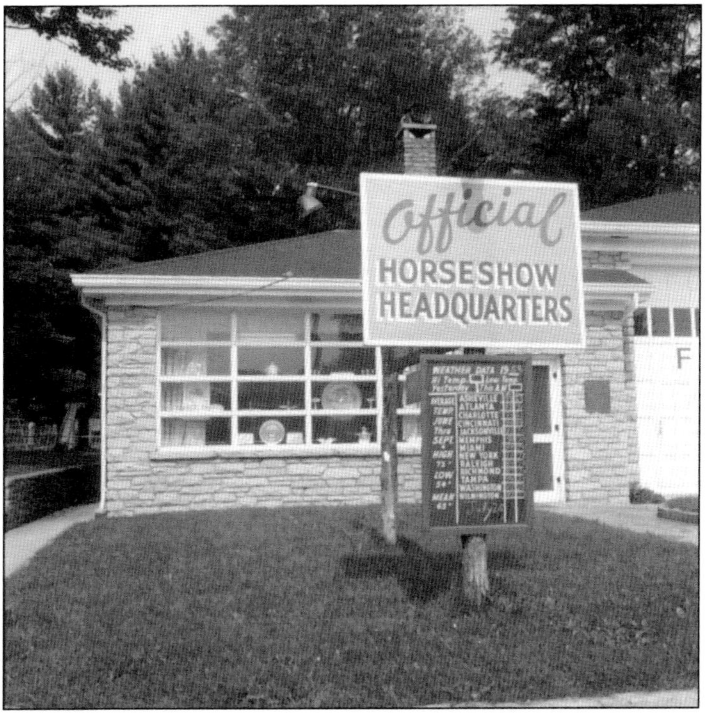

In the early 1950s, voters approved a referendum to permit the town to collect a percentage of the appraised value of property to be used to support a chamber of commerce. The mission of advertising and accommodating visitors to the village included the horse show. The chamber has since moved, as have the fire and police departments. The current town hall and offices remain in the building.

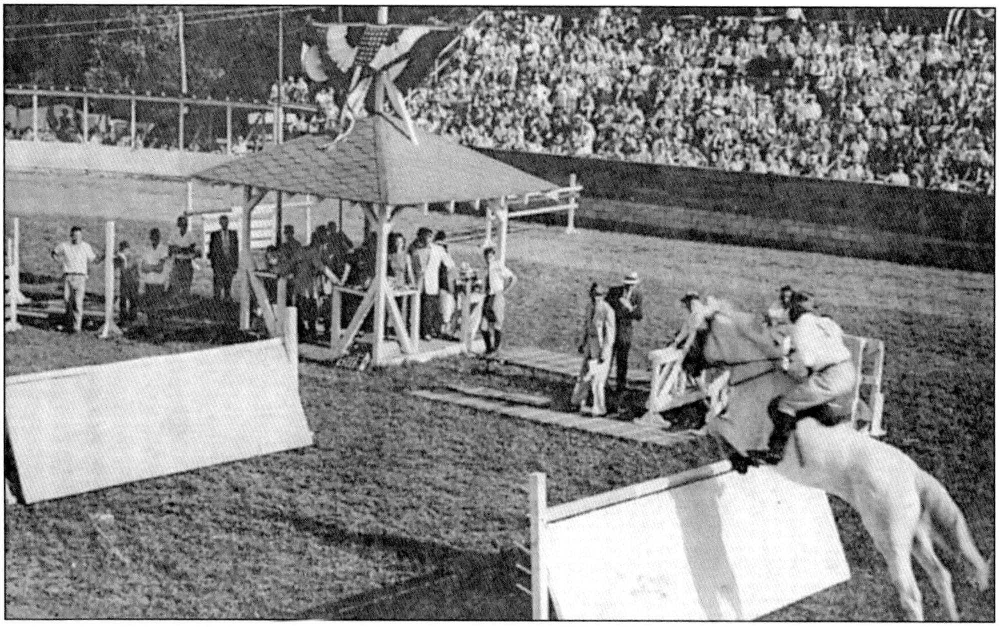

Mary Ann Tate and the Tate family are one of the many generations of family riders. In August 2000, four generations of one family were represented when Lauren Silver competed in a class. During the first years of the horse show, it was her great-grandmother Kathryn Crull that performed, and in between came her grandmother Kay Silver and her aunt Ann Griggs.

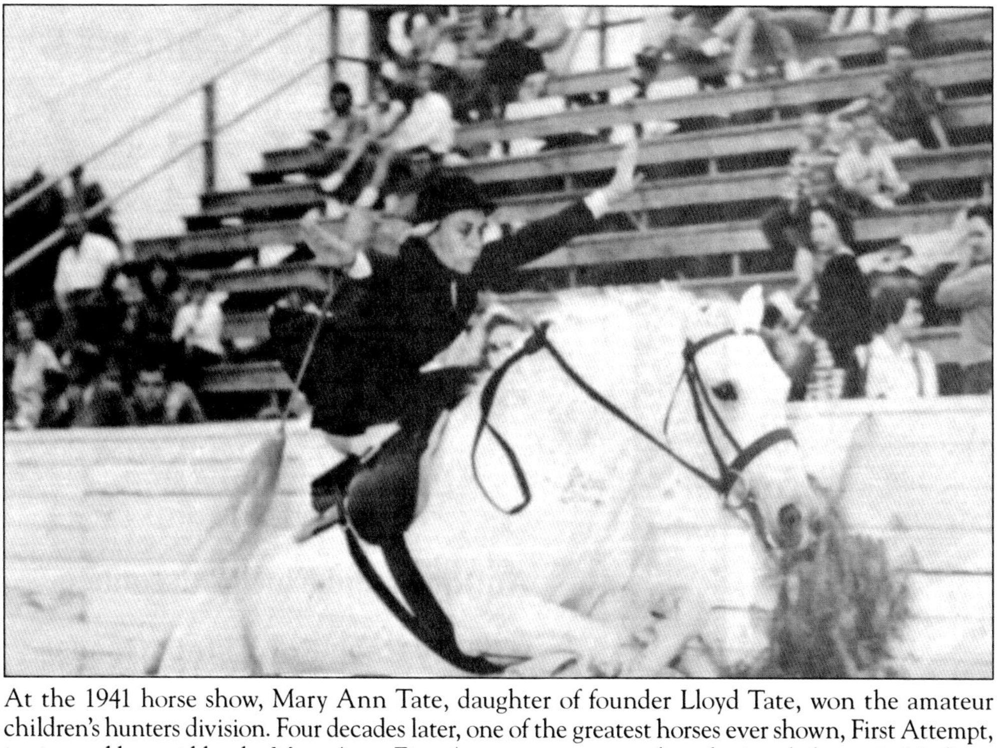

At the 1941 horse show, Mary Ann Tate, daughter of founder Lloyd Tate, won the amateur children's hunters division. Four decades later, one of the greatest horses ever shown, First Attempt, is pictured here ridden by Mary Ann. First Attempt won several professional classes in Madison Square Garden, where the grand championship of the sport is held annually.

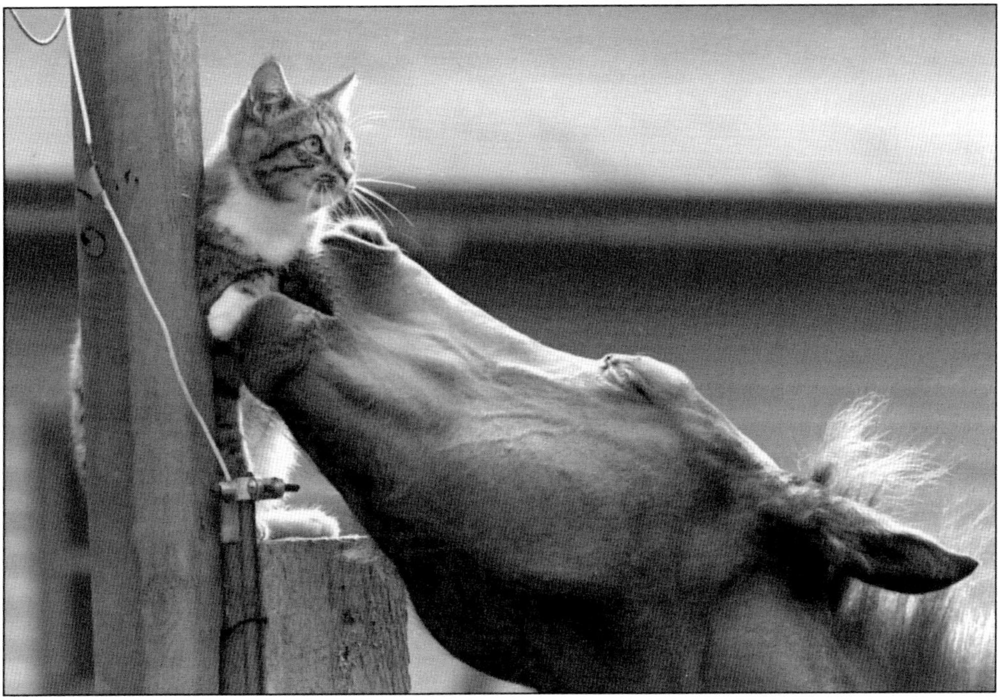

There is a long history of other animals making use of the horse show grounds. In 1938, a pet show was held, including prizes for "most unruly, best mannered, most appropriate, most unusual, ugliest pet, prettiest pet, and a grand champion considered from all viewpoints." Pets registered at the Blowing Rock Drug Company for the competition, and entries included turtles, ponies, goats, white mice, and pigs.

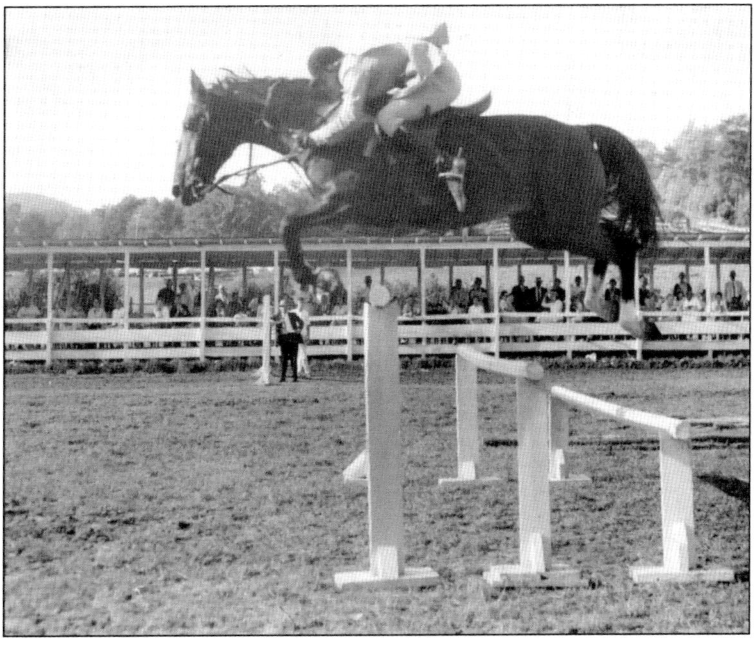

In August 1964, Mary Fisher clears a hurdle as a judge observes closely. The community club was consulted in July 1924 about establishing an annual riding contest, with plans to share the proceeds. They agreed and also set up a concession stand staffed by their volunteers, a project that netted them substantial profits for their many other undertakings.

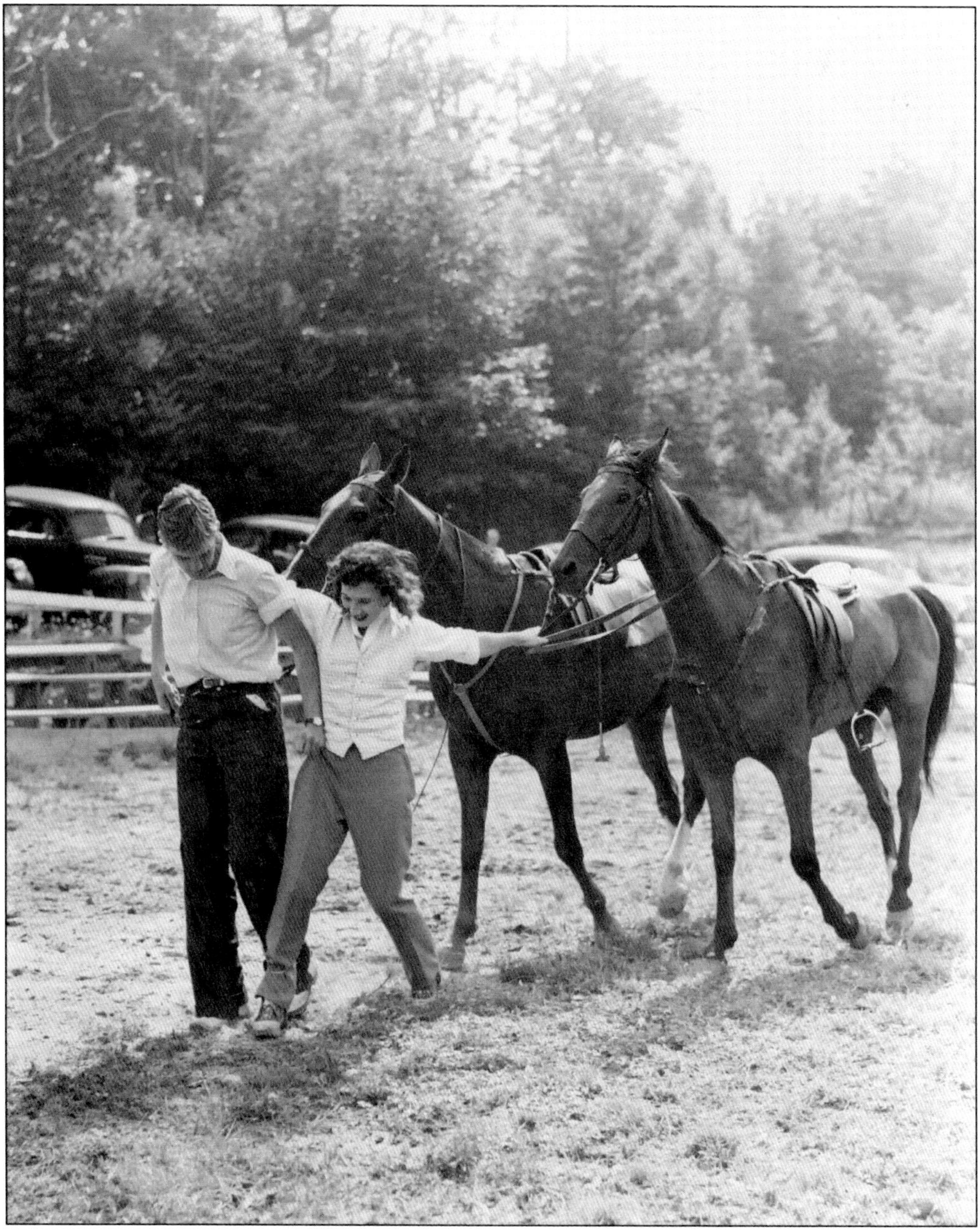

It is always wise to watch one's step around the horse show grounds and riding trail areas of Blowing Rock. The carriage roads of the Moses Cone Estate continue to be utilized for recreational riding, as they were historically. The Blowing Rock Charity Horse Show Foundation supports the Blue Ridge Parkway Foundation, among other charities, for preservation and maintenance of these roads. For the past decades, horses have not been permitted along the jogging and walking trail around Bass Lake but can access the causeway to the trails up to Cone Manor. From the June 24, 1933, *Blowing Rocket*, "Mrs. Moses H. Cone requests horseback riders in the Cone estate to keep to the main roads in the estate. Otherwise, she says, she will regretfully be obliged to close the estate to the public. No additional word of warning should be needed . . . who are sensible of Mrs. Cone's generosity and courtesy in opening Flat Top Manor to all who love the out-of-doors."

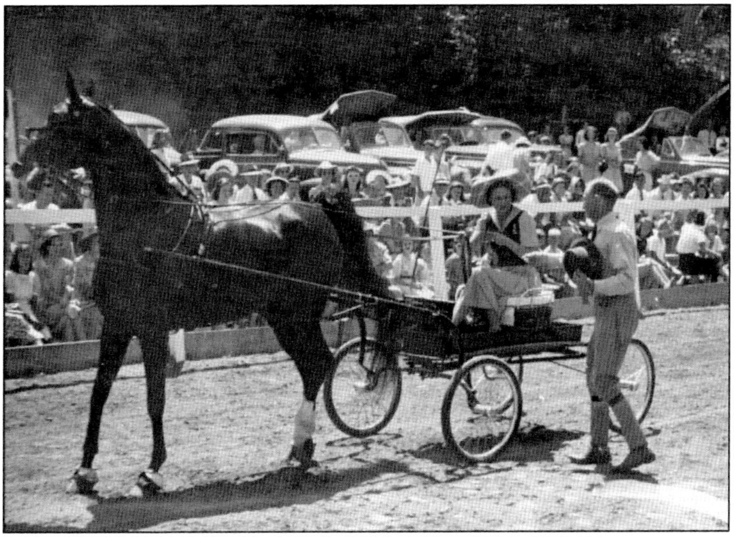

Roadsters became a crowd favorite at the horse show, in both competitions and acting out in small vignettes. In the late 1960s, an overflow crowd often sat on the ground and on small hills surrounding the fenced areas for horse and rider. The close proximity between observer and participant remains a strong appeal of the horse show.

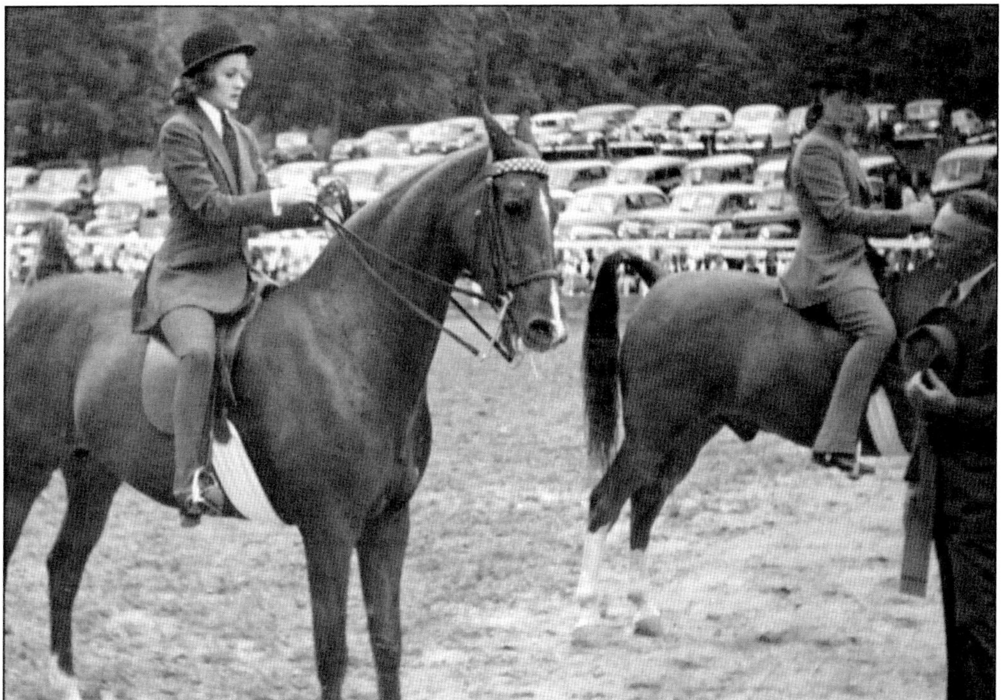

This recollection comes from Martha Rudy Wallace: "My chief joy was accompanying guests to Moonglow Stables for horseback rides on the beautiful trails in the Cone Estate and Chetola. It was a new stable which coveted the business I could bring from the Blowing Rock Hotel. Happy Ann, Easter, Melody and others, who names are long forgotten were good riding horses fitted with English saddles."

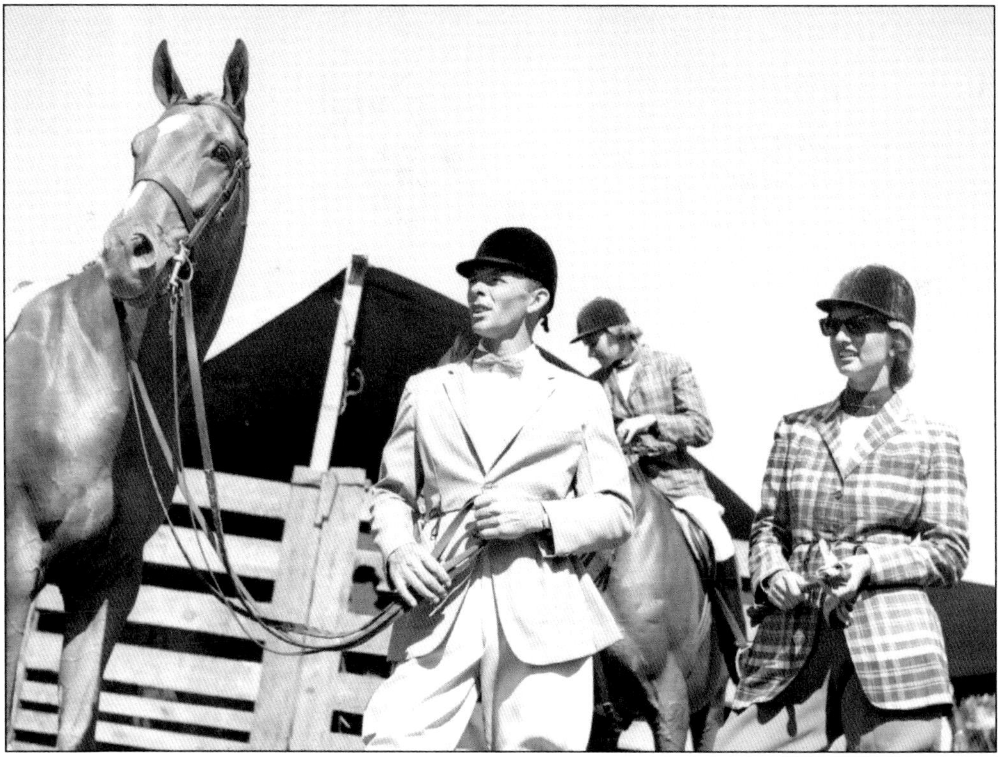

Pictured here is horse Gabriel with Bill Bolick, a horse trainer based in Southern Pines, and Amy Dale. Bolick was raised on a Blowing Rock farm that began his interest in caring for animals. A typical day for a trainer includes three feedings for the horses, cleaning stalls, phased trainings, and putting them to bed.

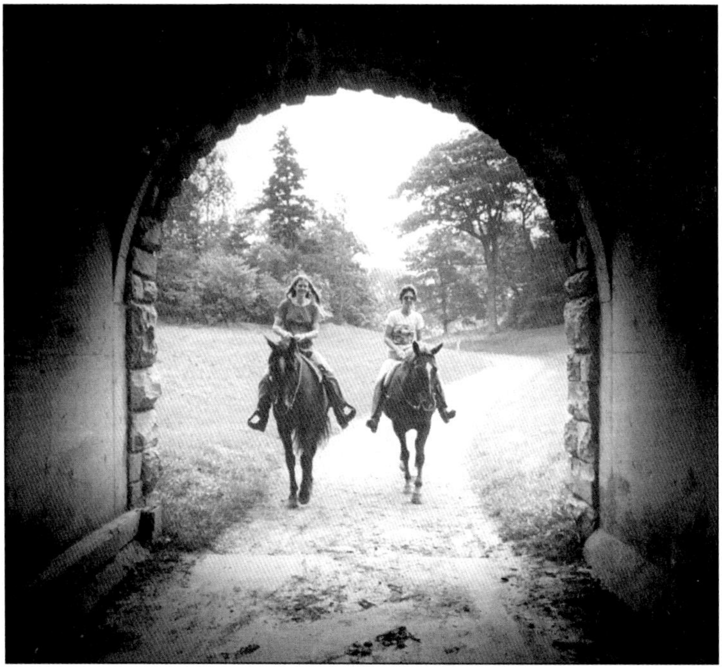

Jean Morgan (left) and Nancy Baker (right) complete the Flat Top Manor trail off the Blue Ridge Parkway. Moses Cone planted extensive white pine forests and hemlock hedges throughout his estate, built lakes stocked with bass and trout, and planted a 10,000-tree apple orchard. Ridership increases significantly on these trails in the summer.

Five

PARADES AND EVENTS

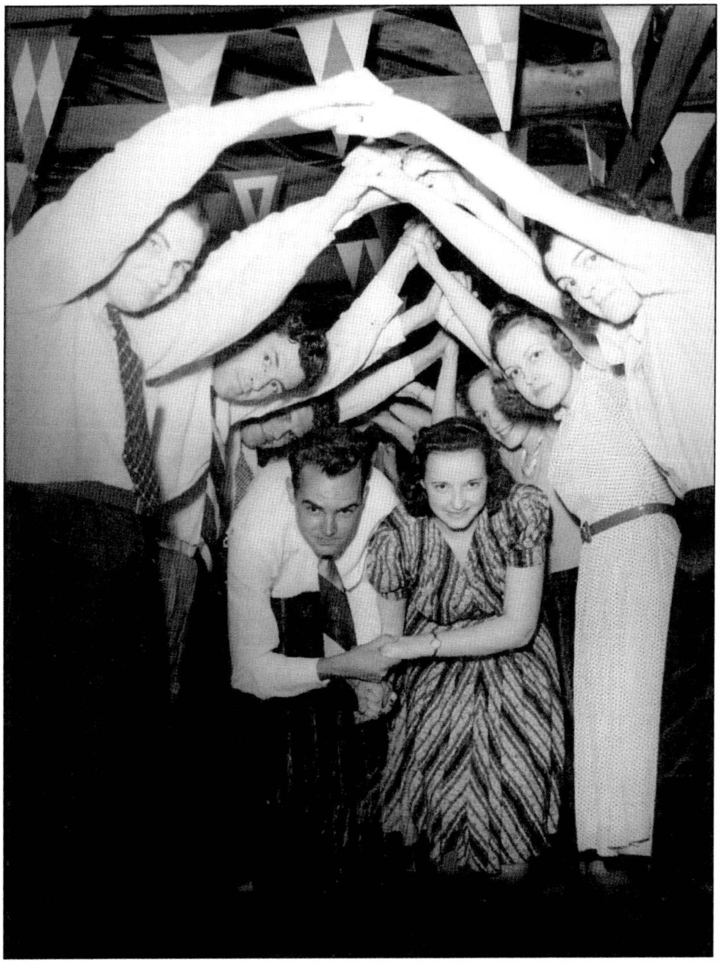

The American Legion Post 256 was established in Blowing Rock in 1946. Square dancing every Wednesday and Friday nights in Legion Hall was a staple of local entertainment in the 1960s. Round and formal dancing took place on Saturday nights. Promenading in this image are some of the younger set of Blowing Rock.

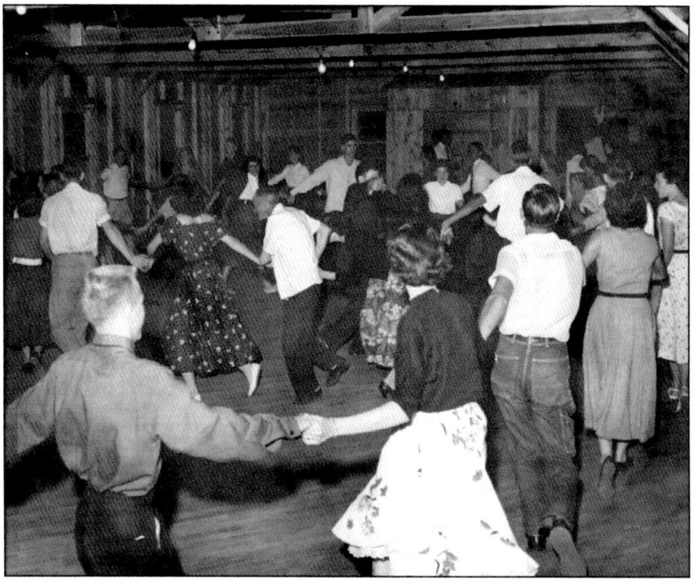

A July 1959 *Blowing Rocket* article states, "It is expected that the work will progress in the next week or so to the stage where the hall can be used for square dances and meetings. One of the main reasons for building the new hall on Wallingford Street is so the Legion can conduct a well-planned program designed to offer year-round supervised recreation for the teenagers of Blowing Rock."

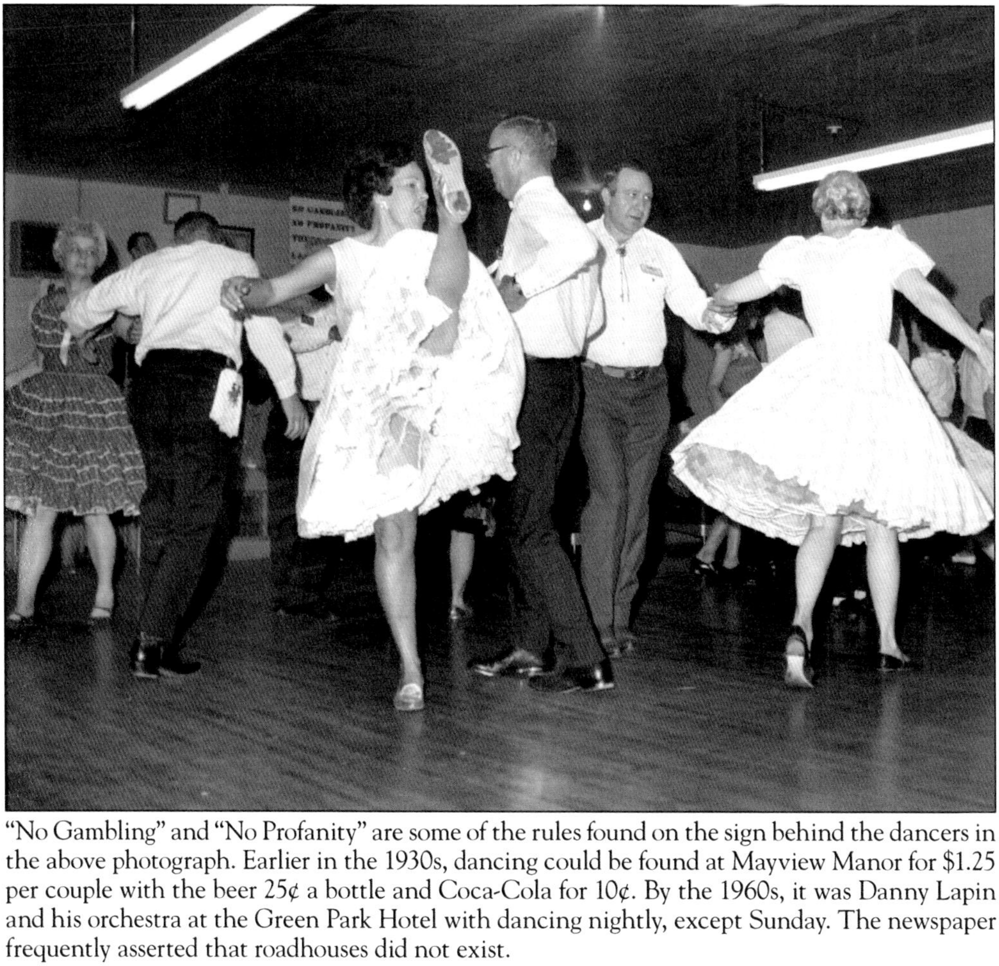

"No Gambling" and "No Profanity" are some of the rules found on the sign behind the dancers in the above photograph. Earlier in the 1930s, dancing could be found at Mayview Manor for $1.25 per couple with the beer 25¢ a bottle and Coca-Cola for 10¢. By the 1960s, it was Danny Lapin and his orchestra at the Green Park Hotel with dancing nightly, except Sunday. The newspaper frequently asserted that roadhouses did not exist.

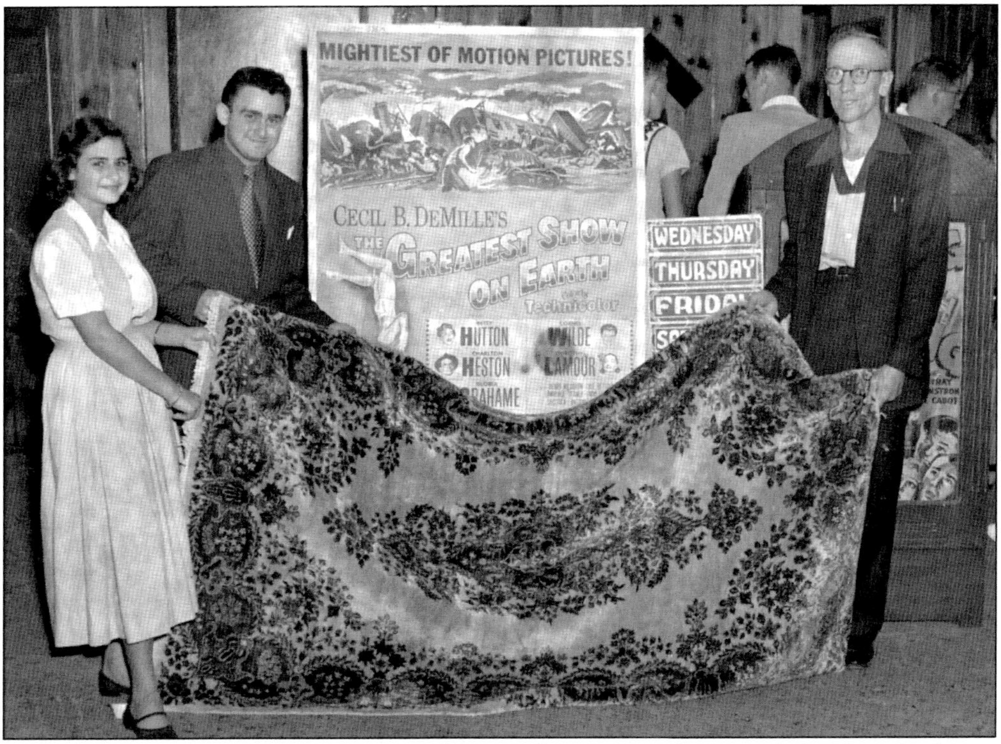

Eugene Koone (right), manager of the Yonahlossee Theater, joins the Hannah family in displaying a beautiful Oriental rug that was used in the filming of *The Greatest Show on Earth*, shown there in 1952. Hannah's was next door to the theater where the rug was displayed. The premiere of the film *Spawn of the North* also took place here and in Shulls Mill in 1938.

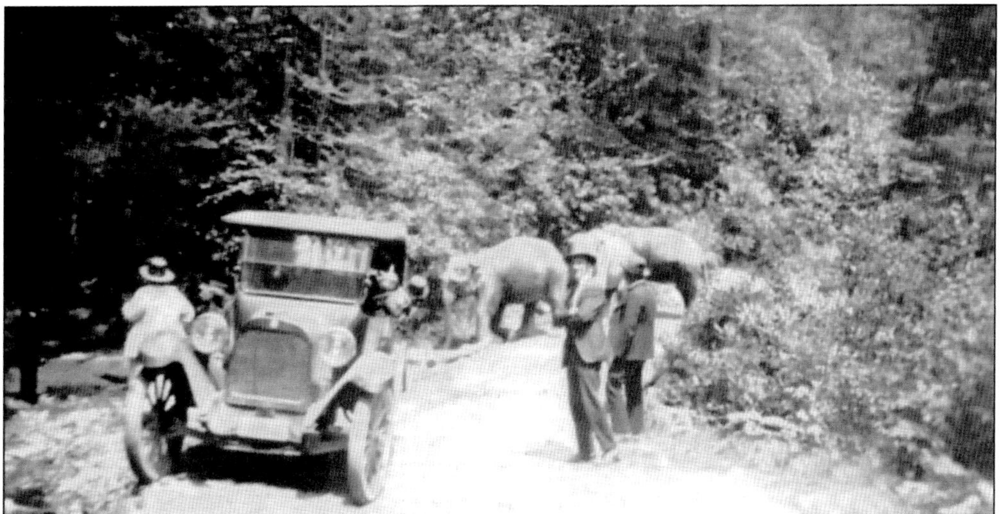

Elephants stop for water just south of downtown Blowing Rock as local citizens look on, possibly heading to a show in Boone, Shulls Mill, or at the Valle Crucis School. There also were reports of elephants from the Haag Circus overturning at Deep Gap on their way down the mountain. The coming of the circus was a notable and heavily promoted event in Watauga and surrounding counties.

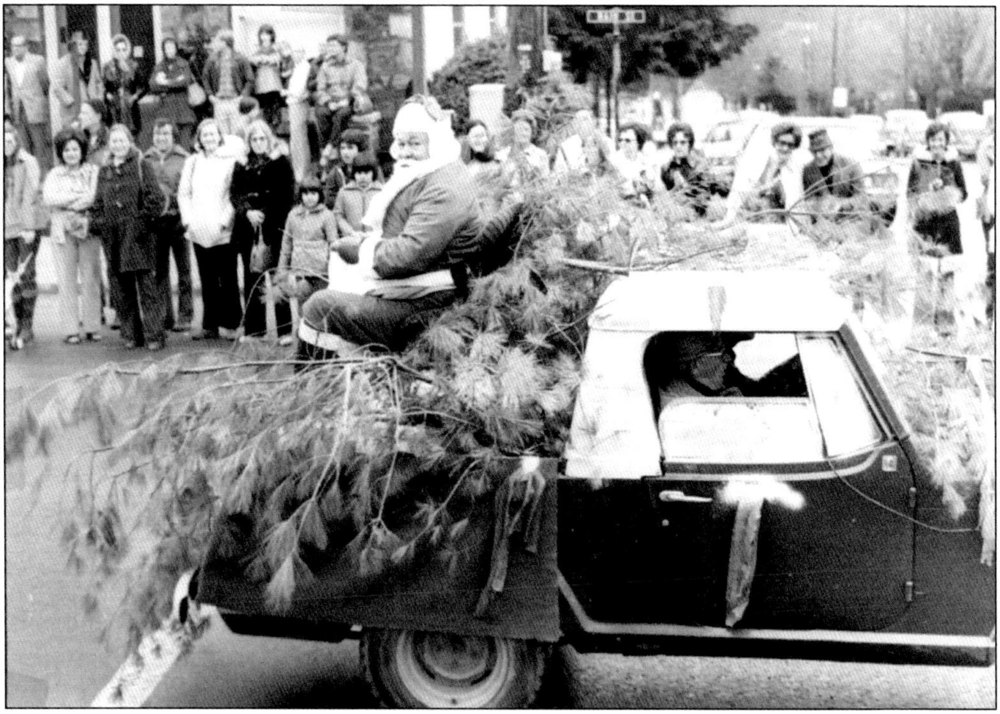

The first Christmas parade took place in 1975 under the direction of the Blowing Rock Recreation Department. Santa has been present at every parade since, though not always atop a fire engine or the vehicle of Sonny Klutz. The lack of significant angles and elevations on Main Street makes it ideal for downtown parades.

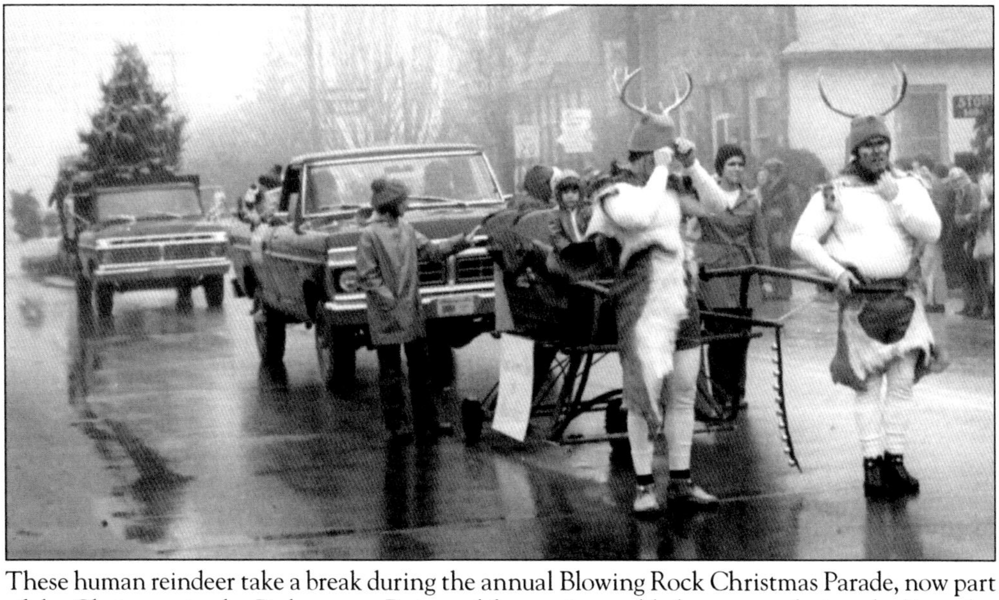

These human reindeer take a break during the annual Blowing Rock Christmas Parade, now part of the Christmas in the Park events. Rain and fog are just as likely as snow during the Saturday afternoon after Thanksgiving. Storie's Soda Shop (Coman's), the auction house, and a speed limit of 20 are found in the background of this image.

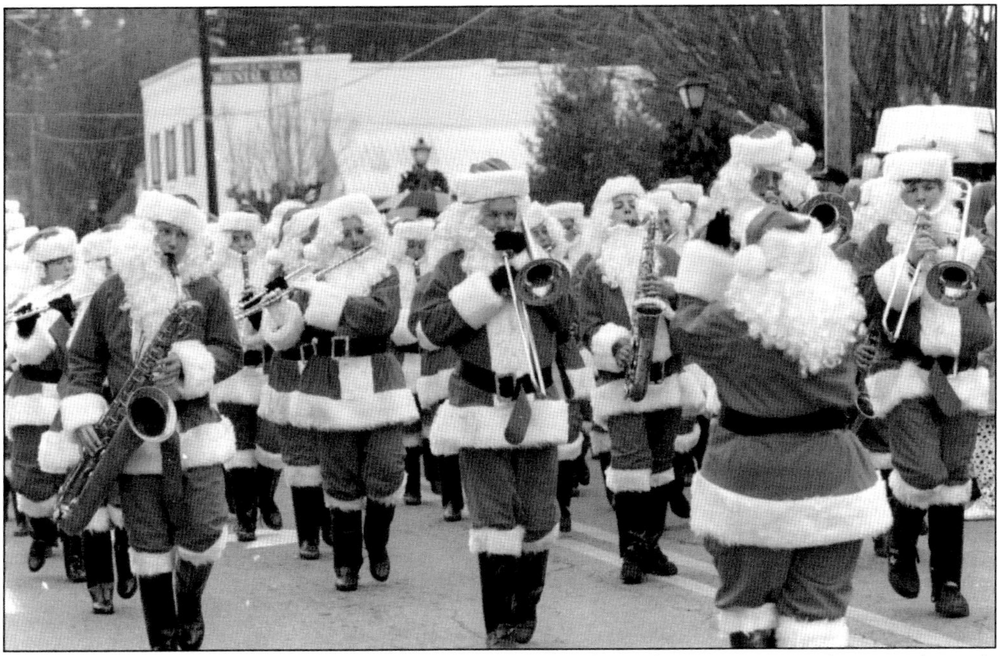

Behind parades and events there is a dedicated group of people organizing and seeing through this work for others to experience and enjoy. Newspaper editor Jerry Burns enjoyed recording these events and promoting them with residents. He received numerous awards for his efforts, including the Order of the Longleaf Pine.

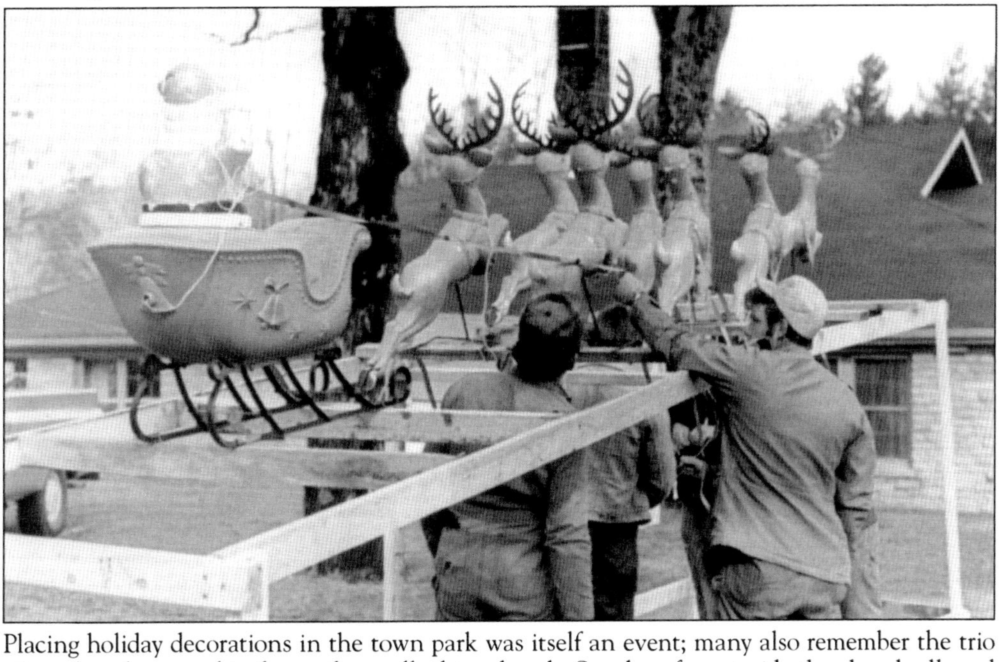

Placing holiday decorations in the town park was itself an event; many also remember the trio of carolers that stood in front of a small white church. Speakers from inside the church allowed town hall to play recorded music, providing the carolers from days gone by. One letter to the editor in 1965 questioning a public nativity scene lead to many miniature displays in local business windows.

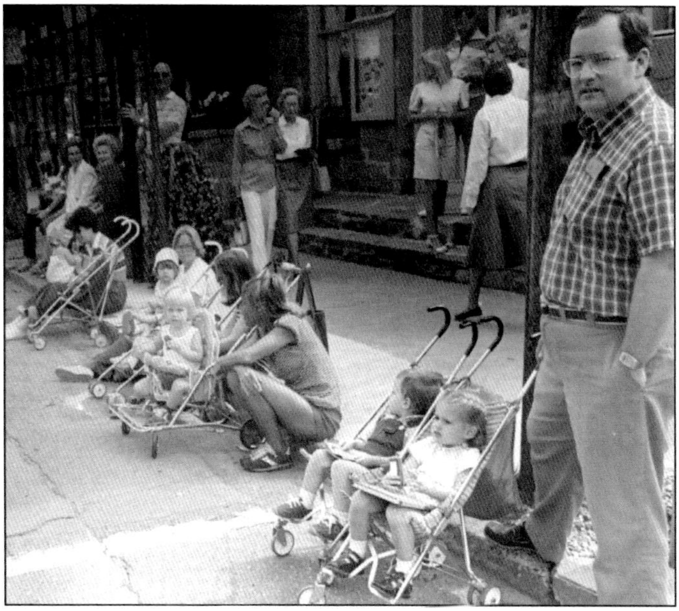

Perhaps those in strollers lined up for the annual Fourth of July parade are catching a glimpse of Grady Barlowe. Barlowe was grand marshal for the parade in 2006 and missed only two of the parades in the decades before, dressed as Uncle Sam. He and his close friend Hal McDaris were also familiar sights on the Cone horse trails.

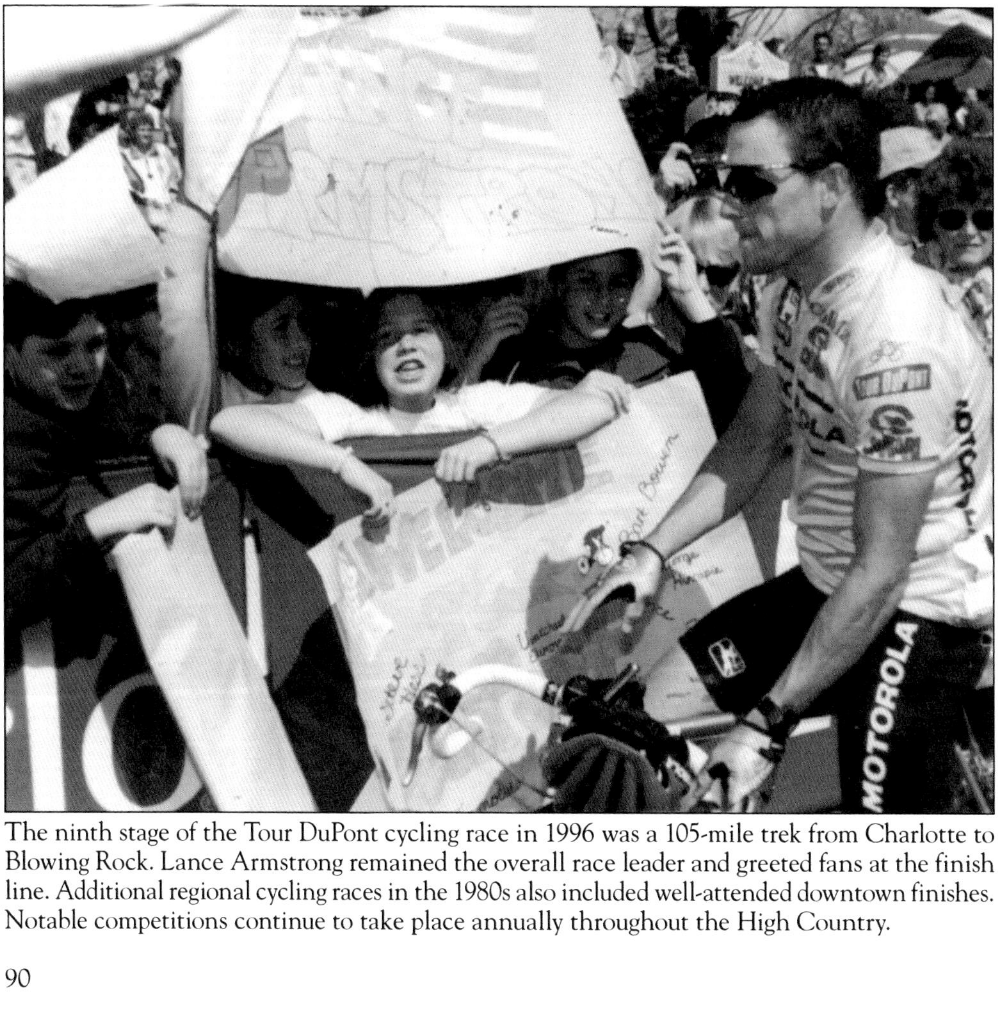

The ninth stage of the Tour DuPont cycling race in 1996 was a 105-mile trek from Charlotte to Blowing Rock. Lance Armstrong remained the overall race leader and greeted fans at the finish line. Additional regional cycling races in the 1980s also included well-attended downtown finishes. Notable competitions continue to take place annually throughout the High Country.

J.B. Lawrence carries and prepares to hand off the Olympic torch in 1987. The torch's 28,000-mile journey, with the help of 8,000 volunteers, passed through Blowing Rock. Lawrence served on the town council for eight years before becoming mayor in 1997. Current town boards include the ABC Board, Board of Adjustments, Blowing Rock Appearance Advisory Commission, Planning Board, and the Tourism Development Authority.

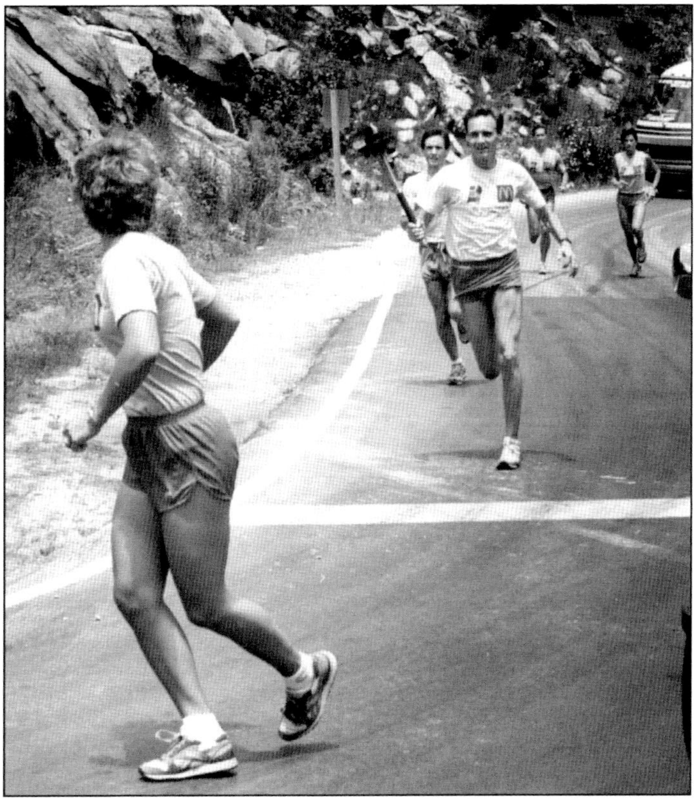

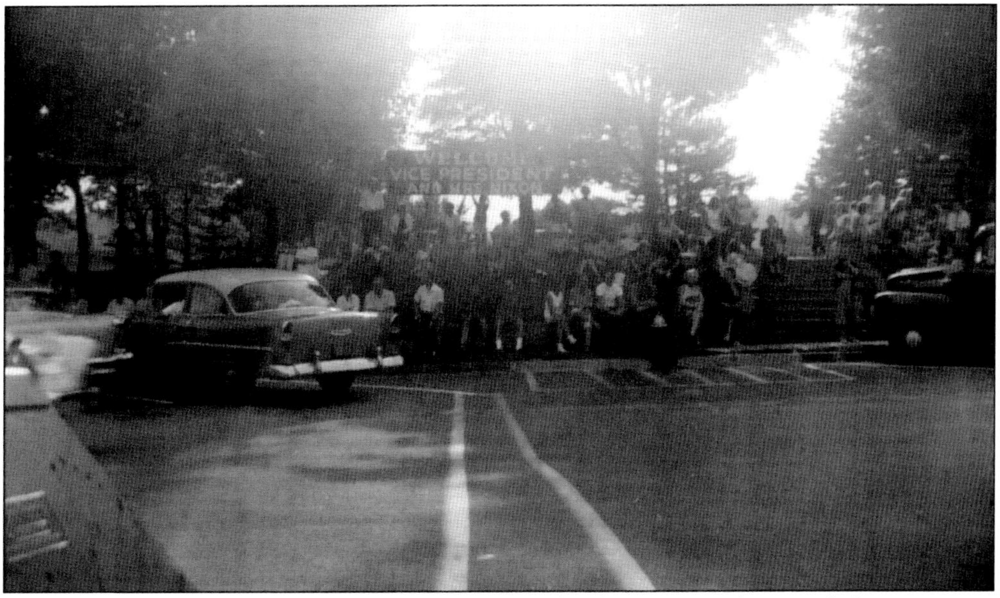

On August 17, 1957, the town welcomed Vice Pres. Richard M. Nixon, who attended a convention of attorneys at Mayview Manor. The future president and family shopped downtown and had coffee at Sonny's Grill. State politicians still stop and present in town, including Emily Preyer, wife of then–gubernatorial candidate Lunsford Richardson Preyer, who served six terms in Congress. She spoke at the Blowing Rock School Auditorium in April 1964.

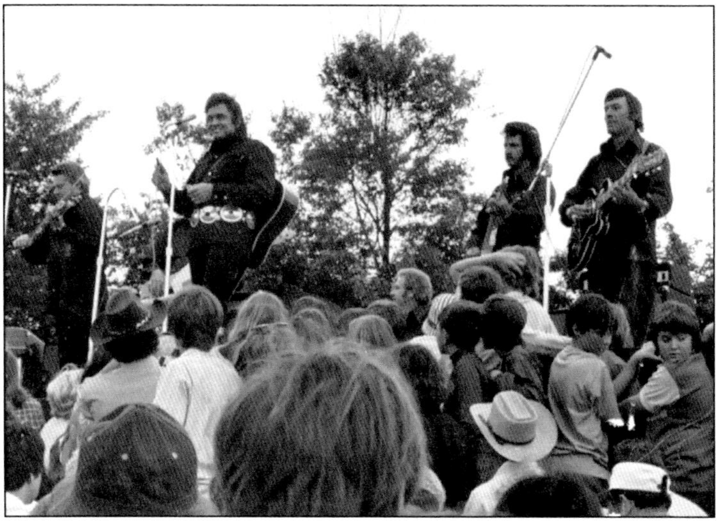

The annual Singing on the Mountain event on Grandfather Mountain included Johnny Cash in 1974; North Carolina governor James "Jim" Holshouser also spoke. The 38th hosting of the event in 1962 had Dr. Billy Graham speaking. Local newspapers noted traffic backed up in all directions, including from Blowing Rock and even down the mountain to Lenoir.

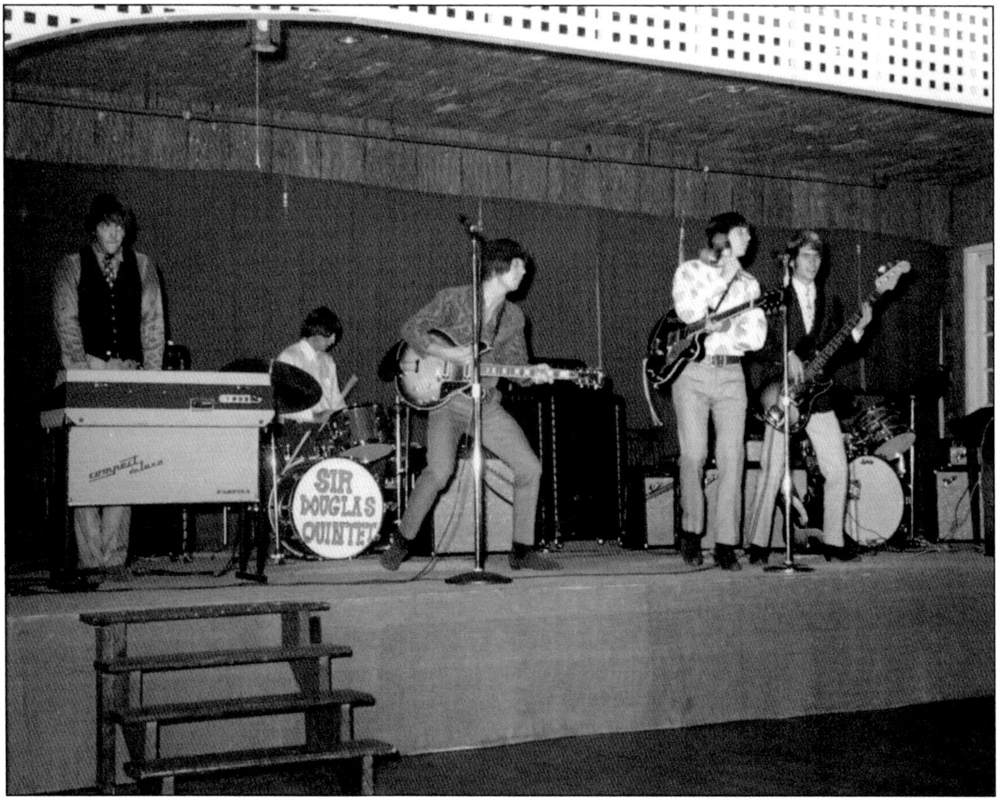

The Sir Douglas Quintet reached national acclaim and here entertain an audience at Mayview Manor. From San Antonio, Texas, the portable organ was part of the signature instrumentation of the band. Fine dining and entertainment were standards of the 138-room hotel, including the Boots and Saddles Ball during the week of the annual Blowing Rock Charity Horse Show.

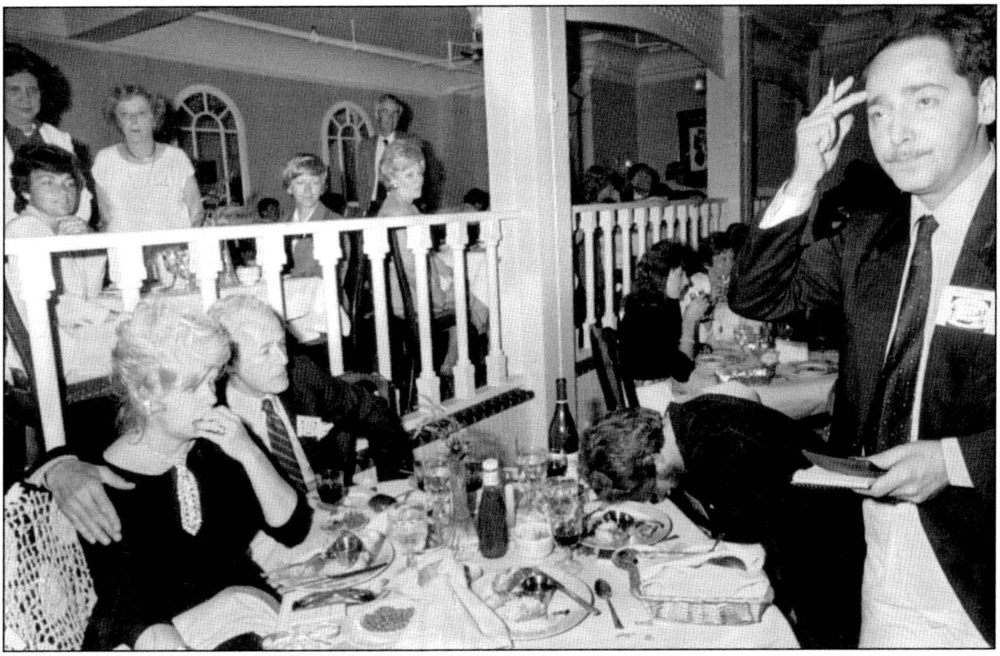

This murder mystery takes place in June 1985 at the Green Park Inn, and the event has returned to this location in recent years. The Green Park Hotel (Inn), opened in 1891 and expanded in 1916, is the second-oldest surviving resort hotel (Woodfield Inn in Flat Rock, now Mansouri Mansion, is first) in Western North Carolina and retains its essential architectural integrity.

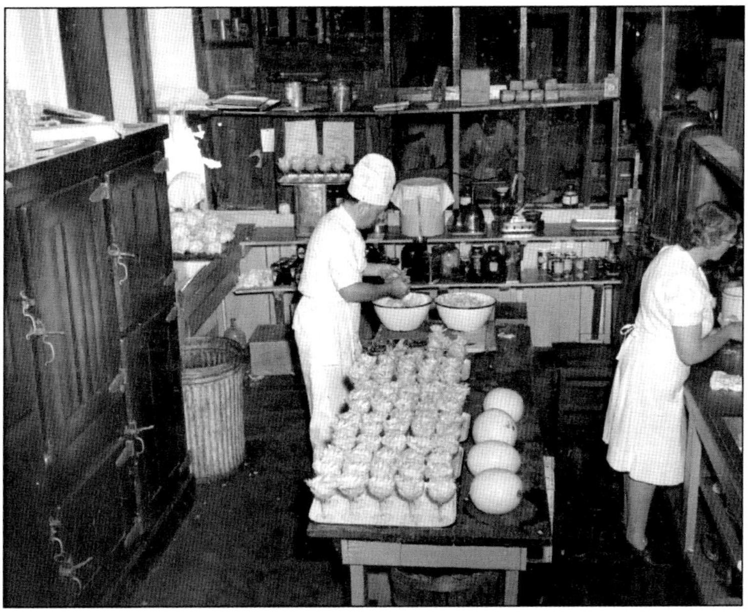

Chef Worrell prepares desserts in the kitchen of the Green Park Inn. The Horse Show Breakfast was noted as hosting chef for a day Francis Bettencourt, who worked at Mayview Manor for 20 summers. Mr. and Mrs. Turner (chef and hostess) were the longtime staples of the Mayview Manor, who came from Florida each season and first prepared the famous breakfast.

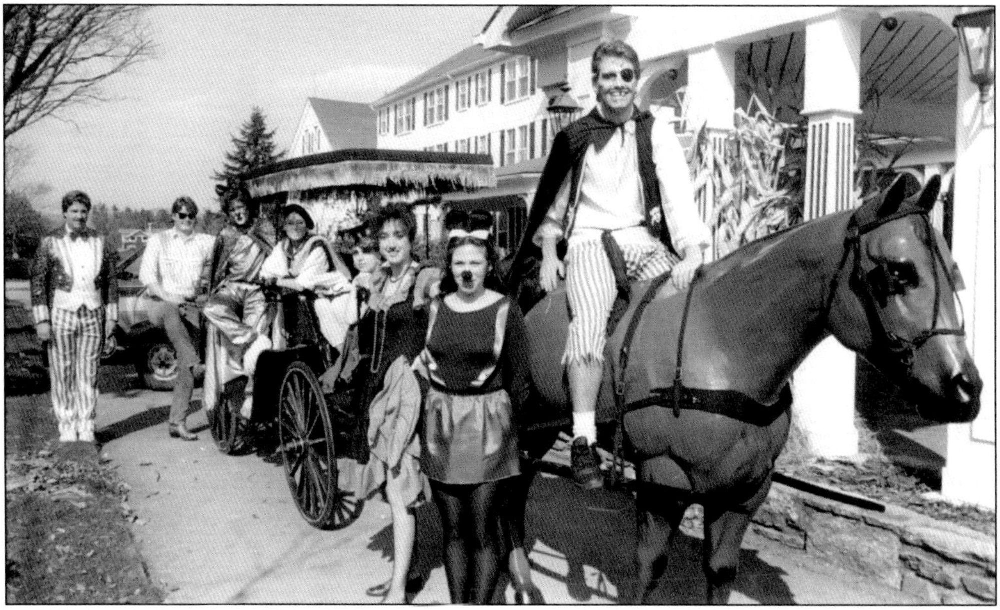

Halloween events for children, college students, and adult guests of the Green Park Inn are common. From 1952 to 1965, the Halloween carnival in the school gym raised funds for the parent-teacher association and included submitting students for the carnival king and queen. Holiday events continue on Main Street, including the monster march of children in costumes, trick-or-treating, and other activities.

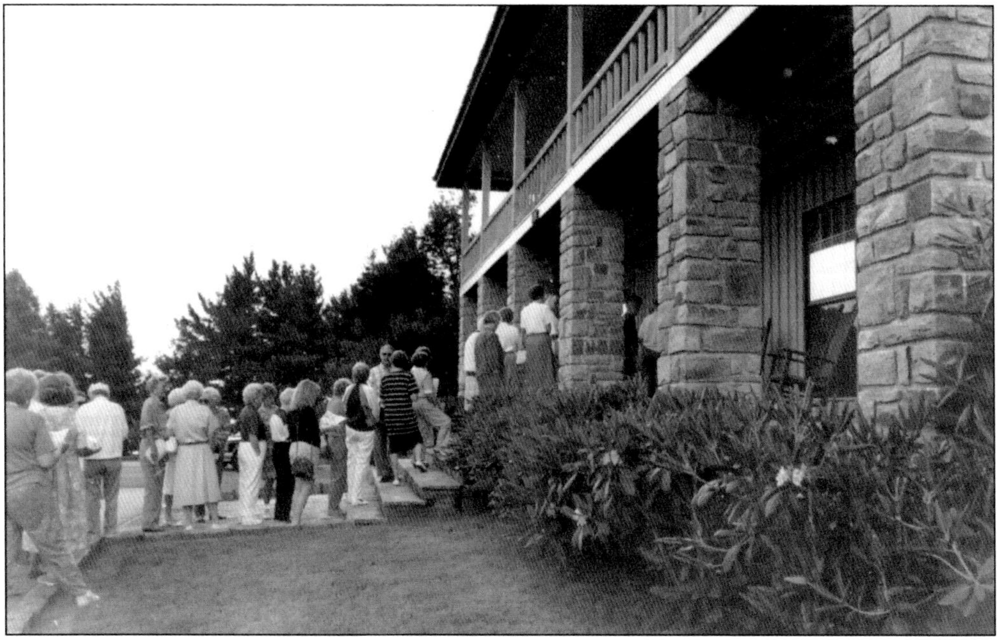

St. Mary of the Hills Episcopal Church has held an annual tour of homes since the late 1950s. There is always a large crowd of residents and visitors, including this 1980s tour of the Weems House. The Blowing Rock Art and History Museum (BRAHM) parking garage has assisted in handling attendance for events, and the museum has highlighted local history.

St. Mary's holds the Blessing of the Animals each October. In 1994, Fr. James R. Harris Jr. blesses this reptile before his retirement. Held in conjunction with the Feast of St. Francis, this annual event is open for all creatures great and small, including dogs, cats, fish, horses, lizards, and insects.

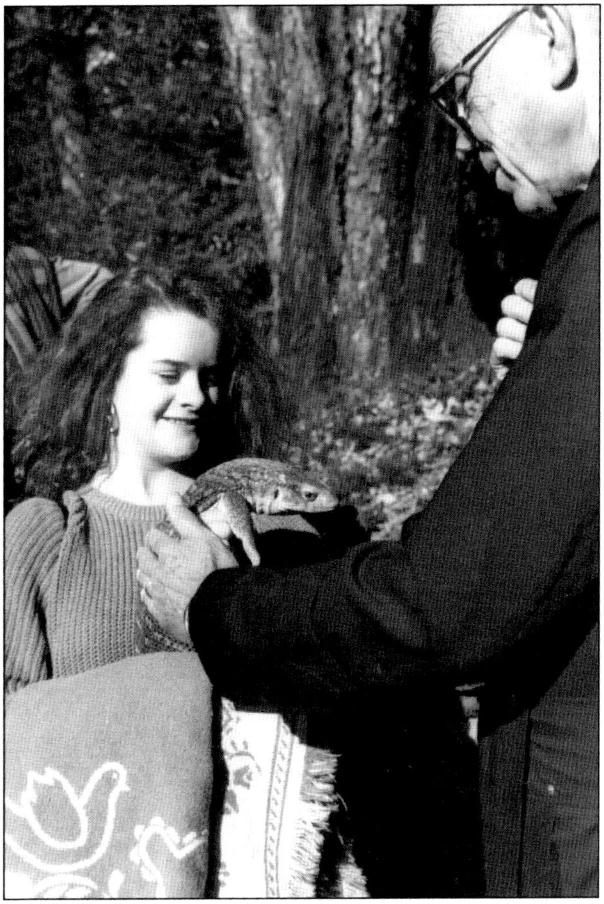

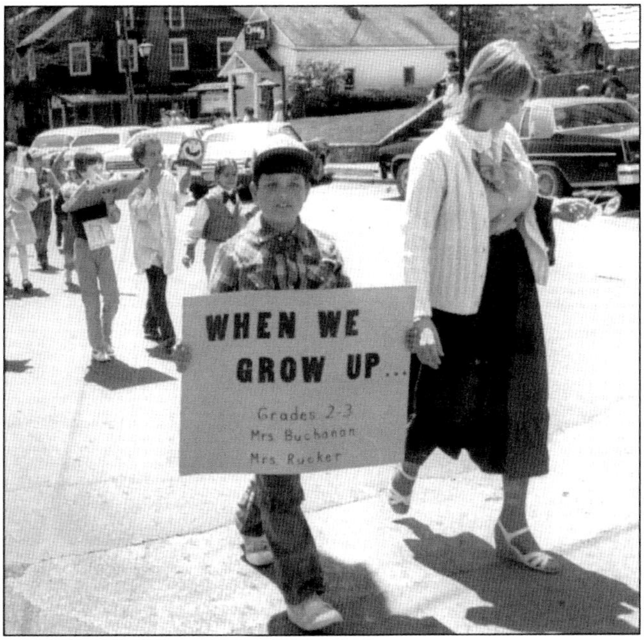

Parades on Main Street have included the Week of the Young Child, usually in April or May. Blowing Rock's community has strived to better meet the needs of all young children and their families. Note the Century 21 office (now museum) and past gazebo structure in the town park. A gazebo constructed for the national bicentennial in 1976 was replaced in May 2015.

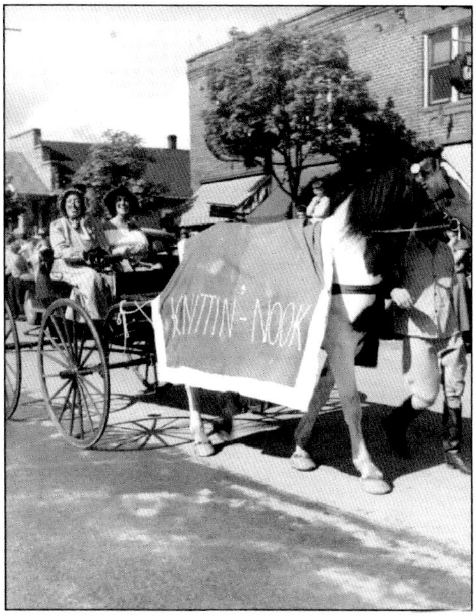

Horses and buggies remain components of local parades, included in past events with "pioneer, heritage, and Blue Ridge" in their titles and promotion. By the 1960s, many of the downtown aluminum awnings may have been manufactured by Miller Industries in Boone. One of the earliest Lowe's stores was in Boone, after its original location in North Wilkesboro, and was heavily advertised in the *Blowing Rocket*.

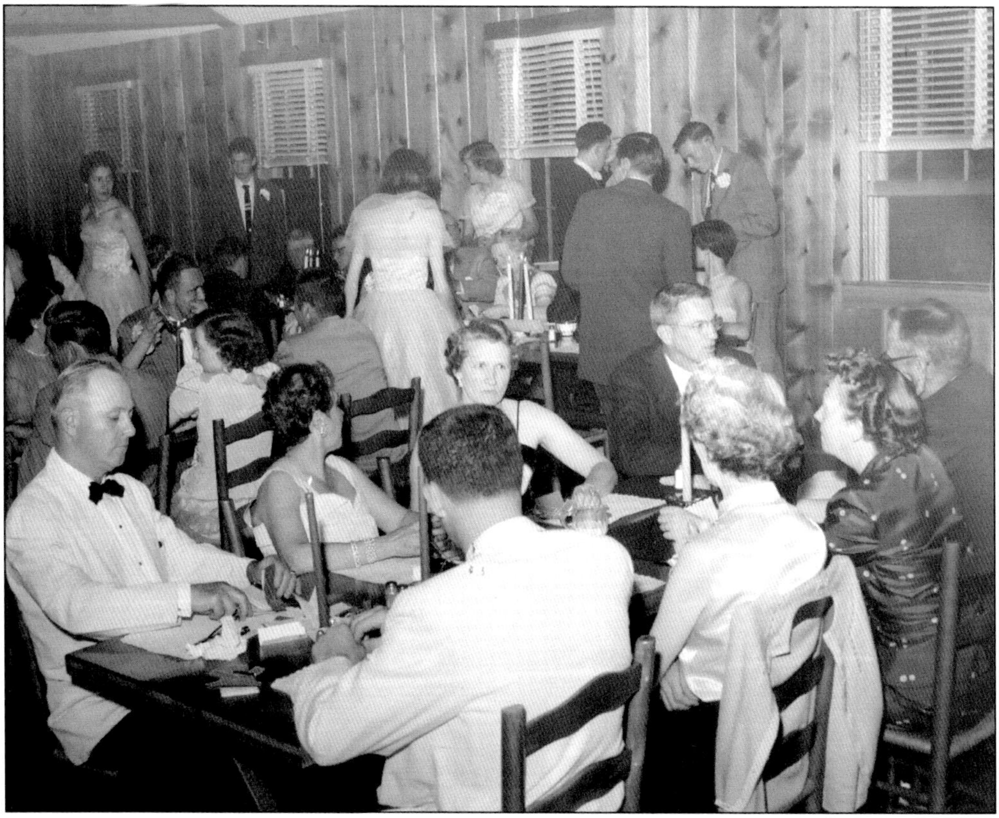

Both students and chaperones attend the school senior banquet. Among those in this 1956 image are Kent and Mary Jane Brown, Joe White, and Bonny Robertson. Yearbooks included photographs from events, poems, and tributes, including that of policeman William "Bill" Dean Greene, a former student who was killed in the line of duty in January 1963.

Mrs. Charlie Coffey presents a beautiful quilt to Mrs. Sud Brown, made by the women of the Blowing Rock First Baptist Church in fall 1976 for a raffle. Annual charity events, large and small, are strong components of local community life. Combined with seasonal residents with available cash, contributions have exceeded expectations at some events.

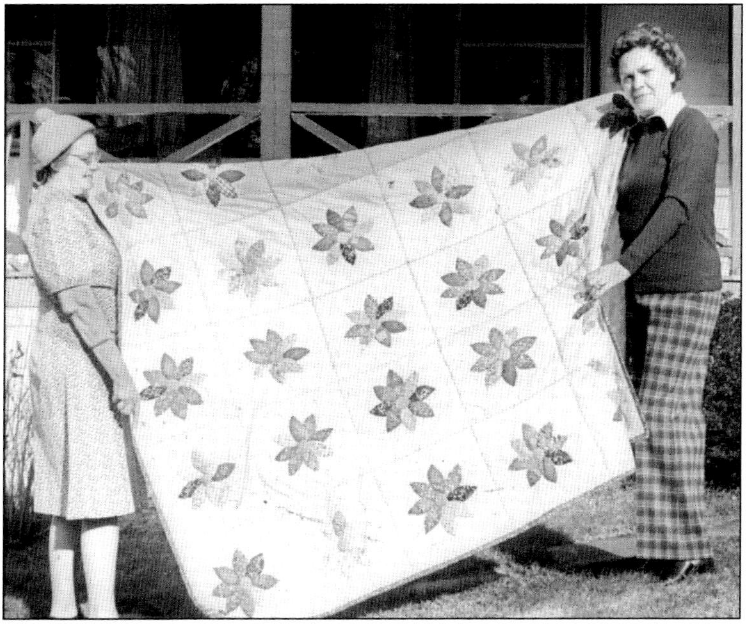

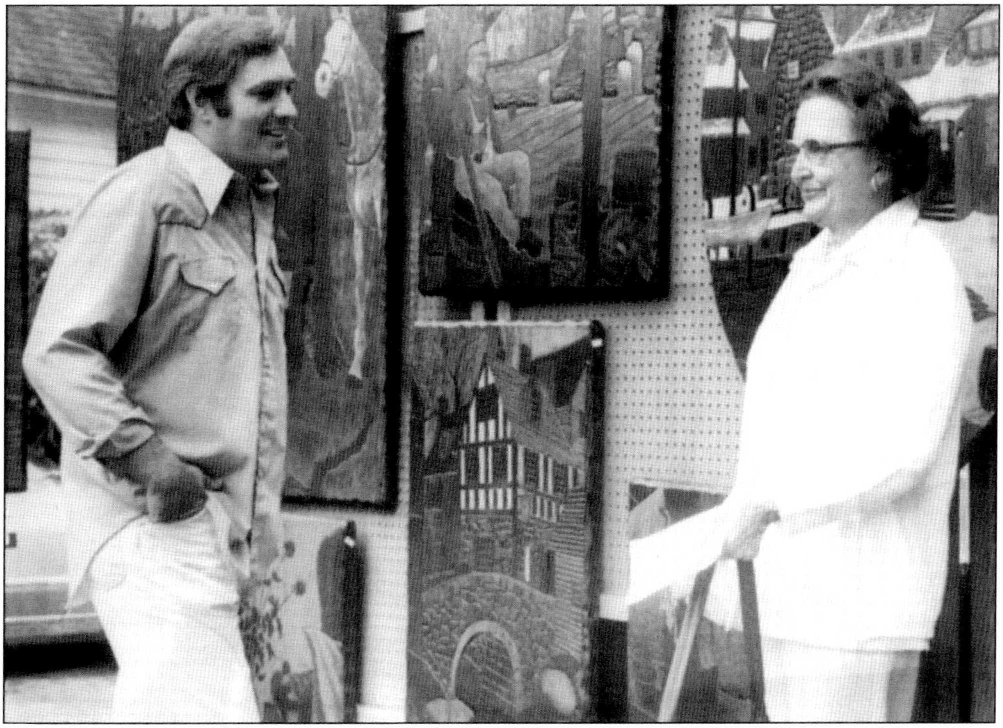

A group of area craftspeople began Art in the Park in 1962 to showcase local artists. Art in the Park's professional jury and high standards attract the best examples of handcrafted jewelry, pottery, glass, fiber, photography, and painting from all over the South. The town park welcomes thousands of visitors and residents for a series of six shows, May to October, through the chamber of commerce.

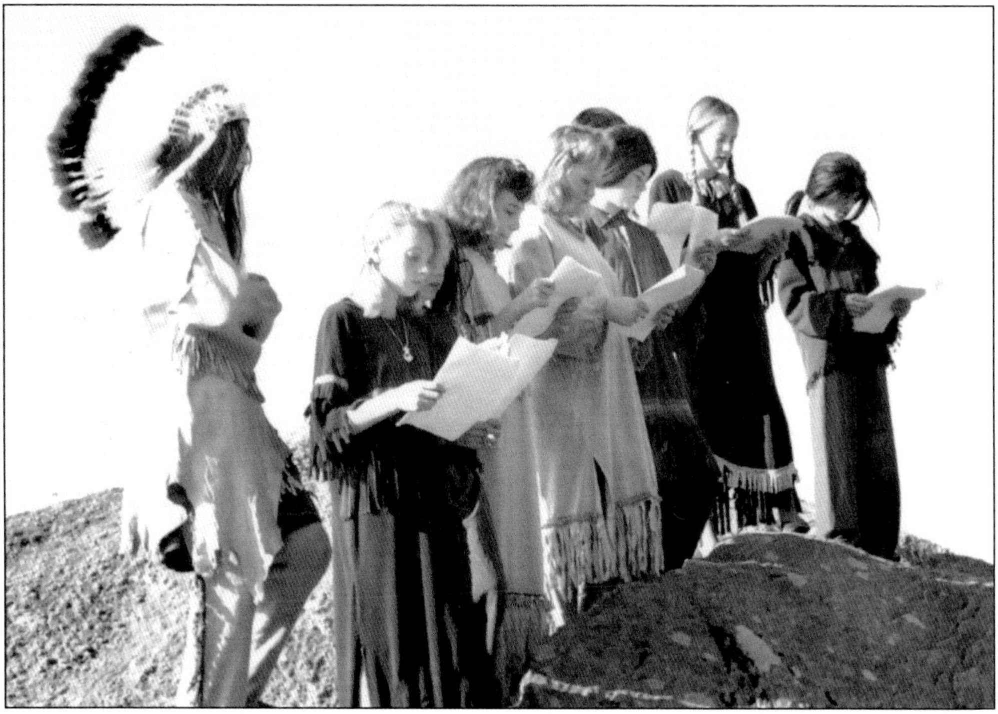

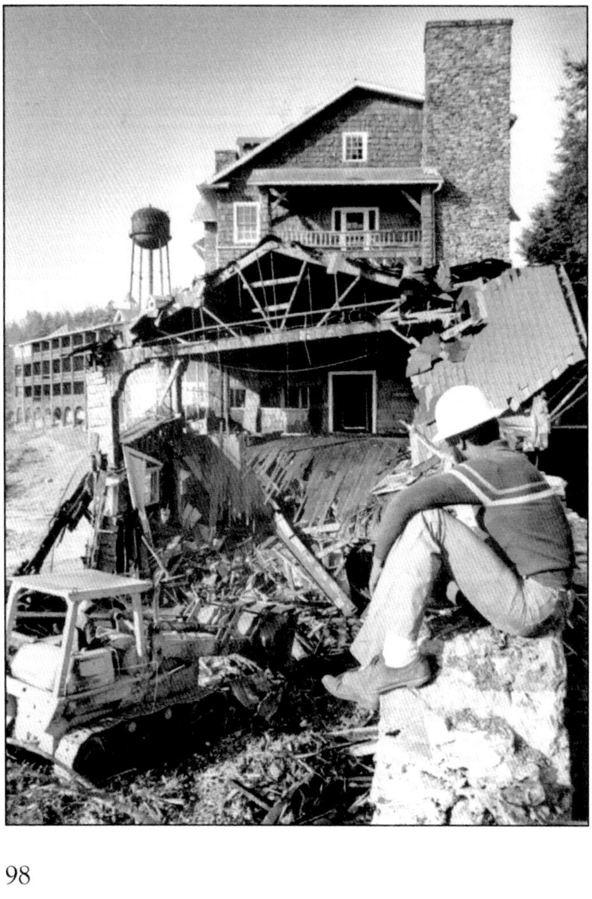

The centennial celebration of the incorporation of Blowing Rock took place in March 1989. Local youth read the legend aloud at the Blowing Rock attraction as part of a larger pageant. The massive celebration included a parade down Main Street, unveilings of special art pieces, and an appearance by the governor.

Mayview Manor's demolition in 1978 marked a significant loss of community heritage. The Blowing Rock Historical Society recognizes the town's birthday annually with cake and a presentation of local historic markers to assist in educating the public, provide atmosphere to the downtown, and add distinction to individual homes, commercial buildings, and sites of significance.

Six

Town Park and Recreation

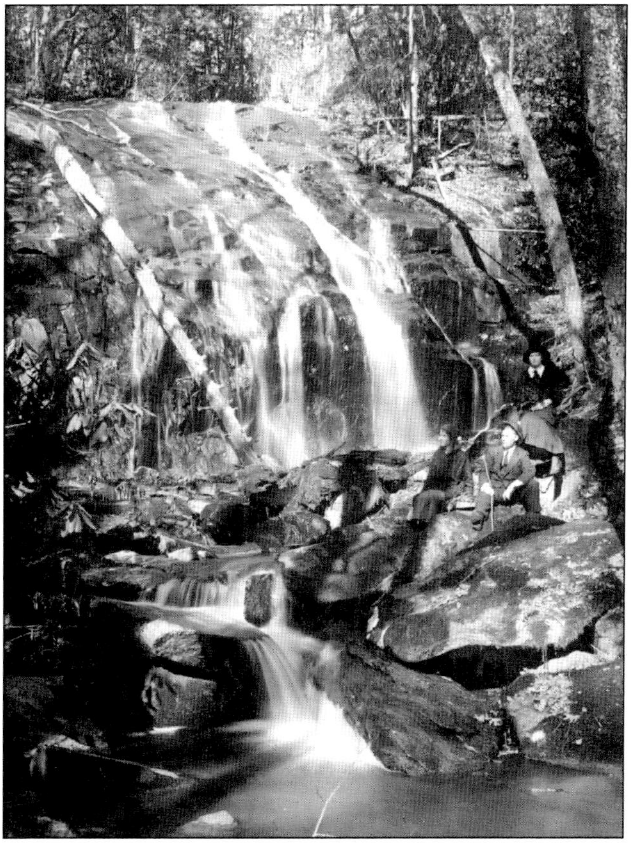

Glen Maria Falls historically has had many additional names, including Mary and Marie. This image is from 1915. Visitors have learned over the years to be cautious of the slippery rocks on this strenuous and steep trail, yet tragic incidents unfortunately continue. The falls are located along the Glen Burney Trail, which descends 800 feet into the rugged St. John's River gorge. A trailhead is located just steps from downtown.

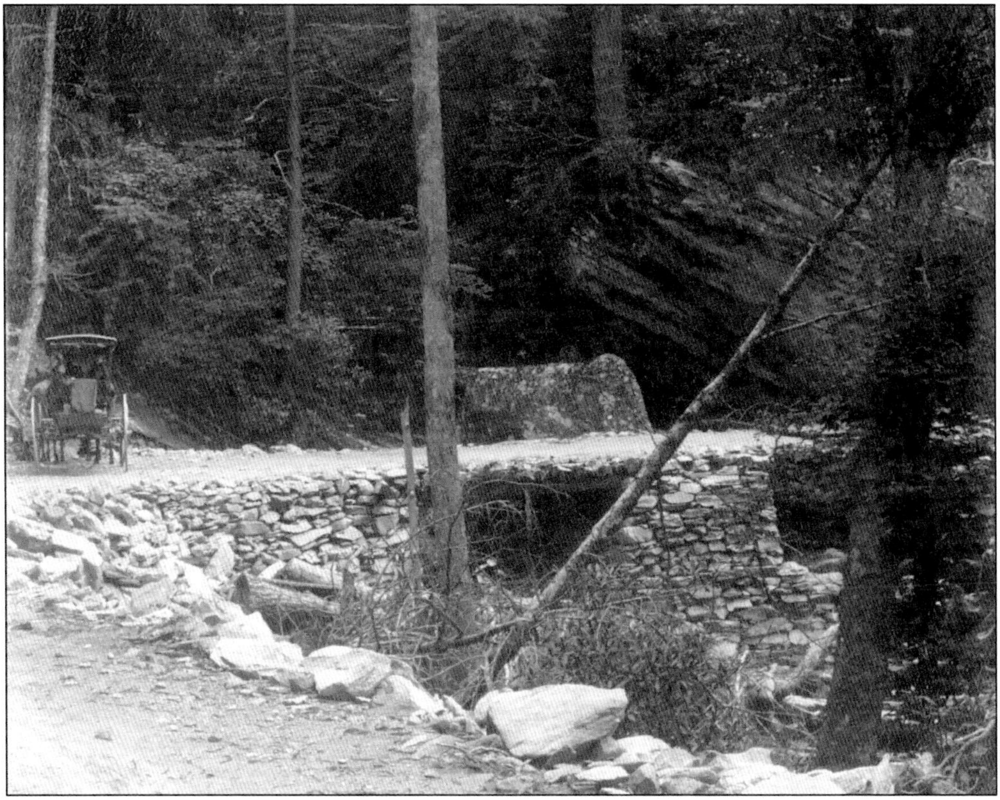

Built by Hugh McCrae in 1889, the Yonahlossee Road (now known as US-221) was originally a toll road designed to open McCrae's Linville resort to Blowing Rock visitors. He used one of the last coaches made by the Wells Fargo Company to transport tourists between the towns. It took two years to build and the labor of more than 300.

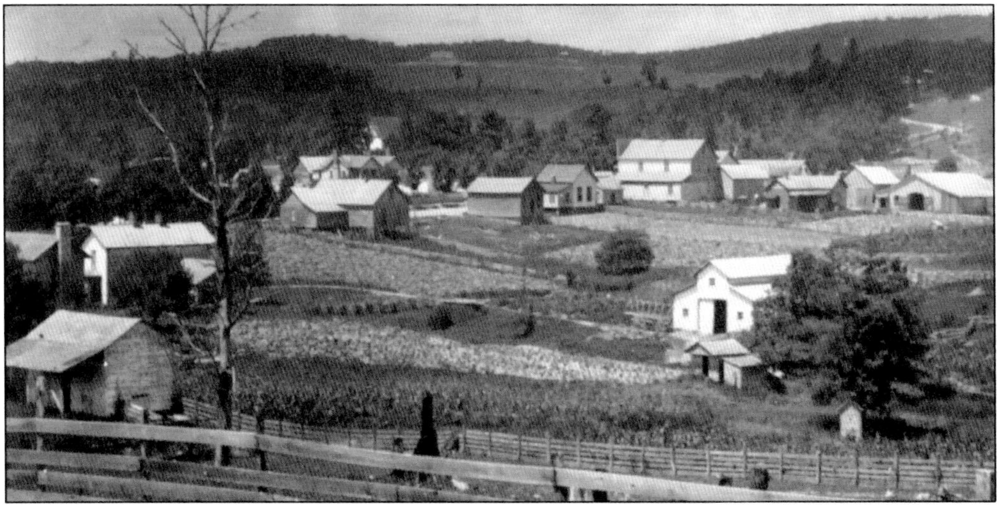

Cone Manor is in the background of this 1920s downtown image. The Cones raised sheep, hogs, chickens, and dairy cows on their estate and experimented with apple orchards; at the estate's height, it had 10,000 apples trees of nearly 20 varieties. The estate supported 30 families total and now allows multiple recreation uses.

Blowing Rock and other areas in the Blue Ridge were a focus of the June 1934 *National Geographic*. The headline of the July 21, 1934, *Blowing Rocket* proclaimed, "Blowing Rock gets Park Highway." Whether on the Blue Ridge Parkway or other surrounding scenic roads, pleasure driving remains a popular form of local recreation.

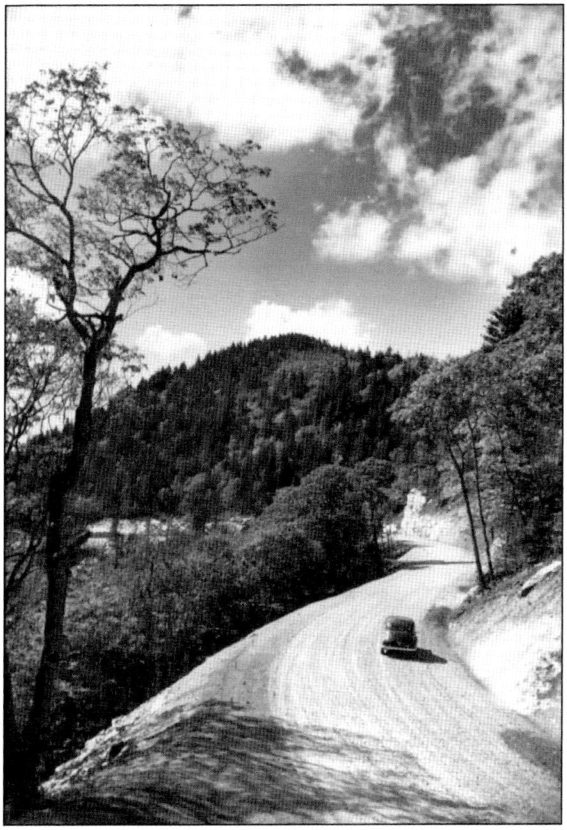

Sunbathers can still be found at the entrance to Julian Price Memorial Park around mile marker 295 on the Blue Ridge Parkway. Access to the Boone Fork trail also begins here where the calm and flat stream turns to plunging over boulders and creating waterfalls to rolling hills, cow pastures, and views of Grandfather Mountain and Price Lake.

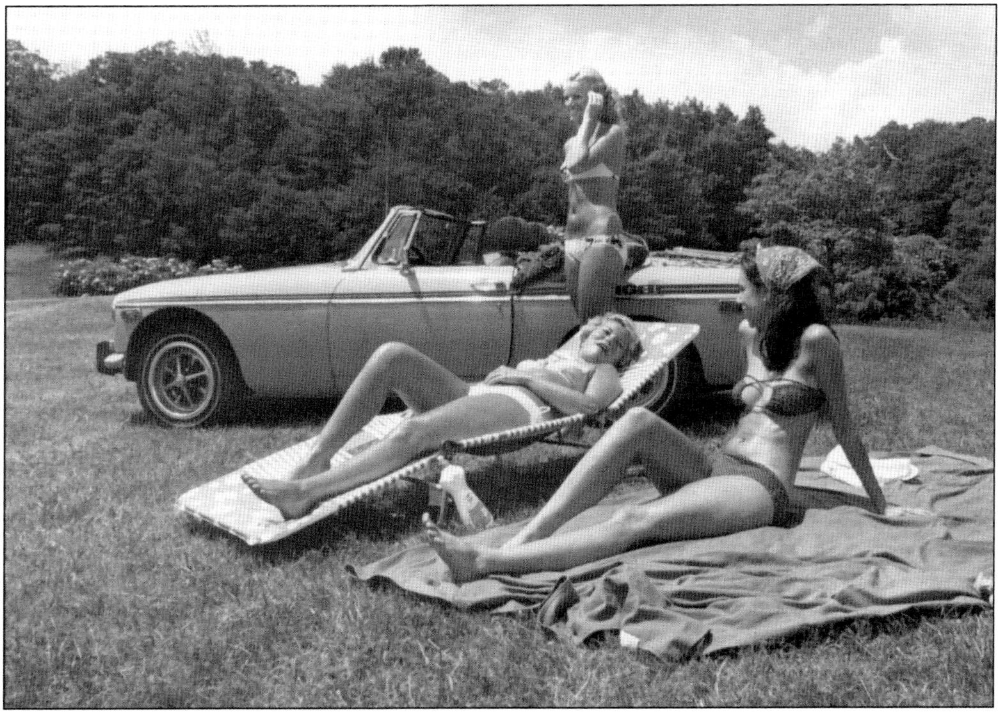

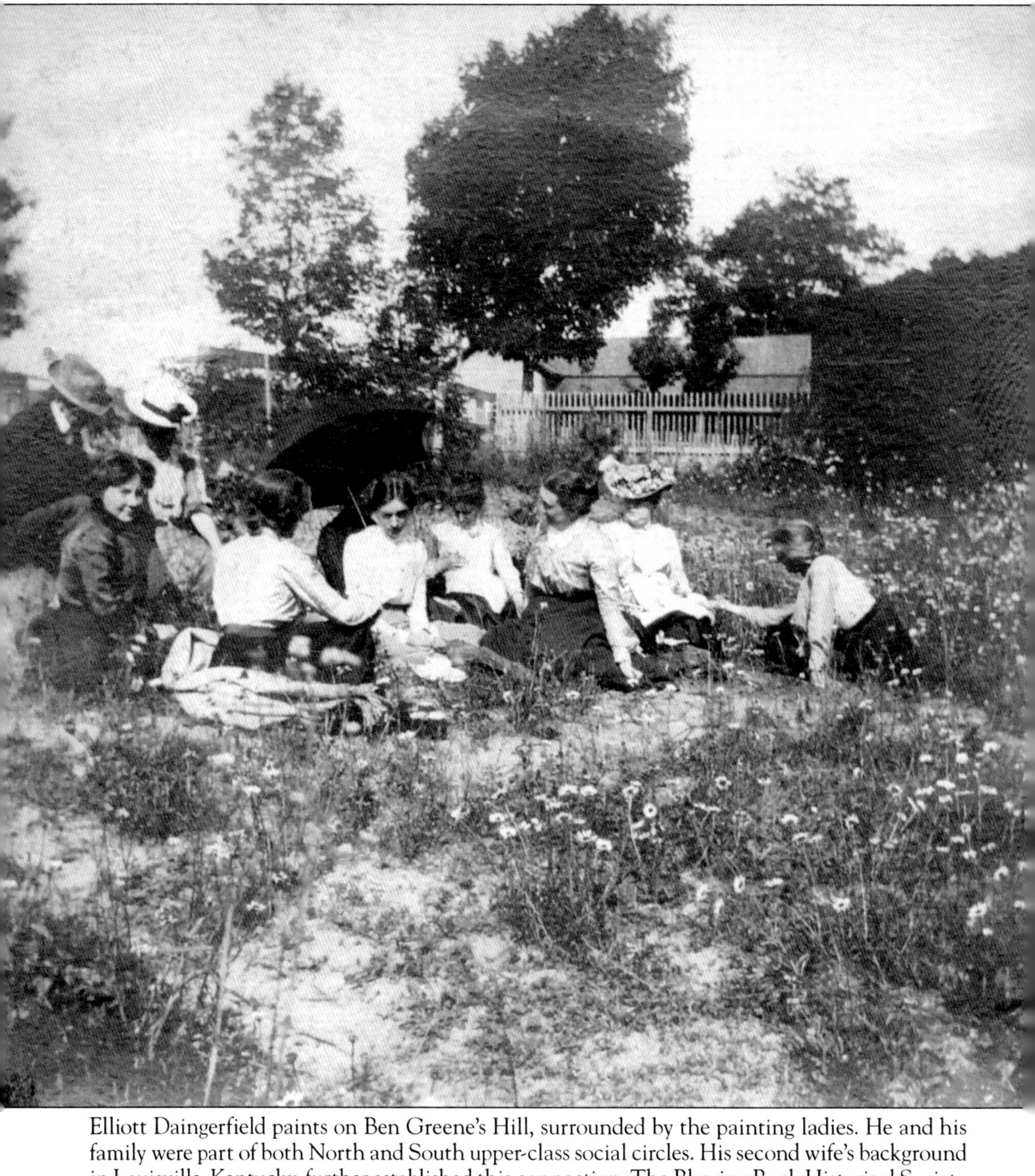

Elliott Daingerfield paints on Ben Greene's Hill, surrounded by the painting ladies. He and his family were part of both North and South upper-class social circles. His second wife's background in Louisville, Kentucky, further established this connection. The Blowing Rock Historical Society utilized the original drawings of Edgewood Cottage and a SWAT (Saving Worn-out Architectural Treasures) team to combat the years of neglect before reconstruction. Among the many unique features is a central chimney with a fireplace in all four first-floor rooms. Each summer, Edgewood Cottage hosts artists in residence and carries on this artistic legacy. Visitors are personally greeted by the artist showing each week, can observe their talent, and are able to purchase works. Information is also on display in the cottage year-round. In the town park and other scenic local areas, artists of all types can be found finding inspiration for their work.

The Dry County Five serves as an example of music as a form of recreation. The band members are students at Appalachian State Teachers College; from left to right are Gail Russell, Phyllis Beam, Carolyn McKennis, Buzz Church (accompanist), Sara Sanders, and Julie Barber (seated). This performance in April 1965 was for the local junior senior banquet. Musical entertainment can be found throughout the town, primarily in the summer.

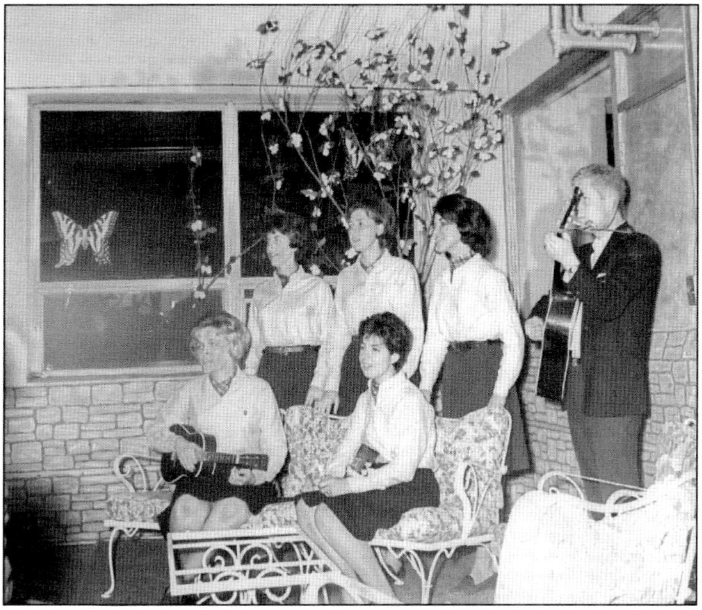

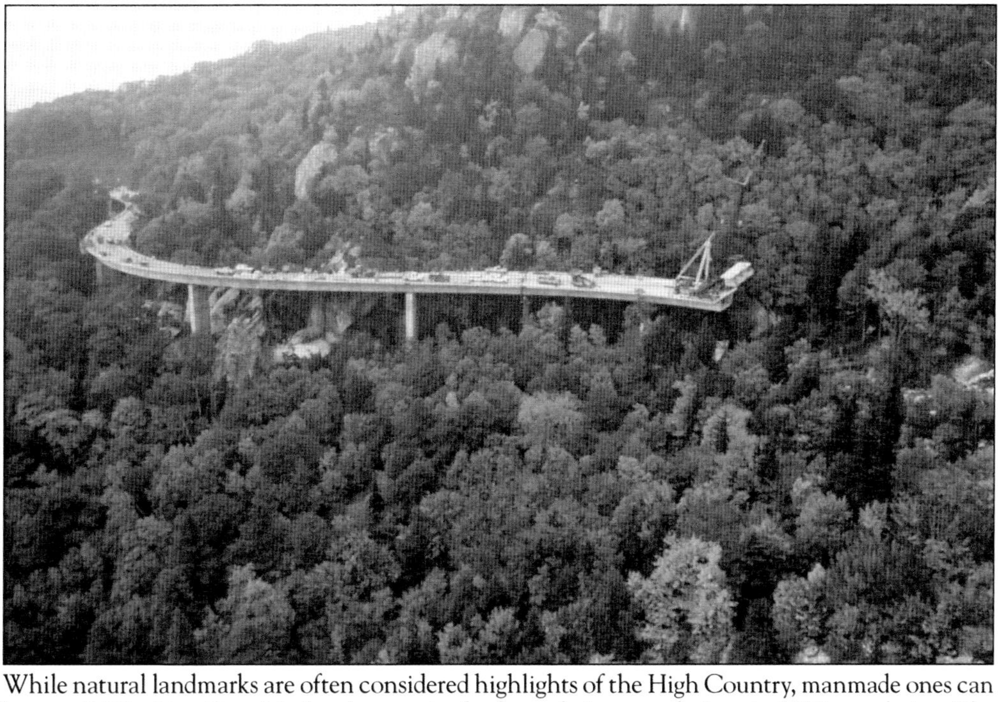

While natural landmarks are often considered highlights of the High Country, manmade ones can be as well. The Linn Cove Viaduct has received a dozen design awards since its 1987 completion. The 1,243-foot-long S-curve utilized 153 concrete segments weighing nearly 50 tons each. This missing link of the parkway allows Blowing Rock visitors easier access to Grandfather Mountain.

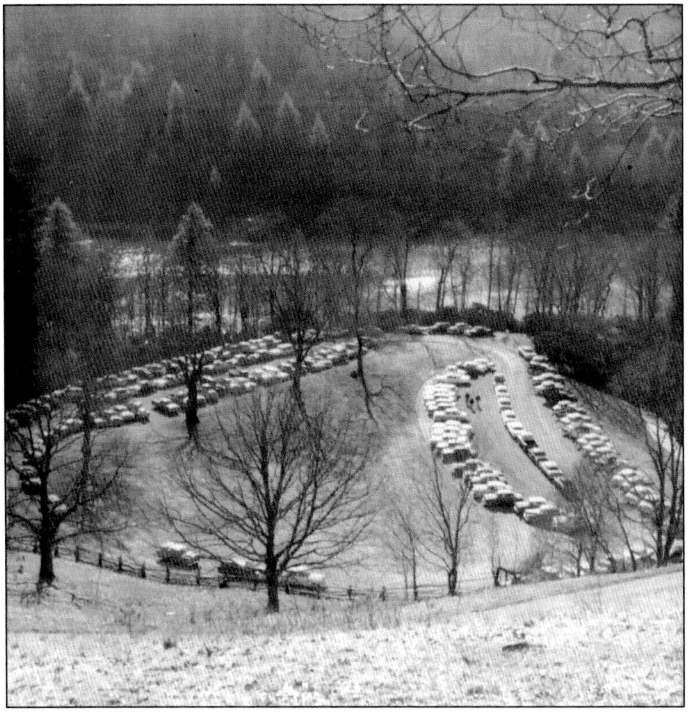

The parking lot at Trout Lake and the start of the Rich Mountain Trail along the Blue Ridge Parkway appear well used. Bass Lake has received far more recreational usage in recent years due to its level trail and waterfowl, and Trout Lake remains quiet, serene, and loved by local residents.

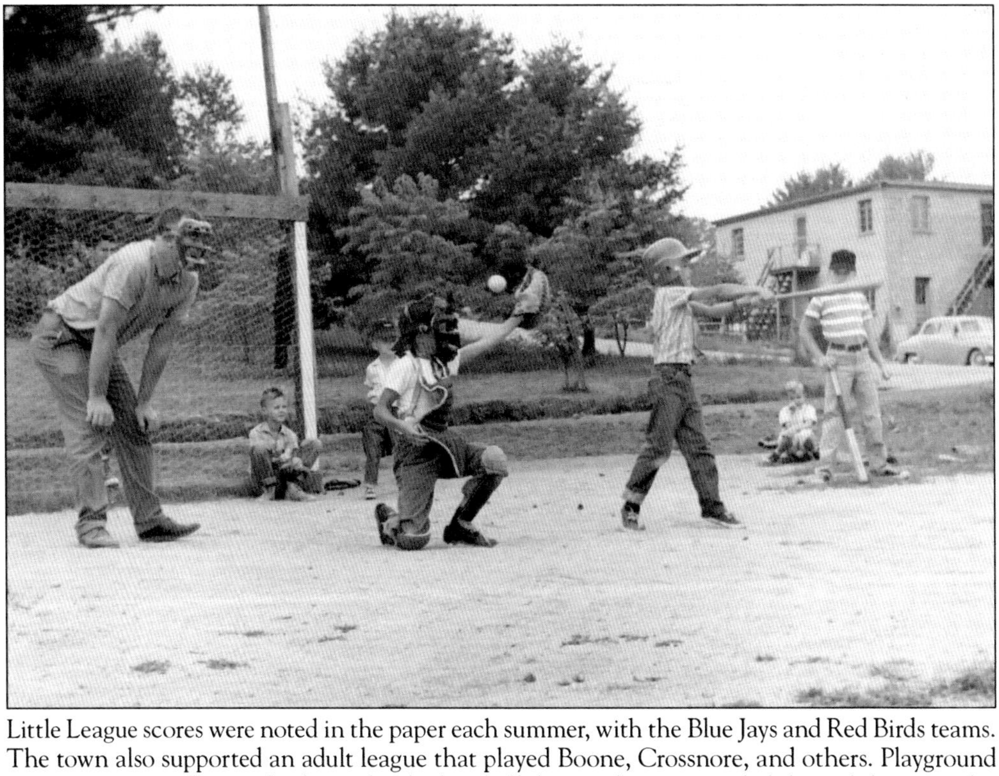

Little League scores were noted in the paper each summer, with the Blue Jays and Red Birds teams. The town also supported an adult league that played Boone, Crossnore, and others. Playground improvements and a new backstop for the baseball diamond were provided through bingo-parlor winnings in 1938.

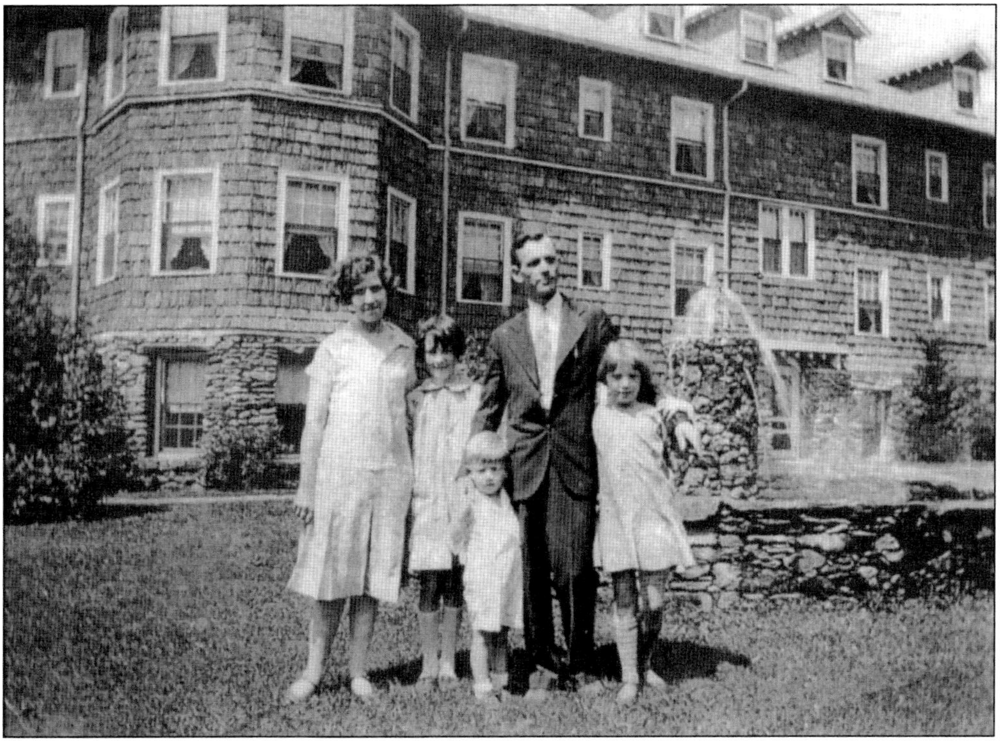

The McNabb family poses in front of the fountain at Mayview Manor in the 1920s. The tennis courts at Mayview also likely led the town to complete their own in the summer of 1937, proclaiming, "Court fees are moderate, tennis carts at a discount, and lessons by competent instructor." The current town park includes a host of recreation opportunities, including tennis.

Fog is a constant in town in nearly all months of the year. The entrance to the town park takes on a particularly eerie feel with substantial fog. Town government is responsible for the landscaping in Broyhill Park, Cannon Gardens, Memorial Park, and other maintained planting areas, working closely with various civic organizations such as the Blowing Rock Appearance Advisory Commission and the Blowing Rock Garden Club.

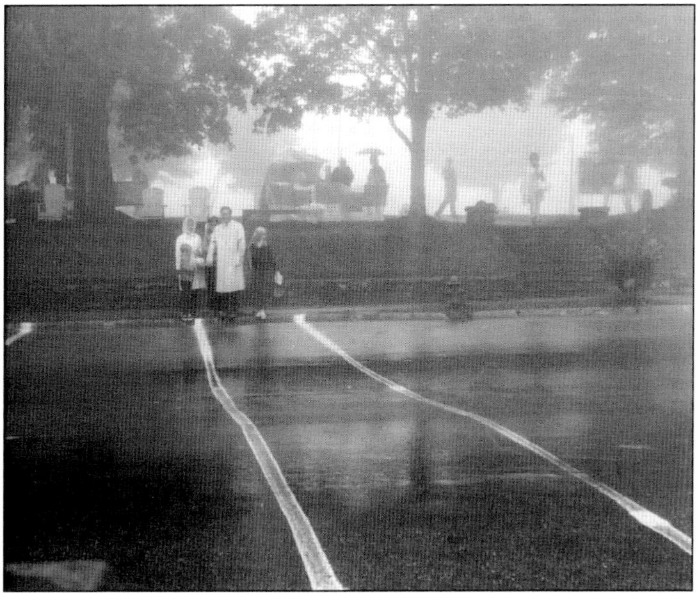

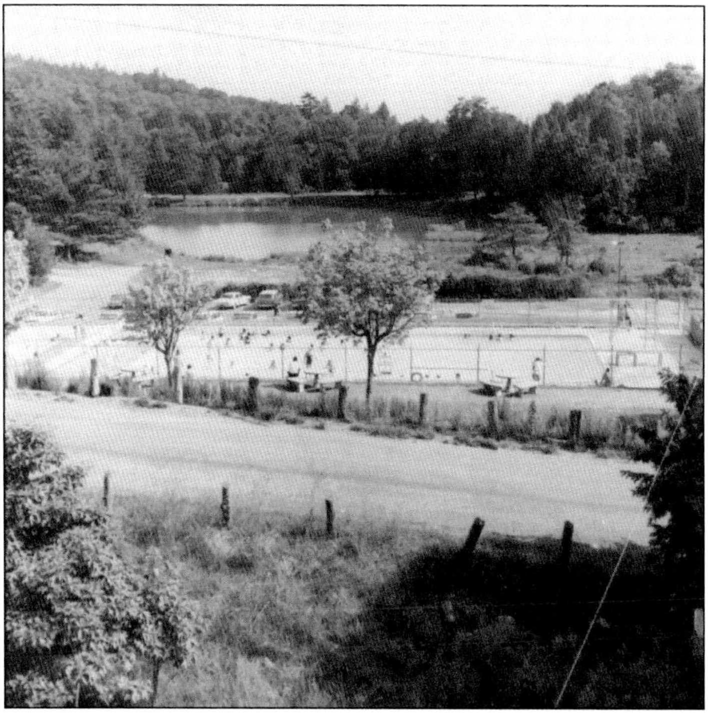

Built in 1957 and dedicated to the memory of Grover C. Robbins, the Olympic-sized town pool is popular each summer. Mayview Lake, as the centerpiece to Broyhill Park, is also well utilized. Five summers after opening, the pool held a swimming meet and contacted Camps Yonahlossee, Broadstone, Rainbow, and Appalachian State Teachers College for competition.

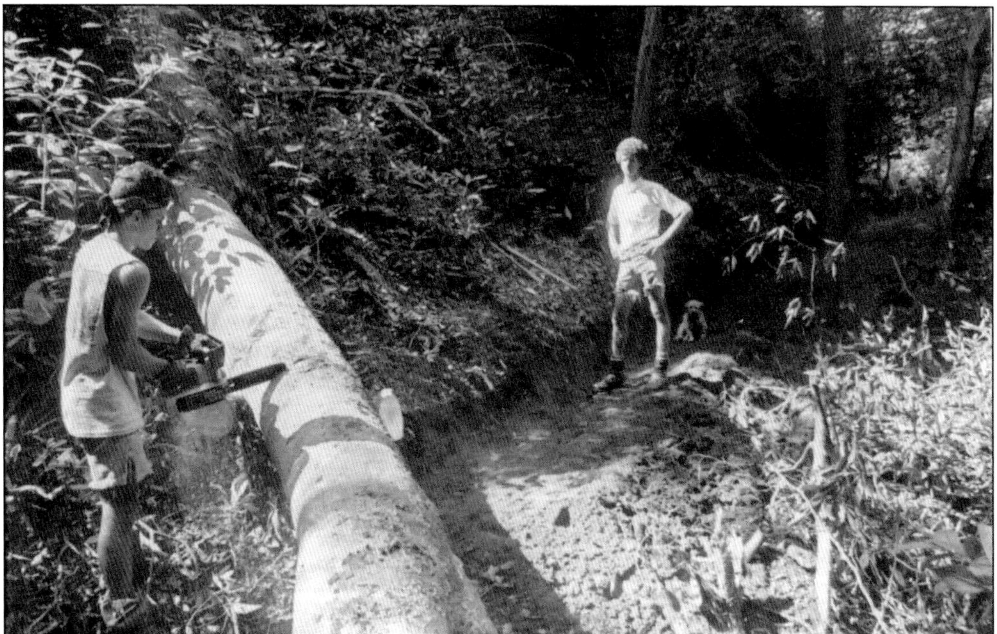

The maintenance of town recreational areas includes the Glen Burney Trail, especially after severe weather downed trees and limbs. A crew of CCC workers in the 1930s improved the trail from Globe Valley to Blowing Rock, which includes only this usable portion remaining. *Ray's Weather Center* remains a popular website to check on local forecasts. Average rainfall remains just below 70 inches, and sudden thunderstorms are not uncommon.

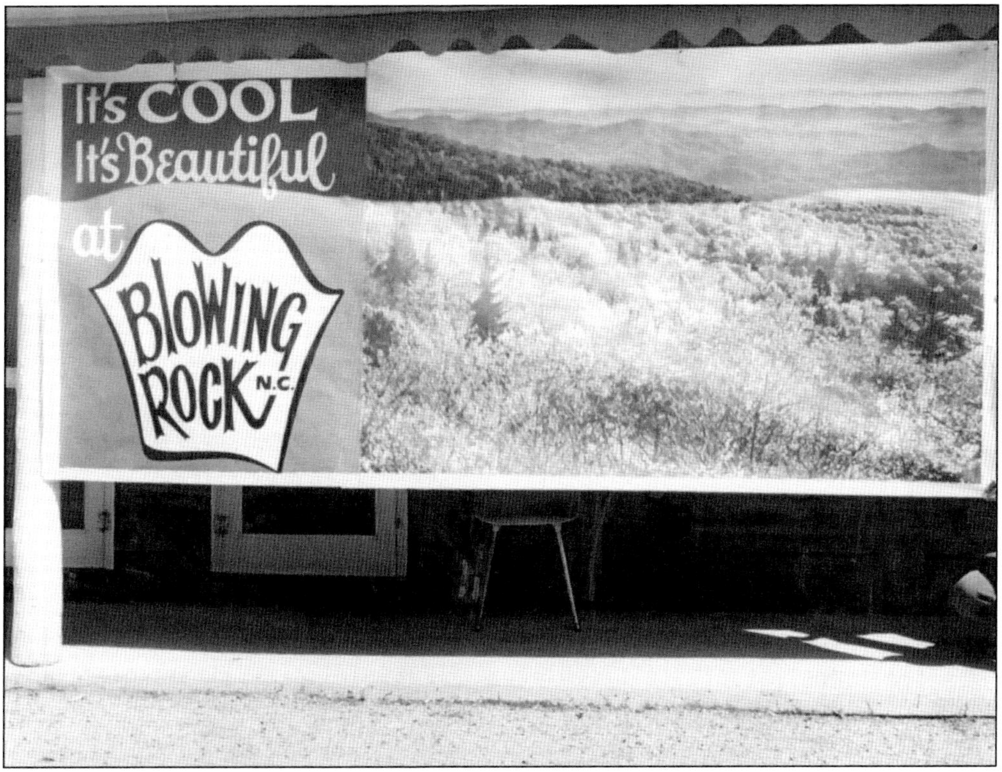

This promotional signage is from 1962, and similar posters were displayed all over the Southeast in the summer of 1969. The Blowing Rock Tourist Development Association's community auction was held in the school auditorium annually in October the following decade, and all proceeds went toward further advertising the area, largely using natural scenery as the main selling point.

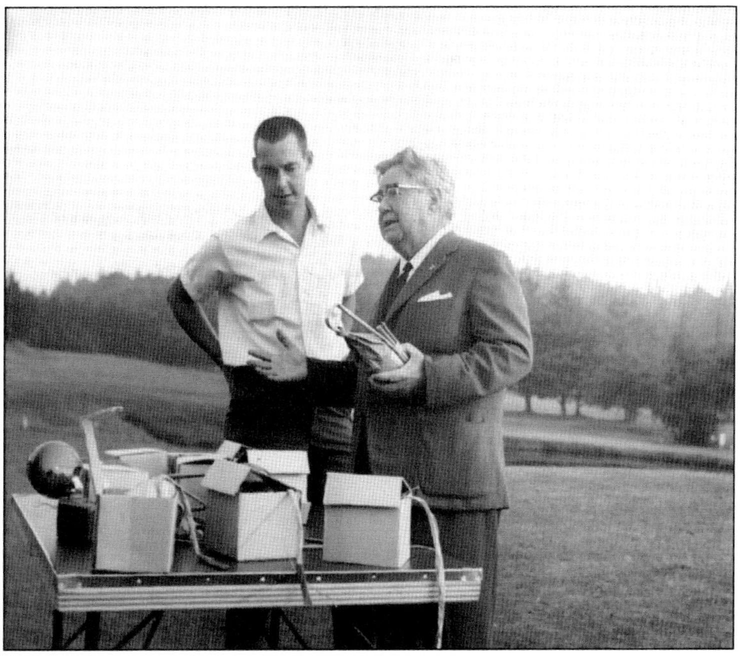

Sid Greene (left) and Dick Pope prepare fireworks for the annual town Fourth of July event. Pope was Florida's premiere showman, owner of Cypress Gardens and one of the state's most successful orange groves. He enjoyed giving Blowing Rock locals "Orange Carpet" passes, good for admission to any attraction in the state. During his years here, he always provided the fireworks.

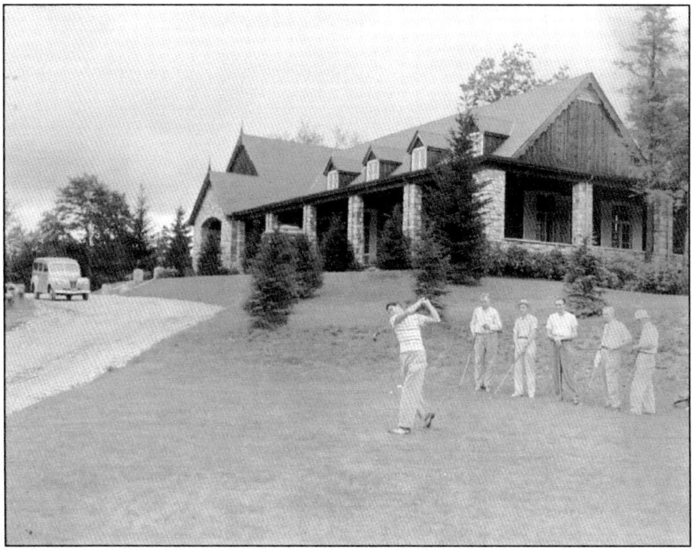

Improvements to the golf course in the 1930s included 12,000 feet of pipe installed for a sprinkler system. The opening of the country club clubhouse in 1941 marked a new phase in local social life, but it burned in 1974. Holes were renumbered to begin and end at the clubhouse instead of the Green Park Inn. Fashion shows, the Gay Nineties costume ball, and guest hosts and speakers increased membership.

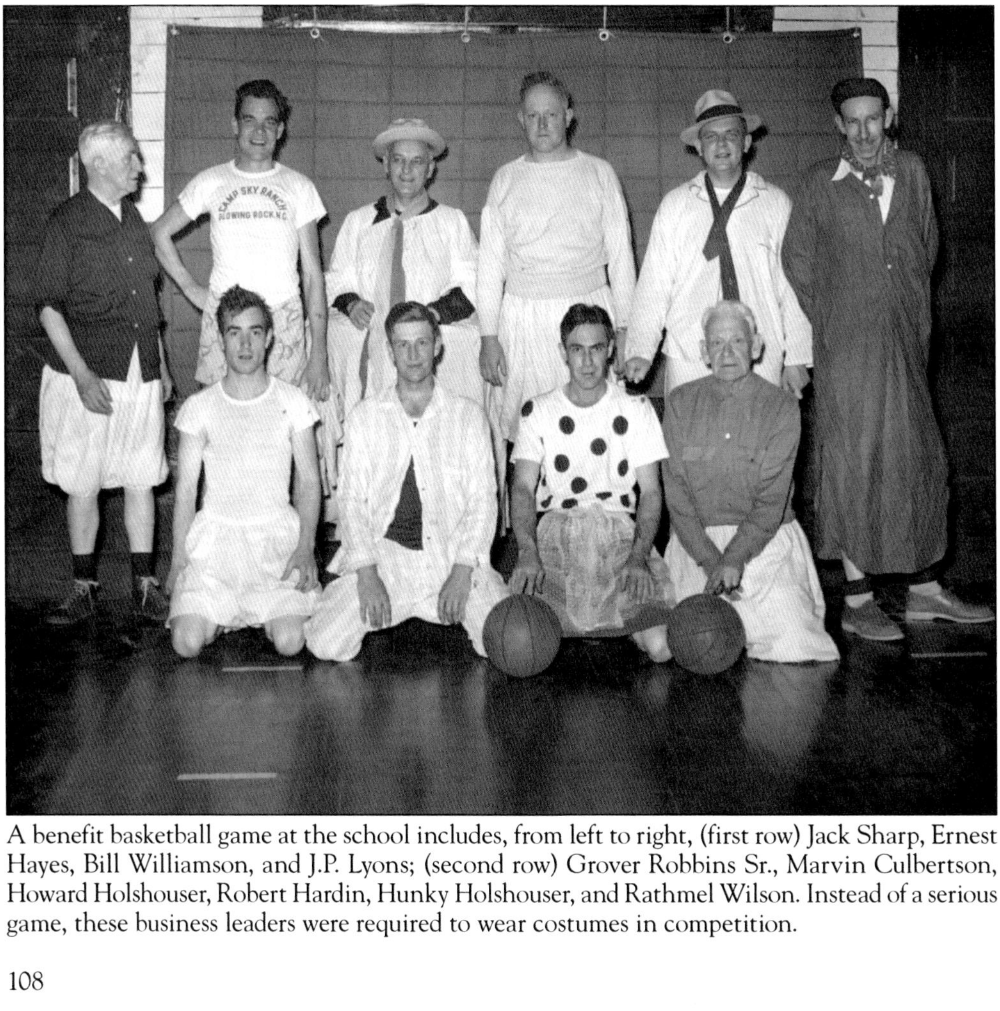

A benefit basketball game at the school includes, from left to right, (first row) Jack Sharp, Ernest Hayes, Bill Williamson, and J.P. Lyons; (second row) Grover Robbins Sr., Marvin Culbertson, Howard Holshouser, Robert Hardin, Hunky Holshouser, and Rathmel Wilson. Instead of a serious game, these business leaders were required to wear costumes in competition.

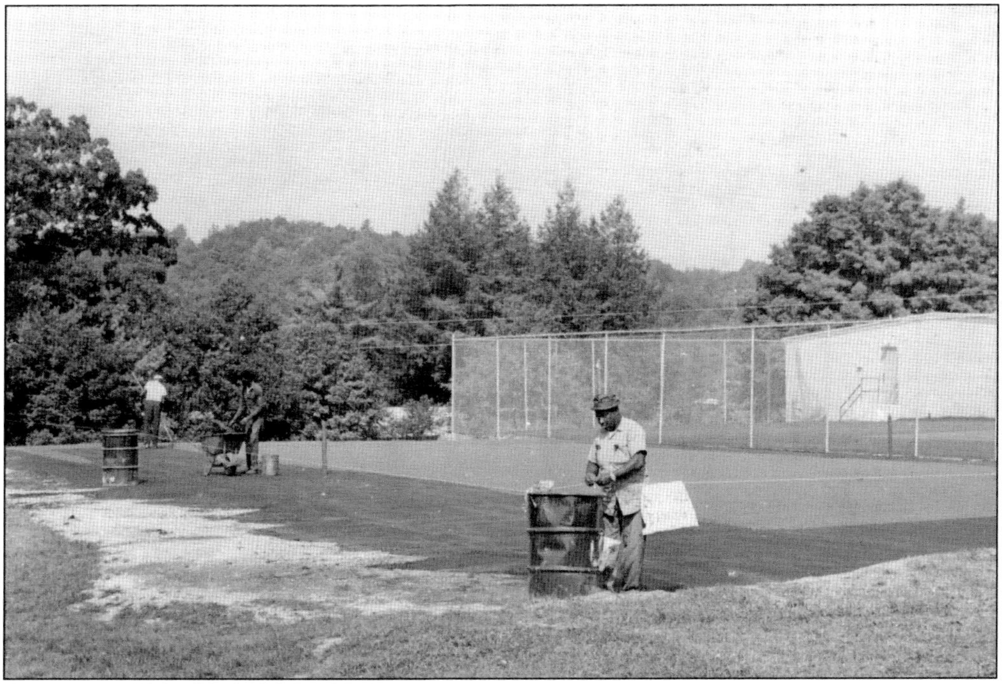

Three new tennis courts were completed in the town park in 1975; two currently exist. Tennis has always been central to recreation here, and summer instruction for girls and boys given by Thomas Buxton made mornings in the 1950s and 1960s memorable. He also ran a program entitled Camp Scamp that included mountain hiking, camping, and fishing.

Playground equipment has changed significantly over the years in the town park, largely due to size constraints and safety concerns. In the 1950s, arts and crafts, baseball, and Dr. Mordecai's nature program in the evening were noted activities. The park, open all day until 10:00 p.m., offered shuffleboard, horseshoes, tennis, checkers, table tennis, basketball, badminton, dancing, swings, slides, and a merry-go-round.

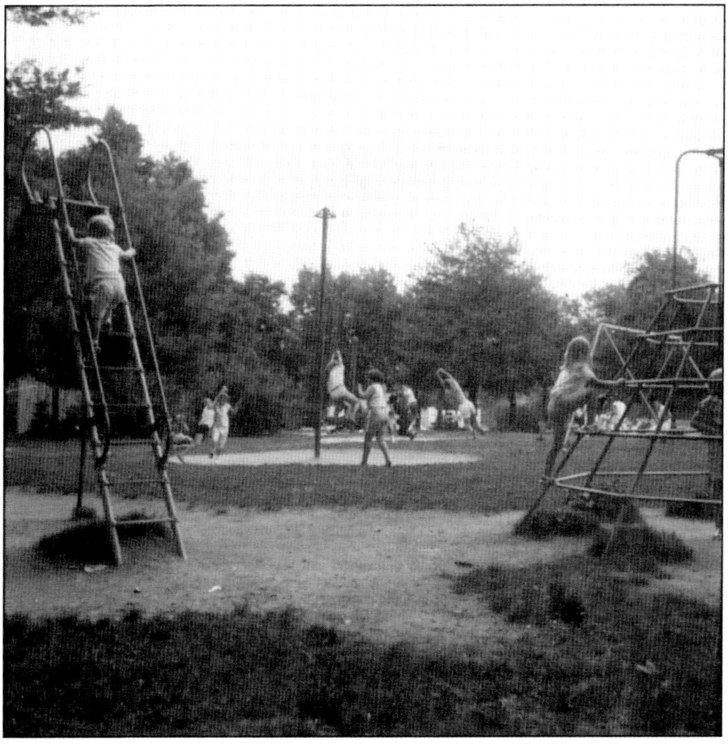

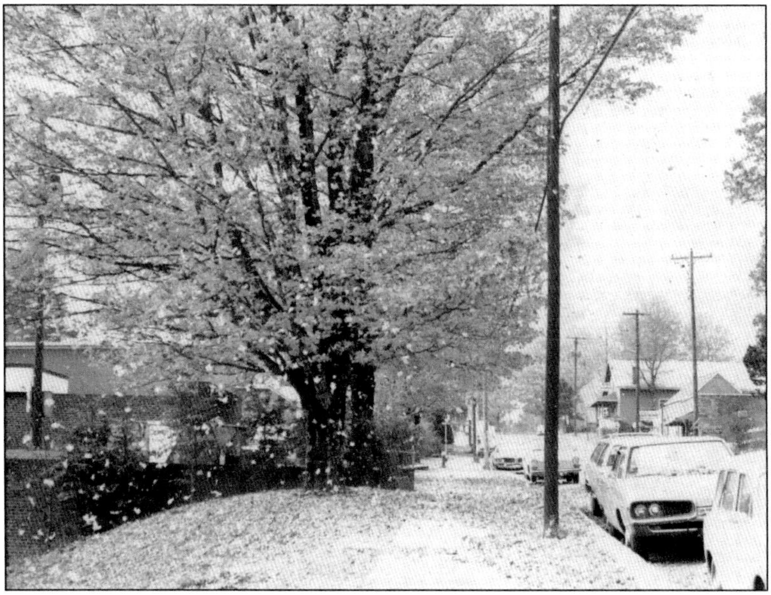

Marketing fall foliage to tourists is a relatively new concept, but Blowing Rock is no exception to those traveling to see spectacular color. Western North Carolina has an enormous variety of trees that provides a broad spectrum. This image along Sunset Drive also shows a laundry and longtime location of Moody's Furniture.

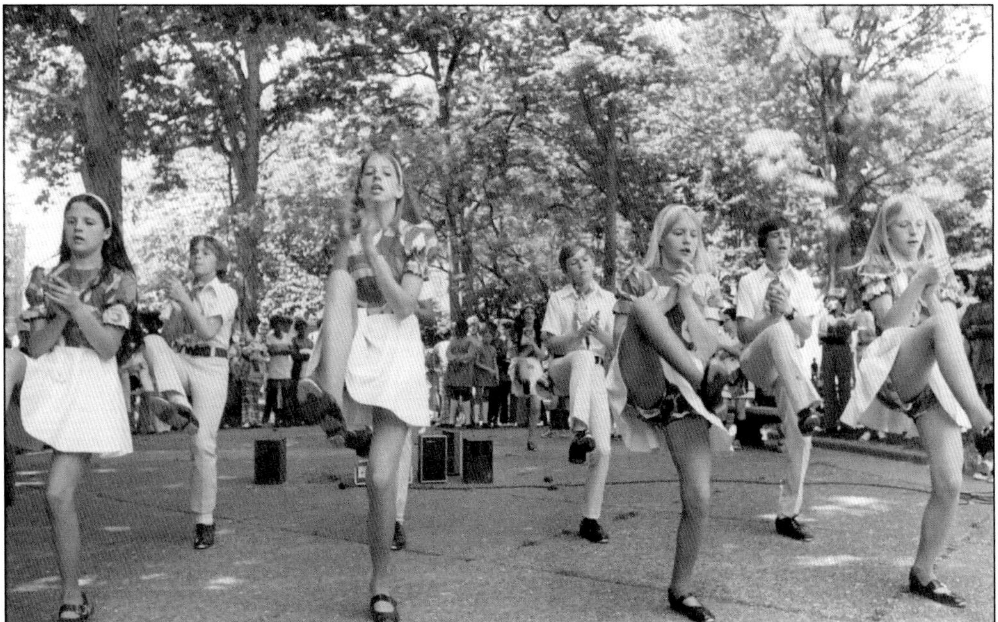

The above photograph shows youth dancers in the town park in April 1974 as a diverse crowd of spectators and performers looks on. The park was created as a living memorial to all who served in the armed forces during World War II, with efforts led by Grover Robbins. In addition to musical entertainment, people-watching from the benches overlooking Main Street is a continued use of the park.

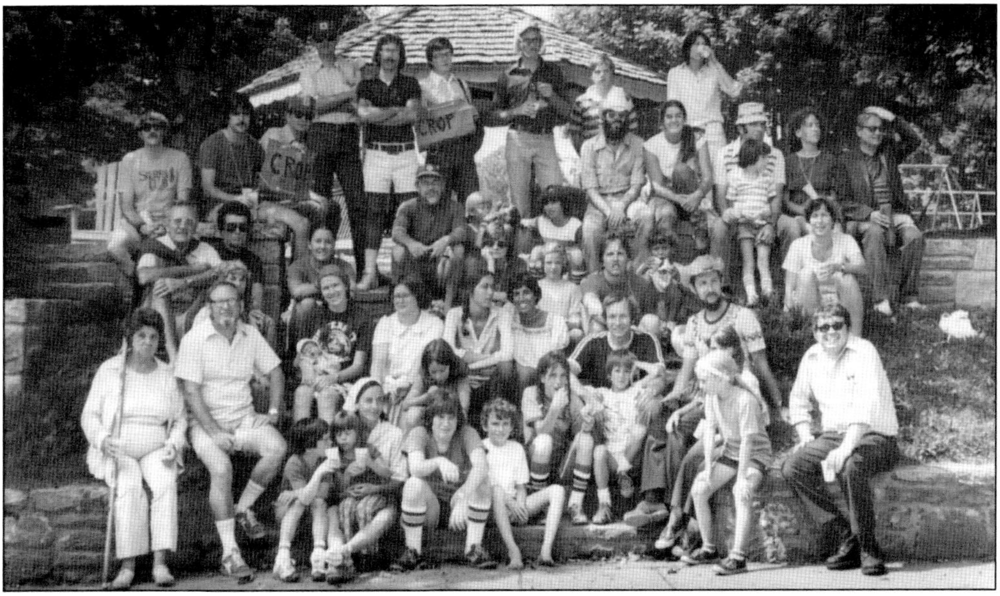

Several times throughout the 1970s and 1980s, nearly 100 citizens of Watauga County, young and old, joined in a Christian Rural Overseas Program (CROP) Hunger March from Boone to Blowing Rock that ended at the town park. Local citizens and merchants pledged to a certain amount per mile for the effort.

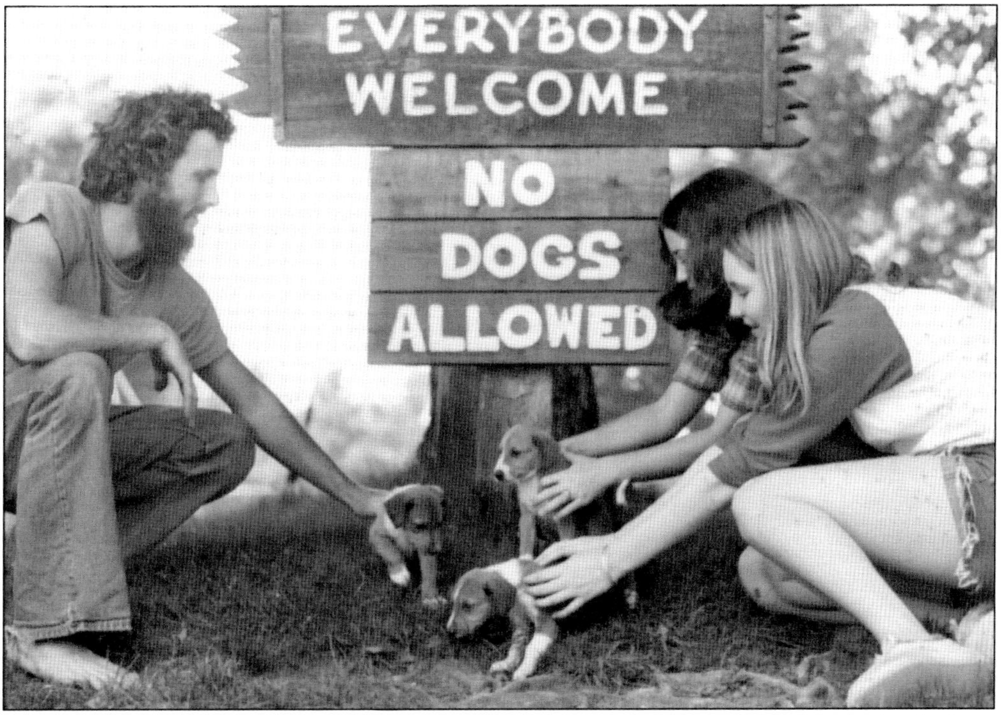

Jerry Burns, photographer, would like to point out irony and maybe suggest even a little rebellion. Animals and children were favorite subjects, but he also documented the accumulation of trash and garbage on local roadways and scenic areas. Burns enjoyed the humanistic aspect of everyday images, close-ups of children and animals, and highlighting parades and events.

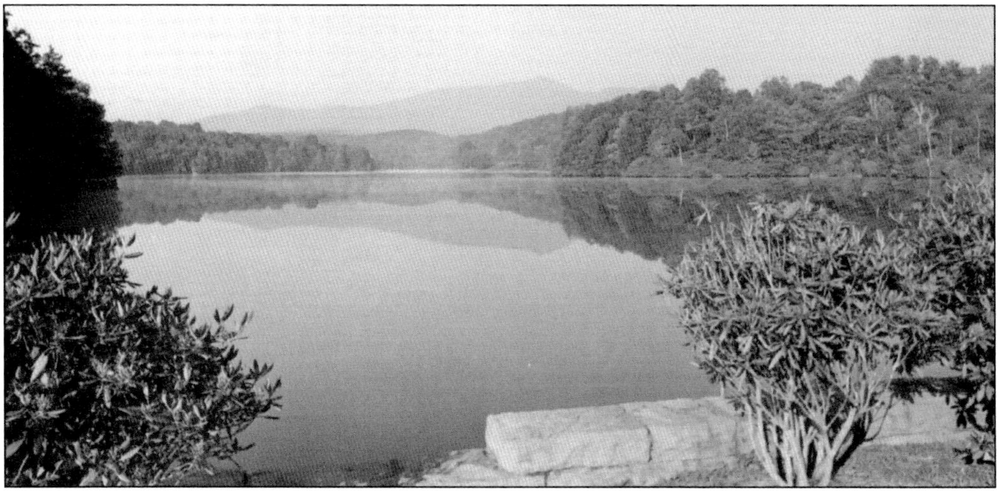

This bridge overlooking Price Lake and Grandfather Mountain along the Blue Ridge Parkway was completed in 1960. It has remained an ideal photo opportunity ever since, with or without reflection. Julian Price was head of the Jefferson Standard Life Insurance Company, and the 47-acre lake was formed by Boone Fork, Gold Prong, and Laurel Creek through the efforts of the National Park Service.

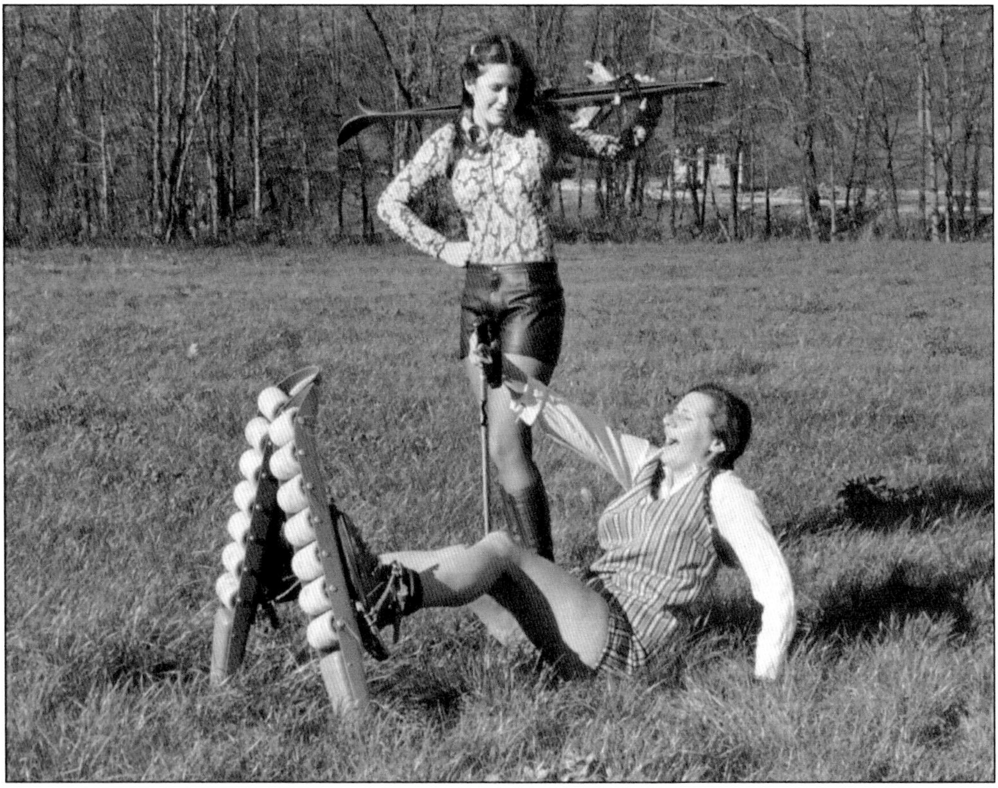

Grass skiing is a method of training for alpine skiing or just a fun way to practice for the local winter slopes. In the late 1970s and early 1980s, grass skiing was a popular summer activity at Beech Mountain and in areas along the Blue Ridge Parkway. Rentals, lessons, and races briefly brought a little bit of the ski season into the summer.

Seven

WINTER WEATHER

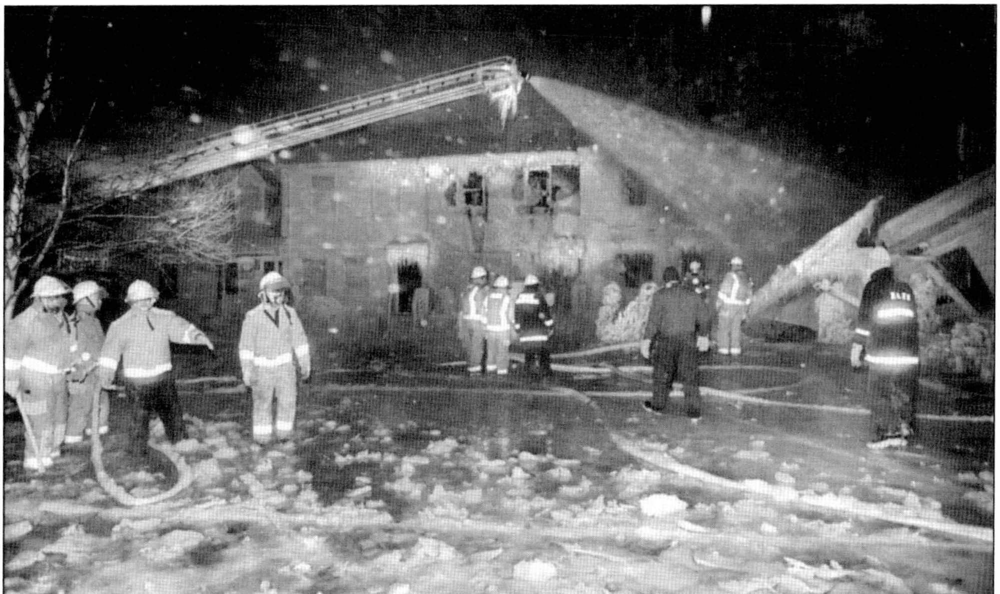

Fire has struck Blowing Rock residences and businesses with great ferocity, including the Glenwood commercial buildings at the end of Sunset Drive. When combined with subzero temperatures, the challenge to local fire crews can be even more intense. Their uniforms are often covered in ice, which builds on the suits as the water sprays backward toward them when putting out fires in the wintertime.

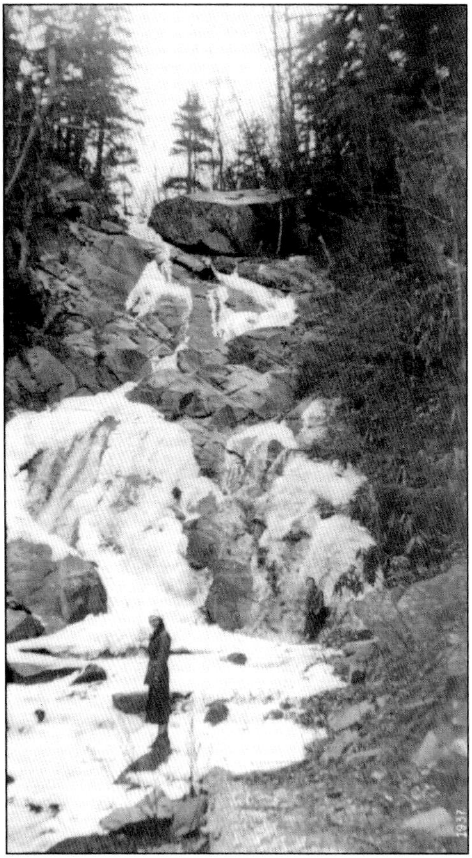

Glen Burney Falls, a treacherous trail in all seasons, is featured here from the bottom in wintertime. Winter weather can bring dangerous conditions as well as unparalleled scenery. Photographers both amateur and professional can be seen around snow, ice, and trees in attempt to get that perfect shot capturing the local landscape.

This group of friends, pictured ice skating on Mayview Lake in December 1929, includes, from left to right, Edward Robbins, Edward Coffey, George Robbins, Ben Greene, and Lloyd Robbins. The families of the individuals pictured played, and would continue to play, a large role in the formation of the Blowing Rock community. Bicycling was also an interest of local youth during all seasons.

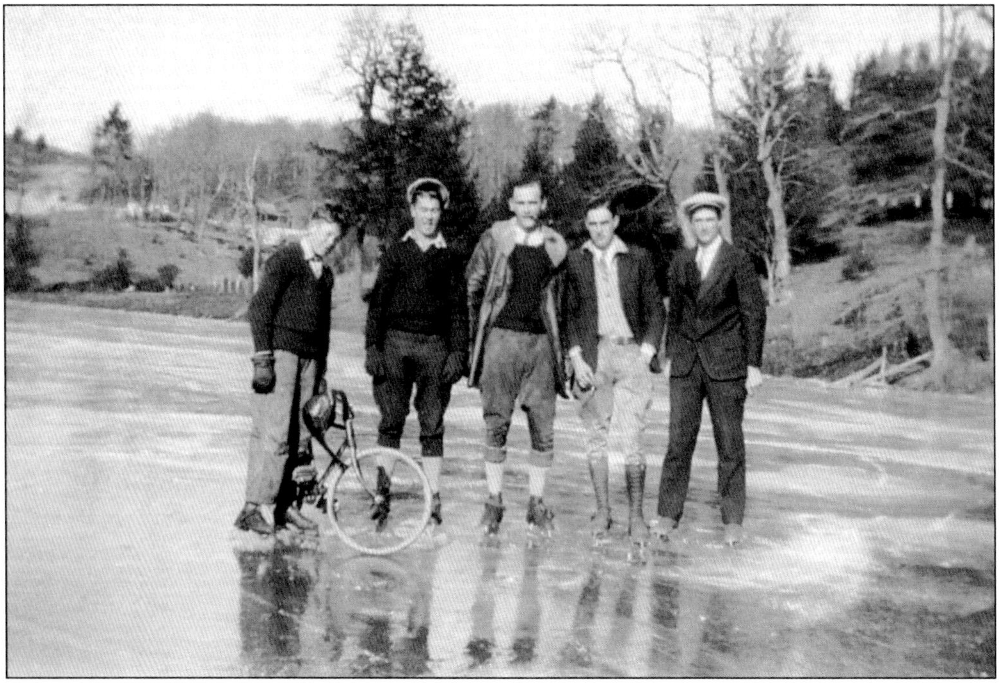

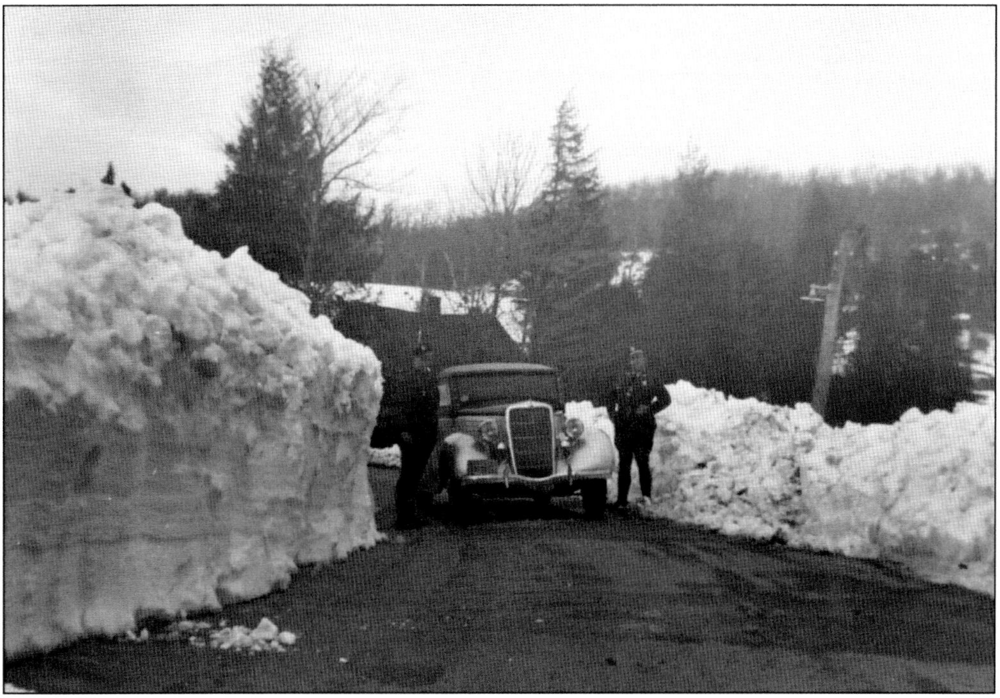

In early March 1936, a significant snowstorm impacted Blowing Rock, and some of the drifts provided photo opportunities. This image was taken just beyond the Green Park Hotel by Velma Cannon Greene. Collaboration between Watauga County and Caldwell County is needed for effective snow removal in this area and all along state highway 321.

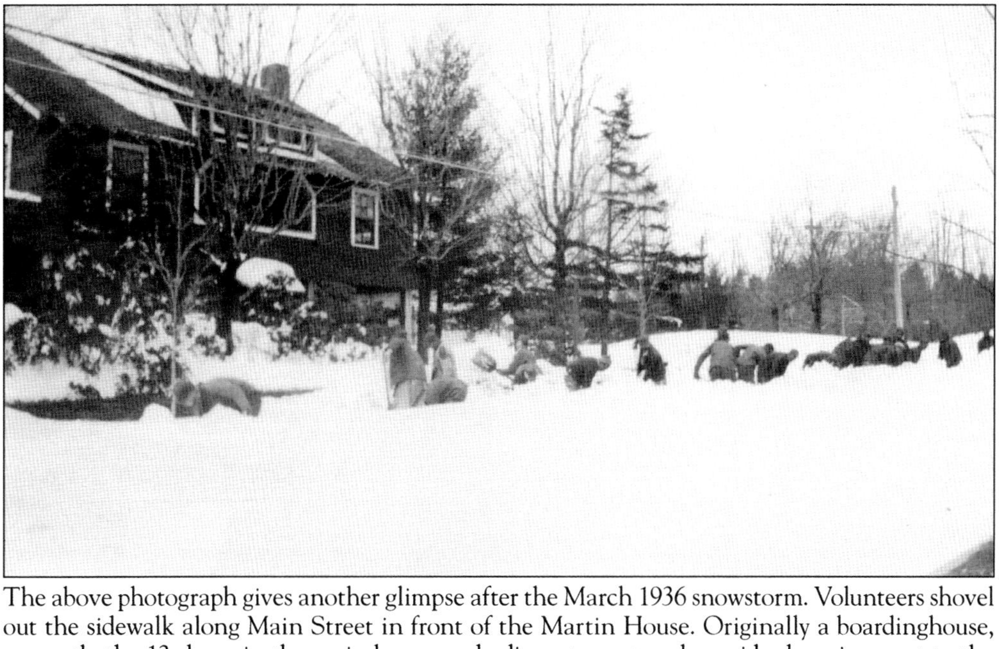

The above photograph gives another glimpse after the March 1936 snowstorm. Volunteers shovel out the sidewalk along Main Street in front of the Martin House. Originally a boardinghouse, currently the 12 shops in the main house and adjacent courtyard provide shopping next to the town park. Like many downtown properties, the building has gone through many alterations over the years.

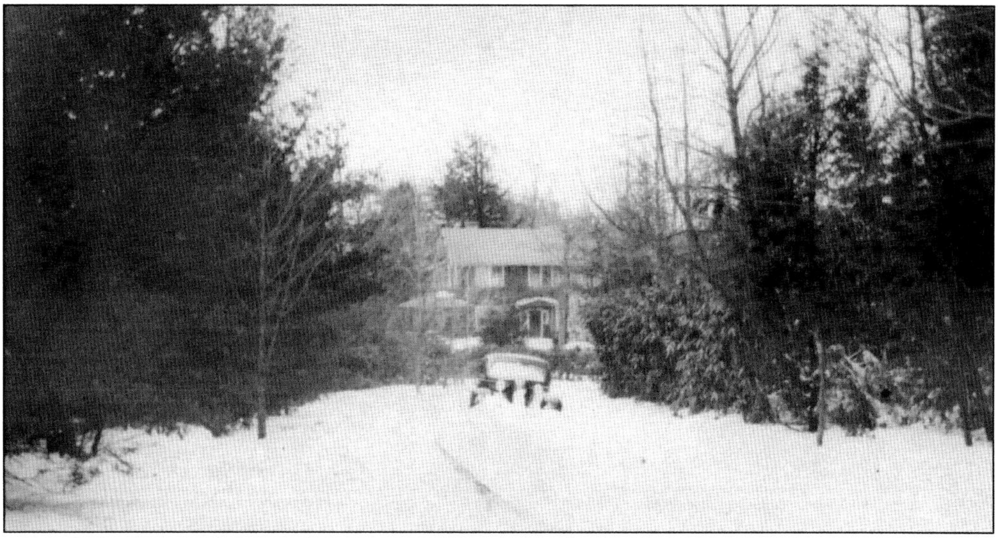

The Chalmers Davidson residence on Laurel Lane, and other driveways in town, could be tricky to get out of after a snowstorm. Dr. Davidson was a summer resident beginning in 1884, and he was knowledgeable of early resort hotel dates of construction. Rhododendrons are found around many residences in town, especially the older ones.

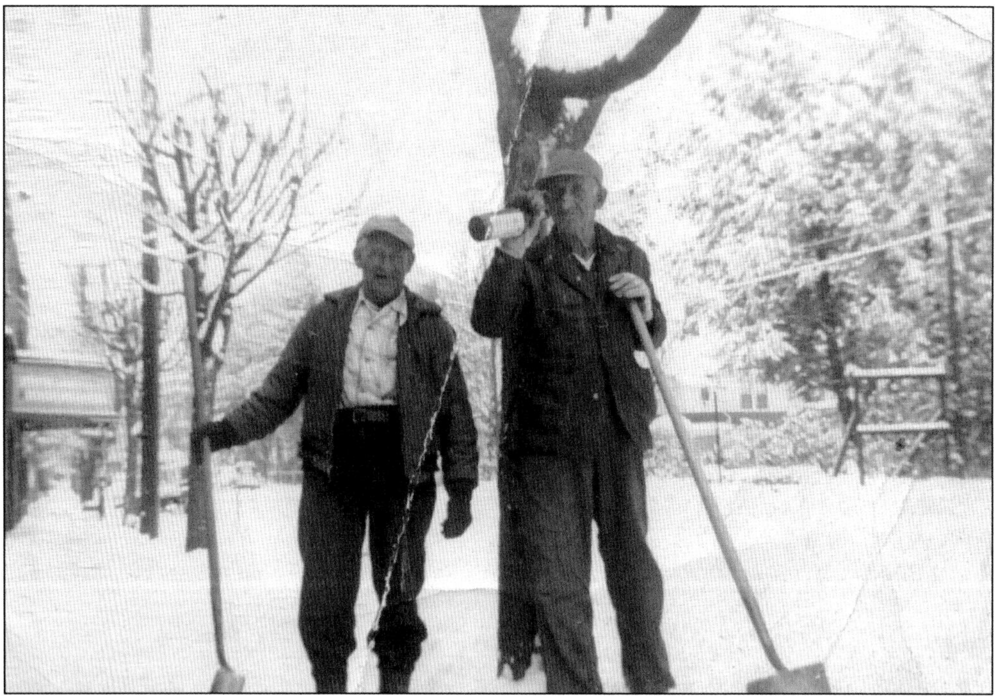

Sometimes a little liquid courage is needed for shoveling after winter's fury. Business owners recall the assistance of many volunteers in clearing the sidewalks, and a shovel could be found right inside the entrances in the winter. The marquee of the Yonahlossee Theater was a familiar landmark downtown for decades, and its letters were changed by leaning out of the second-story window.

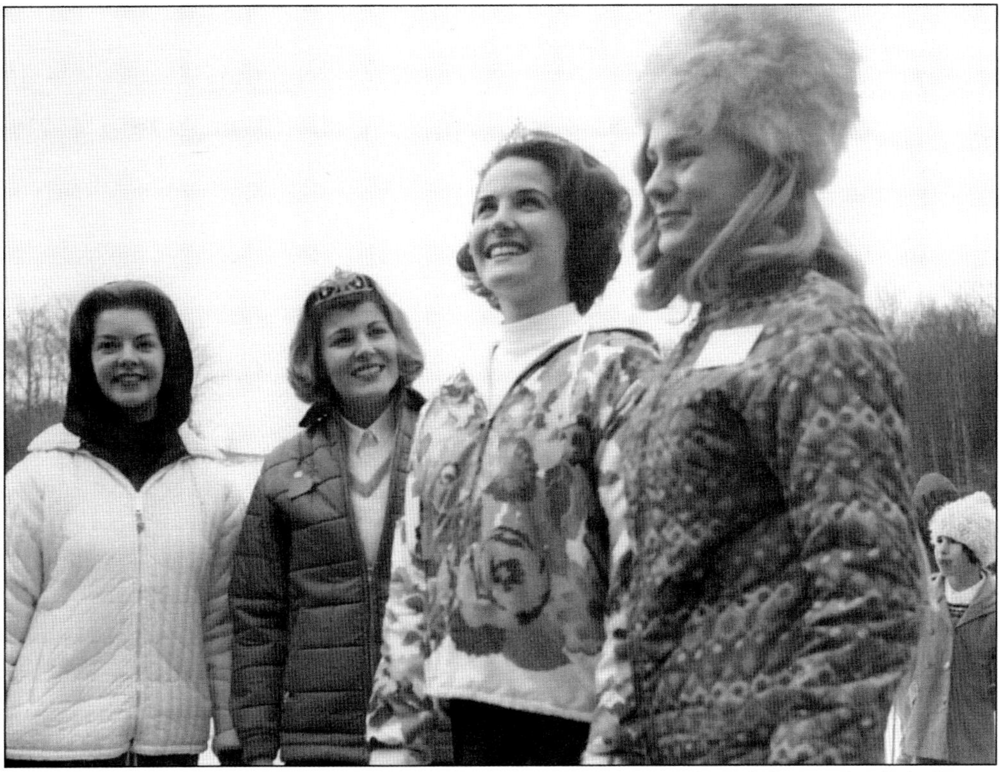

The contestants for the Miss Southern Snow Queen in 1963 are, from left to right, Judy Bower (first runner up), Cynthia Stroupe (Miss Southern Snow Queen 1963), Betty Simpson (who would win in 1964), and Cheri Rose (second runner up). The event took place at the Blowing Rock Ski Lodge with an equal number of local and seasonal observers and contestants.

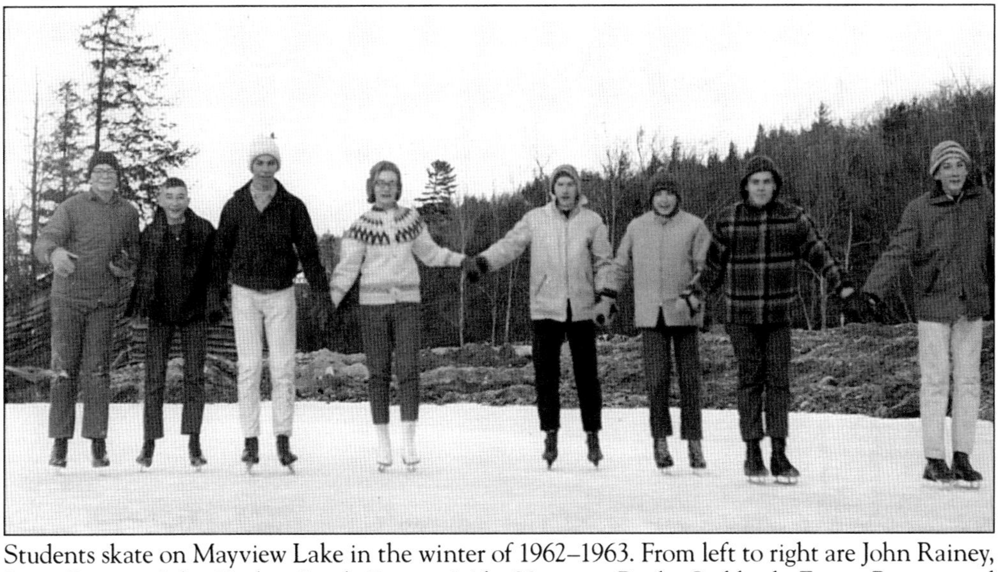

Students skate on Mayview Lake in the winter of 1962–1963. From left to right are John Rainey, Barry Buxton, John Tinker, Linda Rainey, Mike Harmon, Bucky Sudderth, Ernest Bryant, and David Harmon. Buxton would author *A Village Tapestry*, a history of Blowing Rock, and currently is president at Lee-McCrae College in Banner Elk, North Carolina.

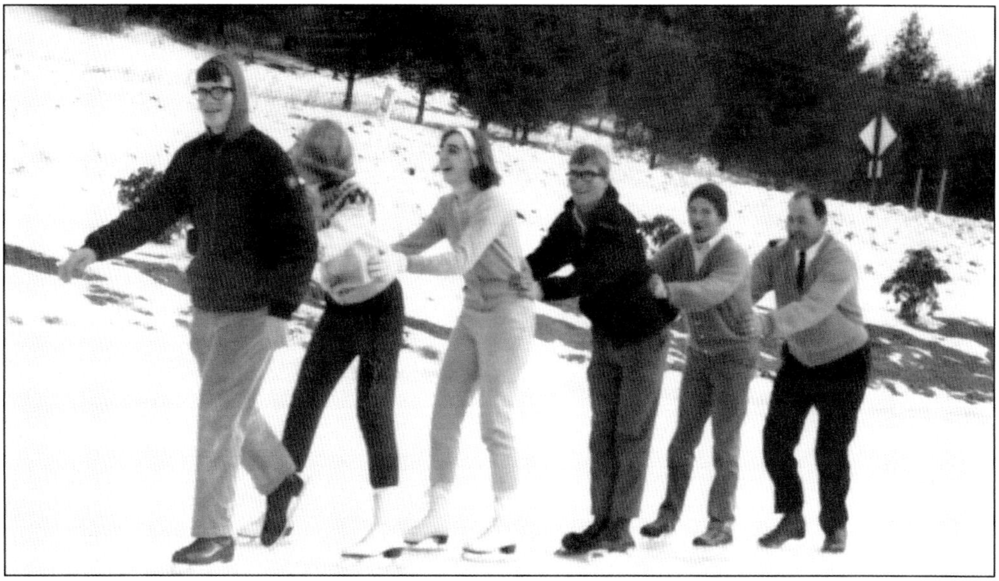

Pictured here is more skating fun from January 1966; many remember multiple ice-skating spots throughout the town. From left to right are Johnny Rainey, Linda Rainey, Pat Sitts, James Broyhill, unidentified, and Ray Critcher. Currently and for the past few decades, Appalachian Ski Mountain has opened its ice rink each winter to accommodate both seasonal visitors and local citizens.

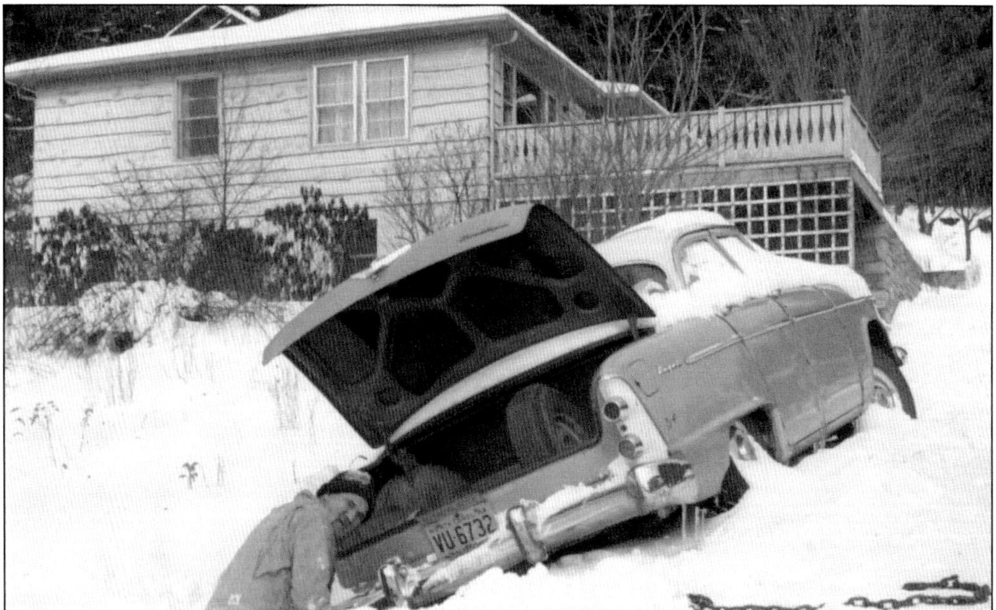

A Monday morning in January 1965 found Rob Greene tunneling his car out of a driveway ditch and hoping that chains would be sufficient to keep it out. It snowed 12 inches the previous Saturday, and all county schools were cancelled that day. The 1977–1978 school year saw 39 days closed, while the 1990–1991 year only four. Snow is predictable, but the amounts each year remain elusive.

Plenty of signage, including Storie's Soda, Warnock Construction, Esso, and "Winter Sports," were displayed above the distinctive chamber of commerce sign after the roads were cleared on Main Street. The slight taste of winter weather in the area by early visitor Bishop Spangenberg in December 1752 may have lead to his settlement near Winston-Salem instead.

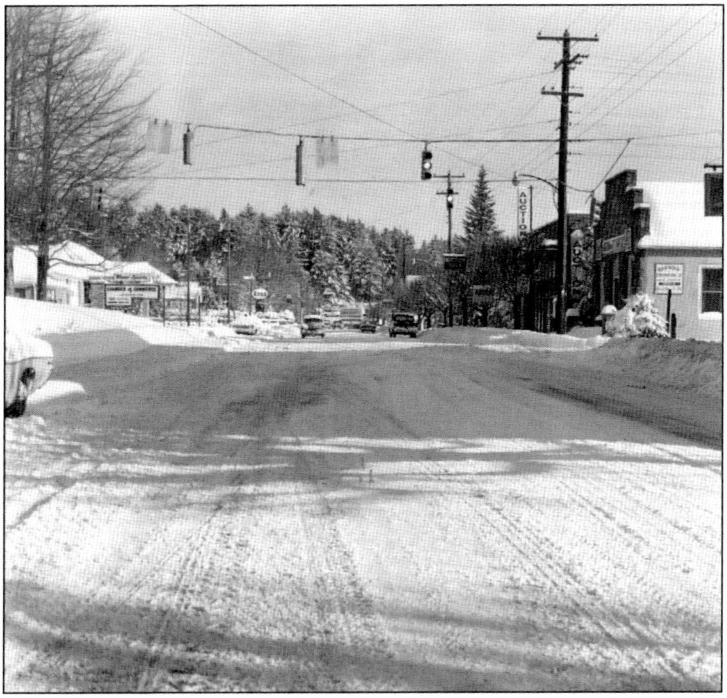

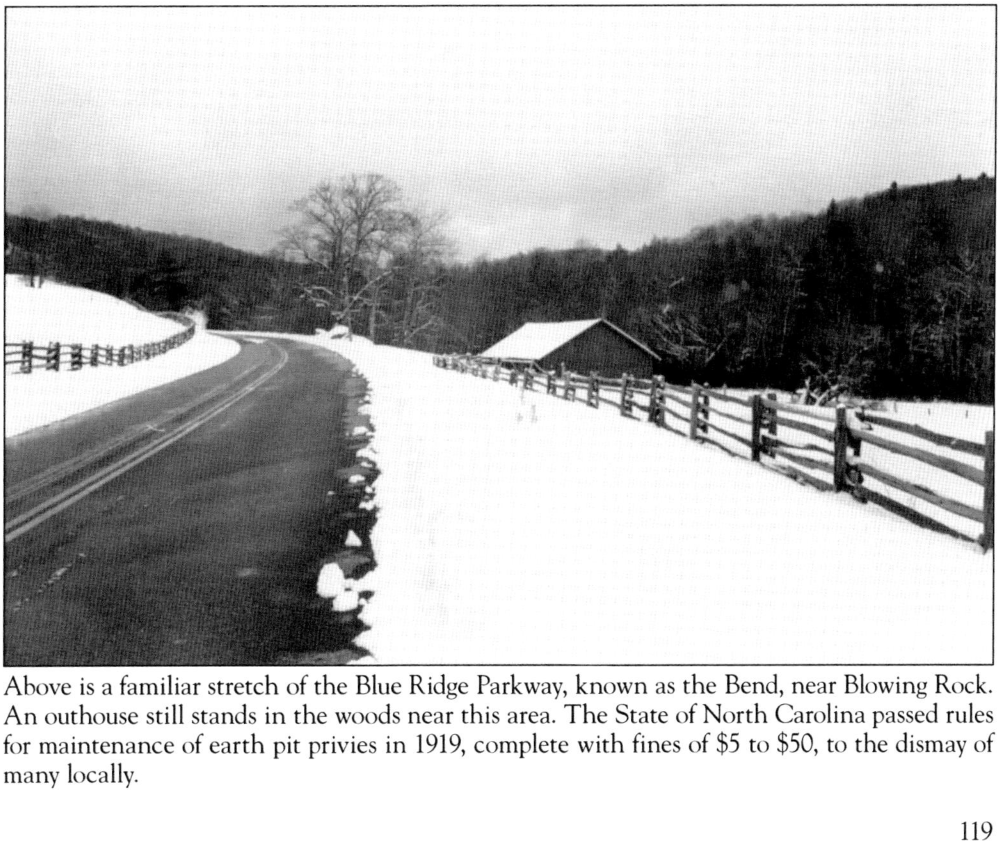

Above is a familiar stretch of the Blue Ridge Parkway, known as the Bend, near Blowing Rock. An outhouse still stands in the woods near this area. The State of North Carolina passed rules for maintenance of earth pit privies in 1919, complete with fines of $5 to $50, to the dismay of many locally.

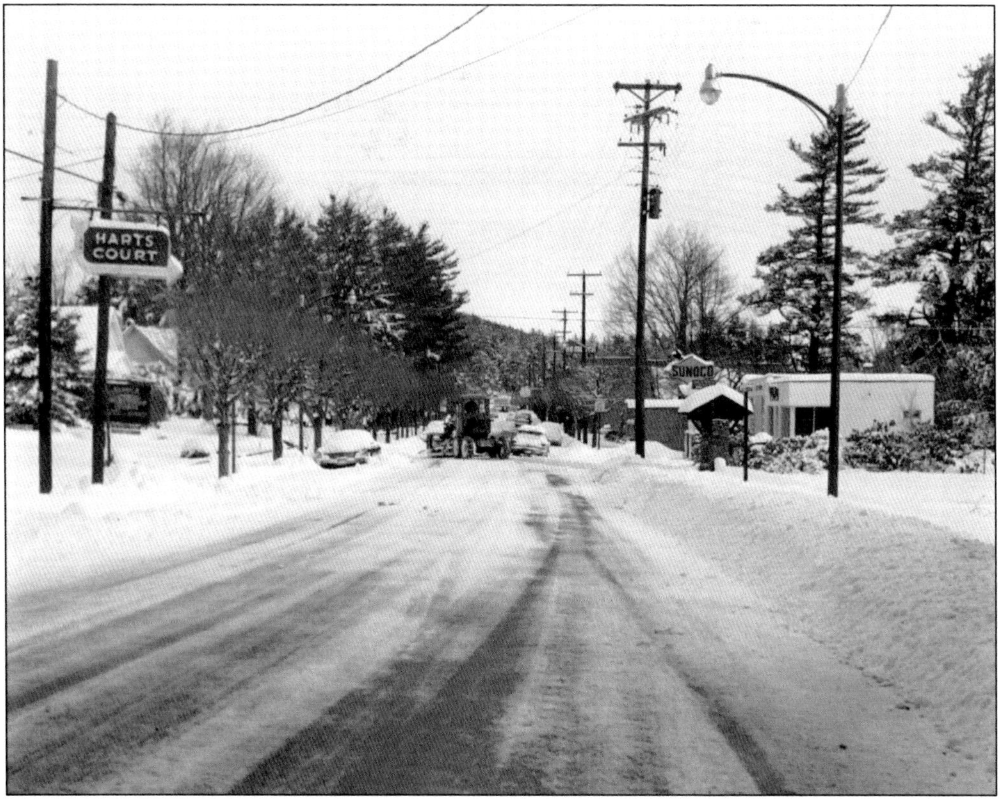

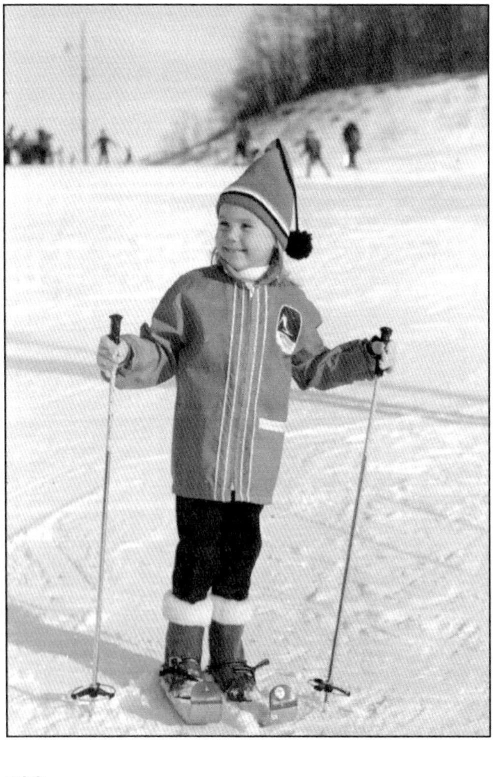

Signage in the above Main Street image includes Harts Court, the Hemlock Motel, and a Sunoco station. The snowplow is also a welcome sign to local residents and businesses. In the 1920s, more Southerners were able to purchase second homes and obtained automobiles to travel to the mountains. By the 1970s, annual winter travel became routine for both longtime and short-stay visitors.

Brenda Moretz happily poses at Appalachian Ski Mountain, with additional skiers coming down a smaller hill. Skiing provided another outlet for youth in the winter; changes in elevation made conditions for sledding attractive, too. Makeshift hills were created each winter, but this local attraction provided the biggest thrill, one that proved to be a success.

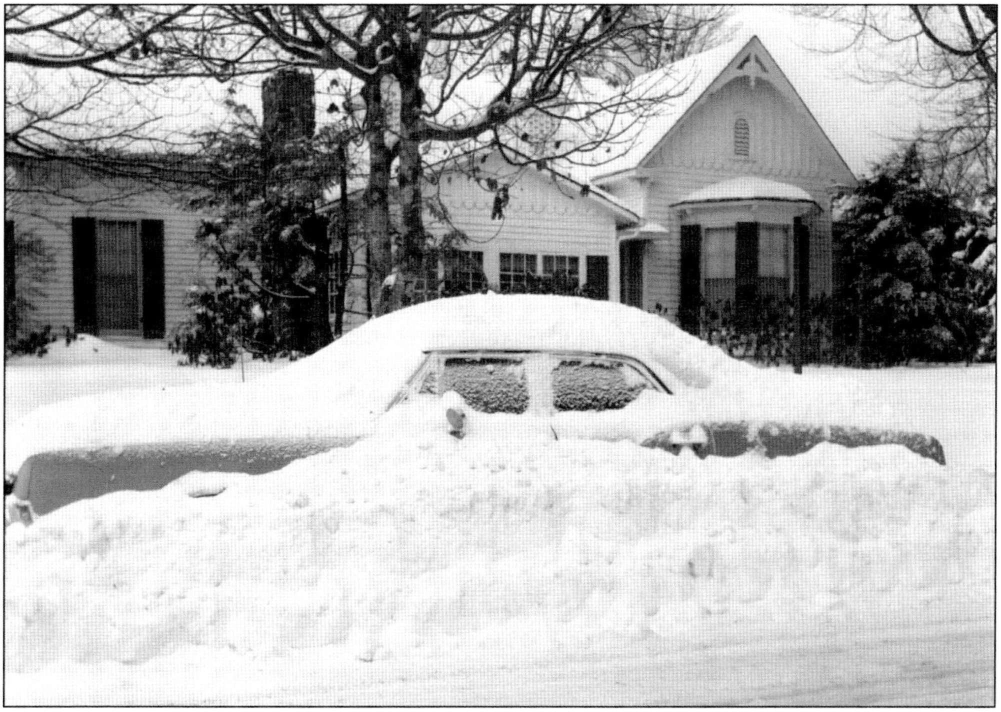

Two-hour parking limits downtown were enforced as early as 1964; in the winter months a consolation was usually ample parking, of course after snow is cleared. The Rumple House was constructed in 1886, also known as the Schenck House. Maj. Henry Franklin Schenck's grandfather built the first cotton mill in the South in 1813. A significant amount of architectural detail has been retained on this structure, including fish scales, pendants, dormers, and bracketing. This image is from January 1968 after a snowstorm accumulation up to 20 inches, the largest since 1960. The newspaper headline ran "most stay by firesides," including the one on what is now called the Rumple House. This structure likely has the same builder as the McBrayer House in Shelby. The facility was extensively refurbished in 2002 by the Rumple Memorial Presbyterian Church and now hosts meetings, Bible study groups, social gatherings, and Sunday school classes weekly.

The lights at the town park are a natural attraction during the winter, singly or in crowds. Since its beginning, Blowing Rock has bustled in the summertime, but gradually it has become a year-round destination. Winter weather combined with elevation makes each event unique—from freezing rain to sleet to snow to sleet.

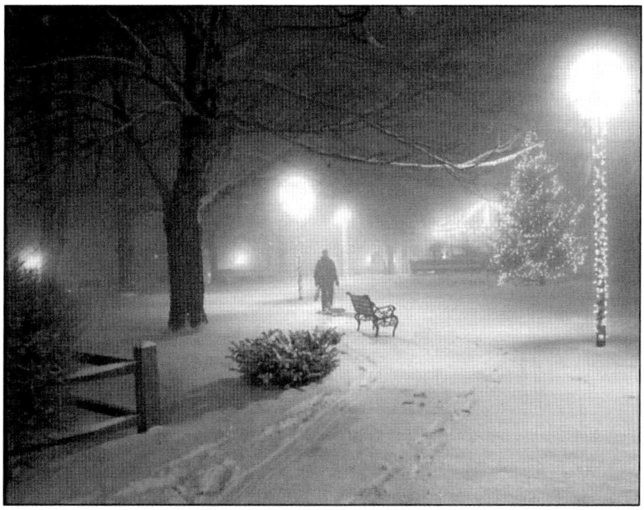

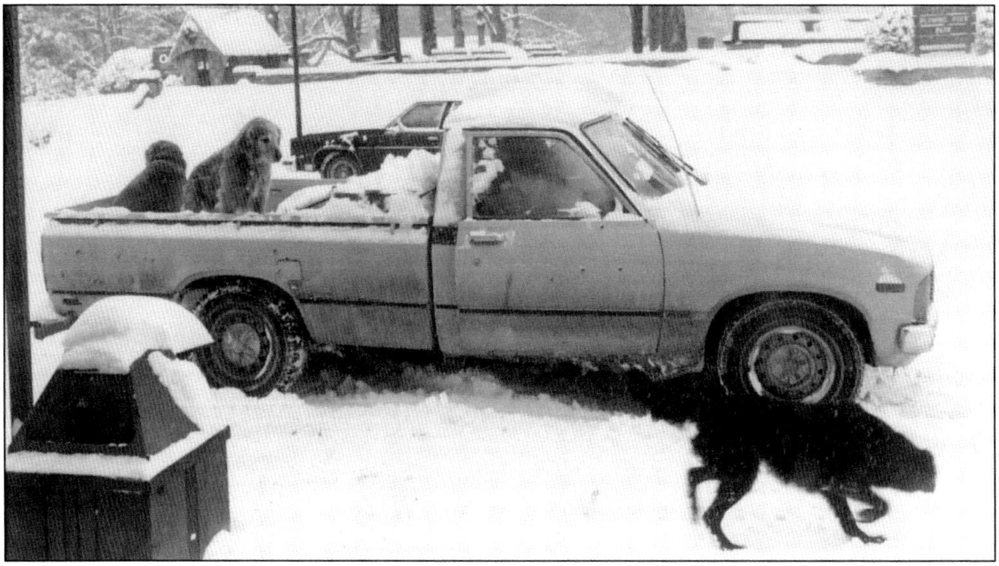

Sometimes the weather is for the dogs—but not always. In 1960, there was a strong concern of stray dogs and that hotel guests are kept up due to howling at night. The town council made a statement that any stray dogs seen on the streets after August 7, 1960, would be exterminated at once.

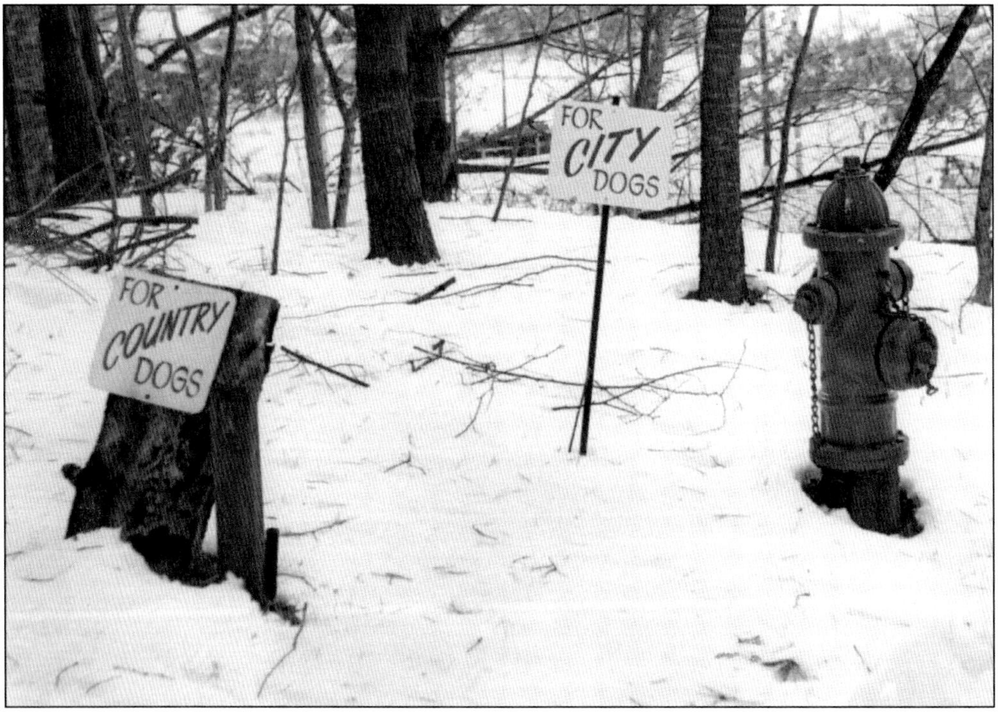

Again, the humor of Jerry Burns comes through; he served on the board of commissioners in 1974 when the zoning ordinance was passed. The ordinance addressed public health, safety, morals, orderly development, panic and other dangers, adequate light and air, overcrowding of land, avoiding undue concentration of population, and the adequate provision of transportation, water, sewage, schools, parks, and other public requirements, all in accordance with a comprehensive plan.

The icehouse on Maple Street was constructed of Grandfather Mountain granite, built for the purpose of storing ice harvested from Chetola Lake. The property has served many uses, including as an automobile service station, electrical repair shop, and the offices of the local newspaper. The Coffey barn behind the icehouse was taken down in the 1960s.

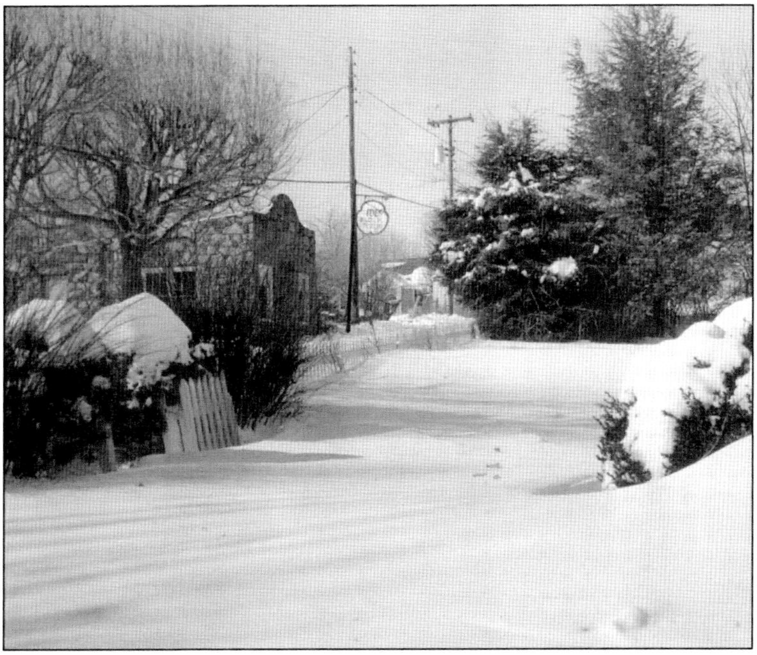

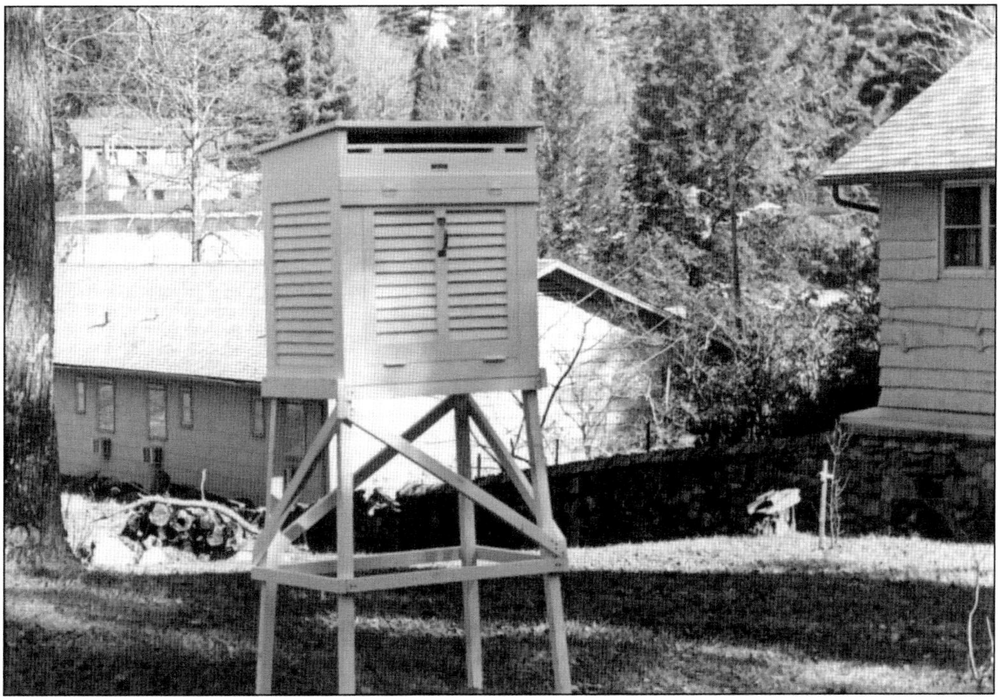

Located near the house of Jerry and Janice Burns on Maple Street is an early version of a weather station. He checked and called in the readings daily and also frequently took images of winter weather right from the house. Jerry also fought and documented fire for the fire department. Department volunteers in the past have included mayors, members of the council, and employees of the town.

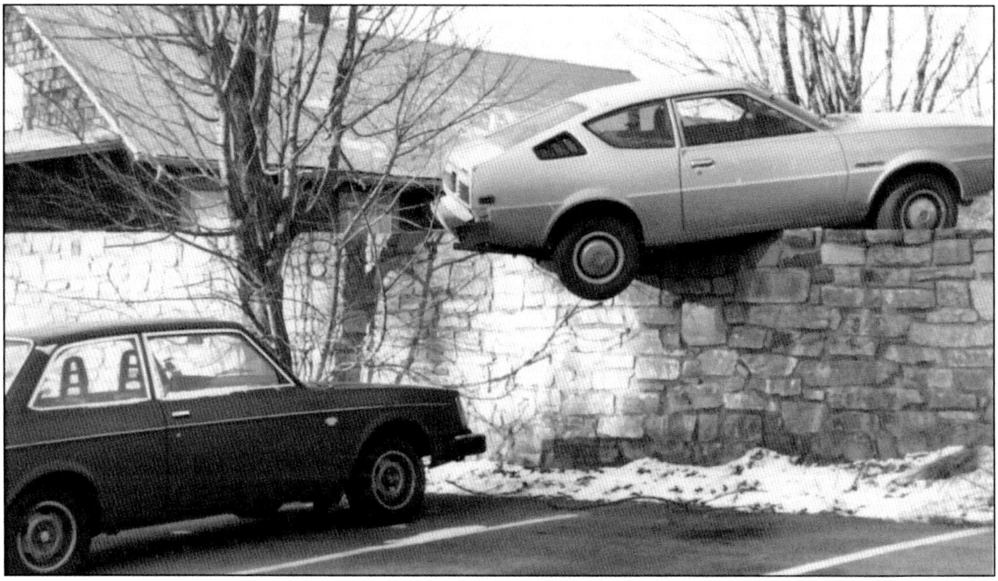

The crashing of cars and trucks into downtown business buildings and similar incidents do occur. Accidents received frequent coverage in the local paper and specifically on Highway 321 toward Boone. Fatal accidents within town limits were less frequent, with one in 1952 and two in 1969. In Watauga County, the years 1968 and 1969 each had over 10 fatalities in car accidents.

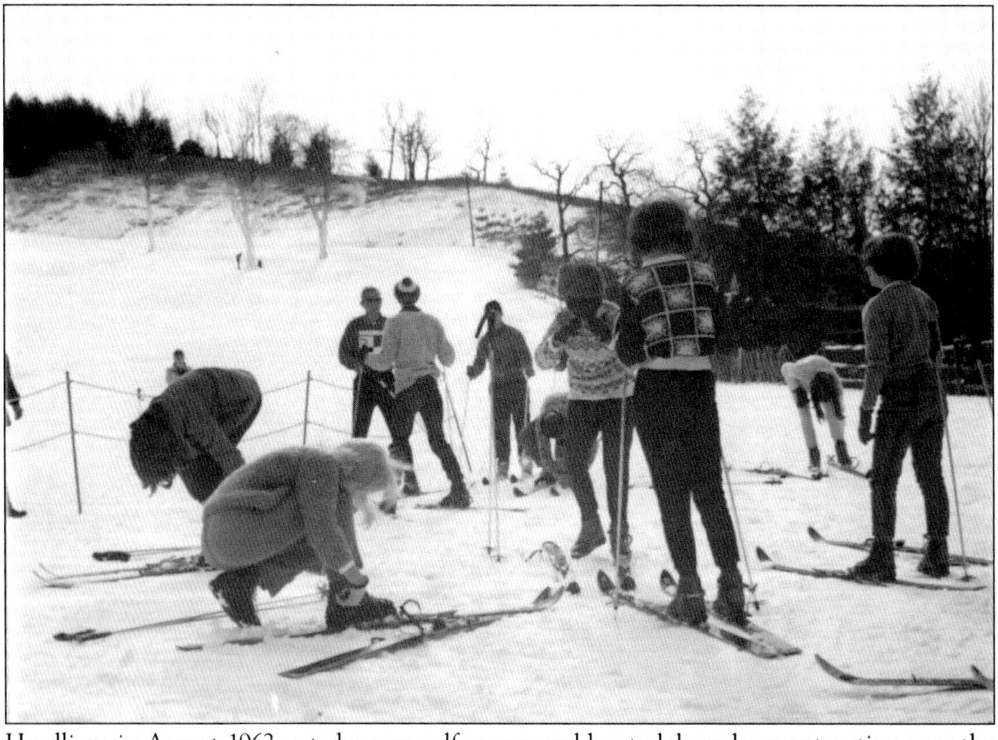

Headlines in August 1962 noted a new golf course and hunt club under construction near the former location of Shulls Mill. The Carolina Mill and Lumber Company developed the Hound Ears Club, which also included a skiing hill. This photograph shows newcomers putting on skis for the first time ever.

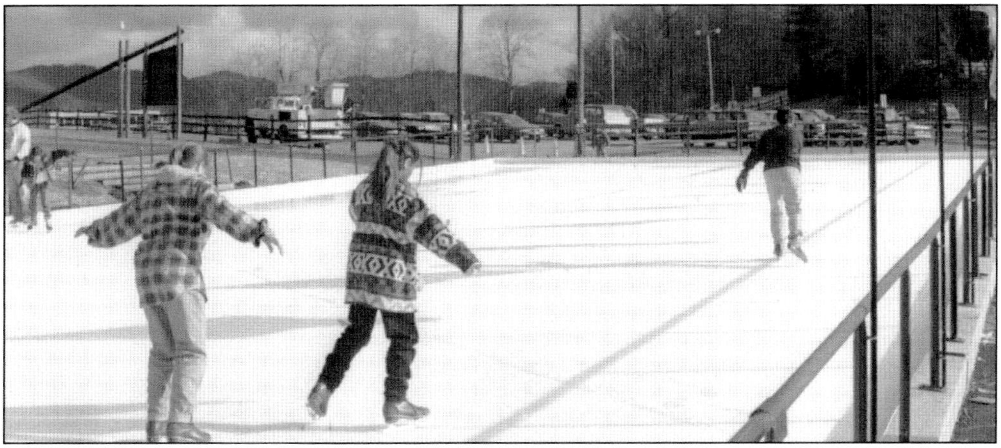

Ice skating at Appalachian Ski Mountain remains popular, North Carolina's only Zamboni-maintained outdoor ice rink. Wherever there was water in the winter, once it froze, ice skating was frequent, including on the small pond in front of the Appalachian Motel along Highway 321. A roller-skating rink was also noted starting in the summer of 1938, directly behind the Carolina Theatre and operated by G.M. Sudderth.

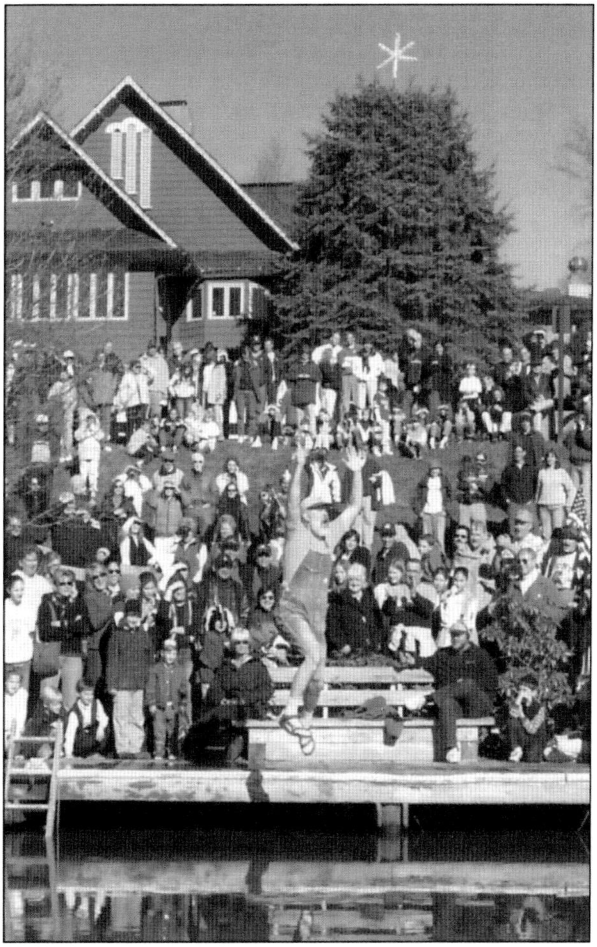

The polar plunge has become one of the highlights of Winterfest, with or without ice and snow, and a community fundraising event. In 1926, J. Luther Snyder purchased the property now known as Chetola; he paid $36,000 for 36 acres. Snyder was a self-made man who started his career by traveling the streets of Charlotte in a one-horse wagon selling Coca-Cola to merchants. Eventually, he operated 10 Coca-Cola bottling plants in the Charlotte area and came to be known as the "Coca-Cola King of the Carolinas." Snyder expanded the estate, even building a regulation-size bowling alley for his children. Horseback riding trails intertwined the estate, joining those at the bordering Moses Cone Estate, today located off the Blue Ridge Parkway. Chetola Lake was a known local ice-skating spot in the winter, and the harvesting of ice took place once it was at least four inches deep, requiring lots of local labor.

Bibliography

Akers, Donna Gayle. *Blowing Rock*. Charleston, SC: Arcadia, 2004.

Akers, Donna Gayle and Brian Lambeth. *Watauga County*. Charleston, SC: Arcadia, 2008.

Altamayer, Bud. *A Family History of Watauga County*. Boone, NC: Minor's Printing Company, 1994.

Arthur, John Preston. *A History of Watauga County, North Carolina*. Johnson City, TN: The Overmountain Press, 1915.

Bate, Ginger Smith. *Walking Around the Lake: Memories of Childhood in Blowing Rock*. San Jose, CA: Ginger Smith Bate, 1999.

Blowing Rocket. June 1932 to present.

Blowing Rock Historical Society. *Post Cards of Historic Blowing Rock*. Boone, NC: Parkway Publishers, 2002.

———. *Post Cards of Historic Blowing Rock, Volume II*. Boone, NC: Parkway Publishers, 2007.

Buxton, Barry M. *A Village Tapestry: The History of Blowing Rock*. Boone, NC: Appalachian Consortium Press, 1989.

Hutchinson, Crete. *In Cloudland, Mayview Park, Blowing Rock, North Carolina*. Washington, DC: Judd & Detweiler, Inc., 1920.

Lentz, Ralph E. II. *W.R. Trivett, Appalachian Pictureman*. Jefferson, NC: McFarland and Company, Inc. Publishers, 2001.

Noblitt, Philip T. *A Mansion in the Mountains: The Story of Moses and Bertha Cone and Their Blowing Rock Manor*. Boone, NC: Parkway Publishers, 1996.

Pezzoni, J. Daniel, editor, and others. *The Architectural History of Watauga County*. Durham, NC: BW&A Books, 2009.

Watauga Democrat. July 1888 to present.

Whisnant, Anne Mitchell. *Super-Scenic Motorway: A Blue Ridge Parkway History*. Chapel Hill, NC: University of North Carolina Press, 2006.

About the Organization

The Blowing Rock Historical Society formed in 1985 to preserve and protect the historical character and charm of the village; it is an active organization of over 300 members and plays a vital role in maintaining the unique sense of place that draws visitors to Blowing Rock. Several examples of accomplishments and activities include the 1890s home of artist Elliott Daingerfield, Edgewood Cottage, which was saved and adapted for reuse for the artist in residence program, and other events and activities. The last remaining cottage of the Watauga Hotel, now the 1888 museum, was refurbished and houses a collection of items from the town's history. The Green Park Historic District was listed in the National Register of Historic Places by the society. In partnership with the Blowing Rock Art and History Museum, a historic marker program recognizes properties with historical significance

The society has published *Post Cards of Historic Blowing Rock, Volumes I* and *II*. These collections of postcards from old Blowing Rock days depict vacations at various hotels and attractions. Hometown Harvest Supper, an annual potluck-style dinner with a dessert competition, is cohosted with the Blowing Rock Fire Department for all residents.

The Historical Society's ongoing efforts include celebrating dates of historical significance to Blowing Rock, serving as a resource for the deposition of furnishings and artifacts, and rallying support to preserve historic buildings and sites. New members are always welcome and encouraged. Future projects include placing the full photographic collection online, a National Register of Historic Places nomination for downtown, and assisting in local preservation efforts such as the recent American Legion building renovation.

Consistent with our mission to preserve history on a local level, this book was printed in South Carolina on American-made paper and manufactured entirely in the United States. Products carrying the accredited Forest Stewardship Council (FSC) label are printed on 100 percent FSC-certified paper.

MADE IN THE USA